Powering Social Enterprise with Profit and Purpose

Trail-blazing social entrepreneurs are tackling the world's most pressing problems that government, business, or charity have failed to solve. They are creating businesses with a primary mission of social change. Scott Boyer is one such social entrepreneur. This 28-year veteran of Big Pharma left a six-figure salary to start OWP Pharmaceuticals and the ROW Foundation. This commercial business and non-profit organization exist in a symbiotic relationship we call a "tandem hybrid social enterprise." This model combines a multimillion-dollar business with a foundation that's on track to become the largest funder of projects serving people with epilepsy and associated psychiatric disorders in the world.

The tandem hybrid incorporates the principles learned by Scott and others for building a truly unique social enterprise from the ground up; one that is:

- Driven by a compelling social mission.
- Financed by commercial success.
- Structured to retain control.
- Scalable and sustainable for the long haul.

Powering Social Enterprises with Profit and Purpose offers a detailed blue-print that has proven commercially and philanthropically successful and that can be replicated in most business sectors.

Scott Boyer is the Founder and CEO of OWP Pharmaceuticals and the Founder and Chairman of the ROW Foundation.

Jeremy Gudauskas taught social entrepreneurship at North Central College in Naperville, Illinois where he founded the Center for Social Impact.

Mike Hamel has helped more than 100 entrepreneurs and C-level business men and women share their stories with a wider audience.

Powering Social Enterprise with Profit and Purpose

The Tandem Hybrid

Scott Boyer, Jeremy Gudauskas and Mike Hamel

Routledge
Taylor & Francis Group

NEW YORK AND LONDON

Designed cover image: Chris Kairos

First published 2023
by Routledge
605 Third Avenue, New York, NY 10158

and by Routledge
4 Park Square, Milton Park, Abingdon, Oxon OX14 4RN

Routledge is an imprint of the Taylor & Francis Group, an informa business

© 2023 Scott Boyer, Jeremy Gudauskas, and Mike Hamel

Library of Congress Cataloging-in-Publication Data
Names: Boyer, Scott (Chief executive officer), author. | Hamel, Mike,
author. | Gudauskas, Jeremy, author.
Title: Powering social enterprise with profit and purpose : the tandem
hybrid / Scott Boyer, Jeremy Gudauskas, Mike Hamel.
Description: New York, NY : Routledge, 2023. | Includes
bibliographical references and index.
Identifiers: LCCN 2022042246 (print) | LCCN 2022042247 (ebook) |
ISBN 9781032352381 (hardback) | ISBN 9781032352374 (paperback) |
ISBN 9781003325987 (ebook)
Subjects: LCSH: Social responsibility of business. | Social
entrepreneurship. | Social change.
Classification: LCC HD60 .B694 2023 (print) | LCC HD60 (ebook) |
DDC 658.4/08--dc23/eng/20221125
LC record available at https://lccn.loc.gov/2022042246
LC ebook record available at https://lccn.loc.gov/2022042247

ISBN: 978-1-032-35238-1 (hbk)
ISBN: 978-1-032-35237-4 (pbk)
ISBN: 978-1-003-32598-7 (ebk)

DOI: 10.4324/9781003325987

Typeset in Bembo
by Taylor & Francis Books

This book is dedicated to the earliest staff and stakeholders of OWP Pharmaceuticals and the ROW Foundation. Your passion, perseverance, and personal sacrifices have resulted in a new kind of social enterprise that's changing lives for the better around the world. And we're just getting started! Thank you!

Contents

Illustrations

Figures

Foreword

Every chapter of history has its share of complex societal issues, but the plot has dramatically thickened in our current era. At every turn there seems to be another inciting incident that challenges the possibility of a more just, equitable and sustainable future for us all: a global pandemic that exacerbates inequities for communities of color worldwide, attacks on democracy that splinter nations along party lines and identity, an unprovoked war that fractures geopolitical stability, and an ongoing environmental crisis that threatens our very existence. At the core of each seismic event remains structural and racial injustice that continue to exclude and marginalize communities crucial for our shared global progress. In our next chapter as a society, we need more disruptive protagonists. We need more social innovators.

Since 1987, Echoing Green has been on the frontlines of addressing the world's most urgent challenges by finding, investing in, and connecting early-stage social entrepreneurs with bold ideas for change. Echoing Green Fellows are leaders disrupting the status quo globally (such as First Lady Michelle Obama; social justice activist and political commentator Van Jones; One Acre Fund founder Andrew Youn; and national service and global education leader and founder of Teach for America Wendy Kopp).

Scott Boyer is this type of social entrepreneur, and he's tackling a global health disparity—access to life-changing medication and treatment typically only available in wealthier countries. His model for a scaled and sustainable social enterprise has game-changing potential. When I joined him on a panel of judges to give feedback for a collegiate social innovation pitch competition in 2021, I knew his story needed to be told. Aspiring social innovators need more than good ideas—they need funding, they need support networks, and they need the tools to scale their ideas for transformative social change.

Since our founding, Echoing Green's community has grown to include nearly 1,000 social innovators and founders who are tackling broken and unjust systems worldwide. In 2020, we launched our Racial Equity Philanthropic Fund to invest millions of dollars into next-generation leaders who are advancing racial equity, with a goal to launch and scale 520 social enterprises by 2024. We understand social enterprises, and we know what they need to succeed.

I have written previously that early-stage social innovators are successful when they do a couple of things exceptionally well: they *mine their personal experiences* and they *hack the current system*. Scott's long career in Big Pharma gave him an insider's understanding of the powerful but profit-obsessed industry that was content to ignore the "rest of world"—those who could benefit from, but not afford, access to life-changing medication. His experience gave him not just the skills, but the credibility, authenticity, and deep knowledge to act within the pharmaceutical industry. As a result, he's been able to hack the system that is notorious for price-hikes and profiteering. His social enterprise has effectively flipped the script by manufacturing profitable medications that meet a need in the U.S. market, and directing the profit to fund global health partnerships in more than thirty lower- and middle-income countries. The power comes from harnessing the benefits of a for-profit and non-profit model working together in tandem.

At Echoing Green, we pay particular attention to the models that help facilitate successful social change. As referenced in this book, our research has shown a significant increase in social enterprises that look to earned revenue as a primary source of funding to sustain and scale their ventures. In fact, we have to look no further than enterprises in our portfolio including BlocPower and Tala. While structural models vary, there is no doubt that the ability for a social enterprise to profit is paramount. This book makes a valuable contribution to the field of social enterprise by showcasing a proven model that is not bound by the either/or question of structure (for-profit/nonprofit) faced by most founders. The both/and approach of the tandem hybrid model provides a blueprint for how to address a social challenge at scale through profit *and* purpose.

We need social innovators to frame the future with creativity, passion, and insight into what works. Whether you are a practitioner in the public or private sector, an educator or student in a university setting, or a current or aspiring founder of a social enterprise, I believe you will be inspired by this book, the perspectives of the co-authors—Scott, a business leader; Jeremy, a social innovation educator; and Mike, an author and leading storyteller, and the examples set by OWP Pharmaceuticals and the ROW Foundation. Use what you learn to structure or support social enterprises for maximum impact and go after today's challenges with boldness. When future generations read our chapter of history, may they find it shaped by social innovators who have made the world more inclusive, more sustainable, and more just.

Cheryl L. Dorsey
President, Echoing Green
1992 Echoing Green Fellow

Acknowledgements

The authors gratefully acknowledge that this book and the organizations it highlights—OWP Pharmaceuticals and the ROW Foundation—exist because of the vision and commitment of so many amazing people. Bruce Duncan, Mark Petersen, and Brett Boyer were key in starting and scaling up OWP. Paul Regan, Lori Hairrell, and Ken Koskela played instrumental roles in launching ROW and shepherding its growth into the ROW Foundation and ROW Global Health.

Many others cheered and supported these efforts, chief among them was Scott's wife, Ruth. Still others added their expertise as board members, including Troy Hammond, Carol Gavin, Kurt Florian, and Jim Milligan for OWP and Mark Petersen, Pat Gibson, Mavin Rossi, Emilio Perucca, Lisa Brown, and Mike deLaroche for ROW. Halftime coach Jim Dean was a valuable resource early on, as was Stephen Fraser, whose strategic calls on the "Bat Phone" at critical times literally saved the day.

Scores of people have worked at OWP and ROW since 2014. Hundreds more have selflessly volunteered their time and money to further our vision of a world "where all people receive the best level of medical and pharmaceutical care regardless of who they are or where they live." Hundreds of thousands of lives have been impacted in more than 30 countries so far. Millions more will have the possibility of a brighter future in the years ahead.

It's the blessing of a lifetime to be part of such a caring community.

About the Authors

Scott Boyer is the Founder and CEO of OWP Pharmaceuticals and the Founder and Chairman of the ROW Foundation. His CV includes eleven years with Abbott Laboratories and fifteen years at Bristol-Myers Squibb. In 2012, he took a job as executive director of business development with InVentiv Health. While there, he noticed that practically all drugs were sold in wealthier countries and almost none went to developing countries. It became harder to overlook or rationalize that most disorders and diseases that could be easily treated by available and inexpensive medications went untreated. "I began to hear a louder 'whisper' to do something about this inequity," Scott recalls, "to find a way to equalize the playing field when it came to medical care. I couldn't accept so many people around the world being left behind." Scott found a partner in Bruce Duncan and pulled together a stellar team to start OWP and ROW. The Tandem Hybrid shares how other social entrepreneurs can learn from their struggles and success.

Jeremy Gudauskas taught social entrepreneurship for a decade during his seventeen year career at North Central College in Naperville, Illinois, his alma mater. Prior to higher education, he had a successful career with a software startup and cut his teeth in business working on product design, marketing, and training. He crisscrossed the world to the studios of high-profile clients and even started a media production business on the side. Jeremy founded the Center for Social Impact at North Central College, which received the prestigious designation as a "Changemaker Campus" by Ashoka U. In his role as Managing Director of the college's Center for Innovation and Entrepreneurship, Jeremy met Scott Boyer. "I had a front-row seat to watch the OWP vision take shape," Jeremy says. "My desire is for more people to have a 'Scott Boyer story;' to use their strengths, discover their purpose, and launch an idea that can change this world for the better." Jeremy now provides social impact consulting for global businesses and social enterprises, including ROW Global Health.

Mike Hamel has written or substantially edited more than forty books. Along the way he's interviewed more than 100 entrepreneurs and C-level men and women for different business books. As a biographer and editor, Mike has helped business leaders tell their stories. These books include autobiographies by C. William Pollard, former CEO of ServiceMaster (*Serving Two Masters and The Tides of Life*), Merrill Oster, founder of Pinnacle Forum (*Conduits of God's Grace*), and Chris Crane, former President of Opportunity International (*A Dream and a Coconut Tree: Transforming Education for the Poor*). Mike has worked with OWP and ROW since 2015. He was the communications director for the foundation and wrote a book about their social enterprise model—*SE 2.0: The OWP Difference*—which is the prequel to this book.

Introduction

This book is a field guide for social entrepreneurs, written by those who are successfully pioneering a new approach to building a large-scale company in tandem with a sizable non-profit organization. By way of illustration it includes the story of Scott Boyer, an executive who left a job he loved, with a solid six-figure income and all the perks, to build a new kind of social enterprise from scratch.

Scott's Story

After more than twenty-five years in the pharmaceutical business with Abbott and Bristol-Myers Squibb, I took a job as executive director of business development with InVentiv Health Incorporated in 2013. While at InVentiv I did analysis on companies and products currently on the market or ready to be launched. As I became familiar with the data, I noticed something that piqued my interest. On the pie charts and graphs, the most common markets were the U.S., Japan, and the wealthier countries in Europe. China and India might be included sometimes. The other 170 or 180 countries would be lumped together in the last column, always the smallest, and titled ROW—"Rest of World." I later learned the descriptive term was fairly common in international business. You focus on the major markets, where profits are the greatest, and throw everyplace else into a big bucket, and that's ROW. This is normal and customary.

It slowly dawned on me that practically all drugs were sold in wealthier countries and almost none went to countries in the ROW column. Patent-protected medications almost never made it to poorer countries, and getting generic medications into them had its own hurdles. Because of those Big Pharma patents, smaller countries were prevented from developing these products themselves. It became harder to overlook or rationalize that most disorders and diseases that could be easily treated by available and inexpensive medications went untreated. The cost to human life and human potential in these situations seemed staggering and inexcusable.

What Scott did as a result of this awakening was start a social enterprise. A social enterprise is a business that has specific social objectives that serve its primary purpose. Social enterprises seek to maximize benefits to society and the environment while maintaining financial viability through earned revenue. "Hybrid organizations that combine social purpose and profit motive appear to have grown significantly in number in the U.S.," notes a recent report cited in the *Nonprofit Policy Forum*. "However, these organizations, which we call 'social enterprises,' face challenges that impede their growth and hinder their ability to deliver greater benefits."[1]

Scott has encountered many of these challenges firsthand as the Founder and CEO of OWP Pharmaceuticals and the Founder and former Chairman of the ROW Foundation. This commercial business and non-profit organization exist in a symbiotic relationship that can serve as a template for other social enterprises. We call it the tandem hybrid social enterprise.

While there are many meanings and models for the term "hybrid," what we are calling the tandem hybrid model takes the social enterprise to the next level. OWP will be a large-scale business and ROW is on track to become the largest funder of projects serving people with epilepsy and associated psychiatric disorders in the world. Launched in the highly competitive world of Big Pharma in 2014, OWP's current revenues are still modest, however OWP has built a strong foundation and is positioned for exponential growth with a number of new products in the pipeline. To date, ROW has worked with more than 75 partners in 35 countries, making $21.7 million in grants and providing 176,589 prescription-months of medication.

This book examines the strengths and weaknesses of profit-driven commercial enterprises, purpose-driven social enterprises, and offers a third way: the tandem hybrid social enterprise, which is:

- Driven by a compelling social mission.
- Financed by commercial success.
- Structured to retain control.
- Scalable and sustainable for the long haul.

There are four sections in this book. Part I ("Commercial and Social Enterprises") gives an overview of why commercial businesses and non-profit organizations are started, how they are structured, and the various ways they can be combined into for-profit *and* for-purpose, social enterprises. It goes on to show how the tandem hybrid model is similar to, but different from, other social enterprises.

Part II ("Building Tandem Hybrid Social Enterprises") drills down into the details of the tandem hybrid. It expands on the four distinctives of the

---

1 Alan J. Abramson and Kara C. Billings, "Challenges Facing Social Enterprises in the United States," www.degruyter.com/document/doi/10.1515/npf-2018-0046/html.

model and uses Scott's experiences with OWP and the ROW Foundation as illustrations of what the tandem hybrid looks like in the real world.

Part III ("Lessons from History") offers an analysis of eight well-known companies that have stood the test of time. Seeing how they met the challenges of changing markets, balanced profit and purpose, and kept on-mission (or not), provides some valuable takeaways for commercial and social entrepreneurs.

Part IV ("A Call to Action") shows why the world needs more social enterprises and why the tandem hybrid model could be a better way to go for many social entrepreneurs.

Whether you are an aspiring or experienced social entrepreneur, this book will help you do well in business while doing good in the world. The world needs you now more than ever. "Social entrepreneurs are the essential corrective force," says Bill Drayton, founder of Ashoka, the world's leading association of social entrepreneurs. "They are system-changing entrepreneurs. And from deep within they, and therefore their work, are committed to the good of all."

"What business entrepreneurs are to the economy, social entrepreneurs are to social change," writes David Bornstein. "They are the driven, creative individuals who question the status quo, exploit new opportunities, refuse to give up, and remake the world for the better."[2]

Ready to get started?

---

2 David Bornstein, "How to Change the World," David Bornstein blog, https://davidbornstein.wordpress.com/books/how-to-change-the-world/.

Part I

Commercial and Social Enterprises

Part I gives an overview of for-profit commercial businesses, for-purpose social enterprises, and the tandem hybrid social enterprise. These chapters trace the transition from business as usual to business as economic engine to bring about social change. Social entrepreneurs are addressing challenges in new ways that go beyond what governments or traditional charities have been able to do. To do this, they are creating new social enterprises that harness the power of for-profit business to the passion of for-purpose mission. These are both/and organizations that pursue profit to fulfill a purpose—making the world a better place.

DOI: 10.4324/9781003325987-1

1 For Profit

Commercial Enterprises

How does one become "the most hated man in America?" In the case of Martin Shkreli, by running a business to maximize profits.

As CEO of Turing Pharmaceuticals, Shkreli made a name for himself in 2015 by raising the price of a life-saving medication from $13 to $750 a tablet—a 5000 percent increase. His critics subsequently made a name for him, "Pharma Bro," immortalized as the title of a 2021 documentary that sought to make sense of his snarky, capitalism-at-all-costs approach to business.

Price-hikes in the pharmaceutical industry are not uncommon, and Shkreli was taking advantage of a system that allowed profit maximization in the absence of competition. However, an antitrust lawsuit finally caught up with his former company in 2020, resulting in a $40 million settlement because of what the Federal Trade Commission called "an elaborate web of restrictions to illegally block competitors from producing a cheaper option."[1] In early 2022, while Shkreli continued to serve a seven-year prison sentence for a separate case involving securities fraud, the ruling was announced in another lawsuit filed against him by the Federal Trade Commission. In a final blow, Shkreli was banned for life from the pharmaceutical industry and ordered to pay $64.6 million in profits gained from the Daraprim price-hike. New York Attorney General Letitia James commented, "Americans can rest easy because Martin Shkreli is a pharma bro no more."[2]

The Shkreli saga included many made-for-TV tidbits: his less-than-mature responses at congressional hearings, dating the journalist who broke the story of his arrest, continuing to run his business behind bars with a contraband cell phone, requesting release from prison to work on a cure for COVID-19

1 Chantel Da Silva, "'Pharma Bro' Firm Reaches $40 Million Settlement as Shkreli Faces Trial," *NBC News*, last modified August 12, 2021, www.nbcnews.com/news/us-news/pharma-bro-firm-reaches-40-million-settlement-shkreli-faces-trial-rcna7990.
2 "'Pharma Bro No More': Attorney General James Scores Court Victory Against Convicted Criminal Martin Shkreli, Banning Him from Pharmaceutical Industry for Life, Ordering Him to Pay Nearly $65 Million," Letitia James, NY Attorney General, https://ag.ny.gov/press-release/2022/pharma-bro-no-more-attorney-general-james-scores-court-victory-against-convicted.

DOI: 10.4324/9781003325987-2

(which the judge called "delusional self-aggrandizing"), and the forced sale of his one-of-a-kind Wu-Tang Clan album to complete a $7.4 million forfeiture. Shkreli's notorious antics led one health institute to honor the imprisoned executive by awarding the ten most egregious examples of profiteering and dysfunction in healthcare with the annual Shkreli Awards.[3] However, beyond the surface-level distractions, the Shkreli case study has sparked a deeper conversation about the obligations of business to society.

This conversation is not new to the pharmaceutical industry, or "Big Pharma," as it's known. From penicillin to vaccines, the industry that can be credited with saving millions of lives is also measured in trillions of dollars. Purpose and profit live in tension. "I could have raised it higher and made more profits for our shareholders, which is my primary duty," Shkreli commented at the Forbes Healthcare Summit. "No one wants to say it. No one's proud of it. But this is a capitalist society. Capitalist system. Capitalist rules. And my investors expect me to maximize profits."[4]

The pharmaceutical industry is known for this type of price-gouging, and the public has grown tired of criminal probes, penalties, and profiteering. This is not the future that drug pioneer George W. Merck envisioned when he said, "We try never to forget that medicine is for the people. It is not for the profits. The profits follow, and if we have remembered that, they have never failed to appear."[5]

It's no surprise that the Gallup Poll's annual trust ranking consistently lists the pharmaceutical industry near the bottom. In 2020, Big Pharma saw a slight bump in positive perception for its role in combating COVID-19, but in 2021 public trust dropped again, keeping the pharmaceutical industry only slightly ahead of the oil and gas industry and the federal government as the least-trusted sector of society.[6] It was in this industry that Scott Boyer sought to launch a new kind of business—a pharmaceutical social enterprise that would maximize purpose through profit, and turn the image of an industry upside-down. We will detail Scott's story throughout these chapters.

Friedman versus Fink

Those who risked coming to the unpopular defense of Martin Shkreli said he was well within his rights to run his business in a way that maximized profits for his shareholders. This, after all, has been the dominant philosophy

3 "The Lown Institute Shkreli Awards," Lown Institute, accessed April 1, 2022, https://lowninstitute.org/projects/shkreli-awards/.

4 Kate Gibson, "Martin Shkreli: I Should've 'Raised Prices Higher'," CBS News, last modified April 12, 2015, www.cbsnews.com/news/martin-shkreli-i-shouldve-raised-prices-higher/.

5 "Our History," Merck, www.merck.com/company-overview/history.

6 Megan Brenan and Jefferey N. Jones, "Image Ratings of Several U.S. Industries Tumble," *Gallup*, September 13, 2021, https://news.gallup.com/poll/354653/image-ratings-several-industries-tumble.aspx.

of business for decades, espoused most notably by economist Milton Friedman. In 1970, Friedman wrote: "There is one and only one social responsibility of business—to use its resources and engage in activities designed to increase its profits so long as it stays within the rules of the game."[7] This doctrine, once held sacred, stated that the sole purpose of business is to generate profits for shareholders. Social responsibility was for the individual, not for the corporation. More than fifty years later, however, the rules of the game are changing. Stakeholder primacy—a broad view that includes employees, customers, suppliers, communities, and the environment—is taking the place of shareholder primacy. Ed Freeman, author of *Strategic Management: A Stakeholder Approach*, writes: "The idea that business is about maximizing profits for shareholders is outdated and doesn't work very well, as the recent global financial crisis has taught us. The 21st Century is one of 'Managing for Stakeholders'."[8]

In 2018, Larry Fink, the influential CEO of Blackrock—the world's largest asset management company with a portfolio of more than $9 trillion—penned his annual letter to CEOs. In what some have called a watershed moment, Fink flipped the table on Friedman, claiming that social responsibility is now an imperative for all businesses. "Society is demanding that companies, both public and private, serve a social purpose," wrote Fink. "To prosper over time, every company must not only deliver financial performance, but also show how it makes a positive contribution to society."[9]

Despite backlash that said Fink was wading into the territory of corporate socialism, he doubled down in his 2019 letter, stating "Purpose is not the sole pursuit of profits but the animating force for achieving them. Profits are in no way inconsistent with purpose—in fact, profits and purpose are inextricably linked."[10] Fink's assessment of purpose in business is consistent with what studies are showing. McKinsey found that 70 percent of employees said their sense of purpose is defined by their work.[11] Deloitte found that 77 percent of business executives said social responsibility is

7   Milton Friedman, "A Friedman Doctrine—The Social Responsibility of Business Is to Increase Its Profits," *The New York Times*, Sept. 13, 1970, www.nytimes.com/1970/09/13/archives/a-friedman-doctrine-the-socia l-responsibility-of-business-is-to.html.

8   Ed Freeman, "Stakeholder Management," Ed Freeman, accessed August 3, 2022, https://redwardfreeman.com/stakeholder-management/.

9   Larry Frink, "A Sense of Purpose," BlackRock, 2018, accessed April 1, 2022, www.blackrock.com/corporate/investor-relations/2018-larry-fink-ceo-letter.

10 Larry Frink, "Purpose & Purpose," BlackRock, 2019, accessed April 1, 2022, www.blackrock.com/americas-offshore/en/2019-larry-fink-ceo-letter.

11 Naina Dhingra, Andrew Samo, Bill Schaninger, and Matt Schrimper, "Help Your Employees Find Purpose—or Watch Them Leave," McKinsey & Company, April 5, 2021, www.mckinsey.com/business-functions/people-and-orga nizational-performance/our-insights/help-your-employees-find-purpose-or-wa tch-them-leave.

important to their company's performance.[12] Edelman found that 76 percent of consumers think CEOs should take the lead on social issues.[13]

In Friedman's world, it may have seemed reasonable to create a hard line between corporate social responsibility and personal social responsibility, leaving the business to focus on profits and the individual to focus on purpose. But now, the lines are blurred—for CEOs, employees, investors, and consumers. The game has changed because the players have changed. Indeed, the culture has changed. In recent years, every business had been forced to grapple with their response to a global pandemic, a racial reckoning in the U.S., and the urgent need for climate action. Some have even used their platform and power to speak and act in response to Russia's invasion of Ukraine, or in response to U.S. Supreme Court decisions. While what companies say and do to address social concerns can be controversial, few today would argue that a business is exempt from social responsibility.

The Responsibility Revolution

While Friedman's doctrine was taking root after his 1970 article, there was another movement brewing. In 1971, the Committee for Economic Development defined the idea of the "social contract" between business and society. Business, it said, has a responsibility to serve the needs of society because it functions under public consent. This "license to operate" should hold business to a higher standard. The social contract provided three tenants that should guide a responsible business—all of which still hold strong today:

1   Provide jobs and economic growth through well-run businesses.
2   Run the business fairly and honestly regarding employees and customers.
3   Become more broadly involved in improving the conditions of the community and environment in which it operates.[14]

What's known today as corporate social responsibility (CSR) can trace its roots back to the industrial revolution in the late 1800s, as some companies started seriously considering their workers' welfare. In the same era, the

12 "Infographic: The Rise of the Social Enterprise, 2018 Global Human Capital Trends," Deloitte, March 28, 2018, www2.deloitte.com/us/en/insights/m ultimedia/infographics/2018-global-human-capital-trends.html.
13 "2019 Edelman Trust Barometer: Expectations for CEOs," Edelman, all fieldwork conducted between October 19 and November 16, 2018, www. edelman.com/sites/g/files/aatuss191/files/2019-05/2019_Edelman_Trust_Ba rometer_CEO_Trust_Report.pdf.
14 "Corporate Social Responsibility: A Brief History," ACCP, accessed April 2, 2022, https://accp.org/resources/csr-resources/accp-insights-blog/corporate-so cial-responsibility-brief-history/.

world's richest businessmen—Andrew Carnegie and John Rockefeller—who made their fortunes from steel and oil, respectively, began to funnel millions of dollars into educational, scientific, and religious causes. By the 20th century, many businesses already held themselves to high standards of responsibility, doing their best to give back to their workers and communities, often through the establishment of charitable foundations. Because of the scale and profitability of their companies, many had the capacity to make a significant impact. You'll read about some of these companies in our "lessons from history" chapters.

Then in 1953, with the publication of *Social Responsibilities of the Businessman*, economist Howard Bowen coined the term corporate social responsibility—earning him the title of "Father of CSR."[15] The CSR movement continued to grow in the latter half of the 20th century and reached critical mass heading into the 21st century, with large corporations like Coca-Cola, Walt Disney, and Pfizer implementing CSR into their business strategy. Over the last two decades the landscape has shifted at an even more rapid pace. While once upon a time private commercial entities could go about their business with little accountability to the public, save for certain governmental regulations, businesses are now being held to a higher standard as it relates to their workers, their communities, and the environment. The private sector is no longer so private.

Businesses now face a new set of questions, driven by the values of their customers, investors, and regulators. Gone are the days when one might simply ask, "How much does it cost?" Now, people are asking: "Who makes your clothes and what are their working conditions?" "Where is your coffee grown and do the farmers make a living wage?" "Can your packaging be recycled or will it biodegrade?" "Can people actually afford your life-saving medication?"

By 2015, 92 percent of the largest 250 companies in the world produced a CSR report to highlight their responsible practices to their shareholders and the public. That was up from 2005, when 64 percent produced CSR reports. In 2018, Global Fortune 500 firms spent more than $20 billion on CSR activities[16]. The need to track, measure, and report on a company's social performance gave rise to even more tools, networks, and movements over the last fifteen years.

15   "Corporate Social Responsibility: A Brief History," ACCP, accessed August 3, 2022, https://accp.org/resources/csr-resources/accp-insights-blog/corporate-so cial-responsibility-brief-history/.
16   Stephan Meier and Lea Cassar, "Stop Talking About How CSR Helps Your Bottom Line," *Harvard Business Review*, January 31, 2018, https://hbr.org/ 2018/01/stop-talking-about-how-csr-helps-your-bottom-line#:~:text=Today %2C%20Fortune%20Global%20500%20firms,for%20attracting%20and%20m otivating%20employees.

B the Change

With all of the corporate do-gooding, it became harder to distinguish between a business making a legitimate social or environmental impact and those who were masters of marketing. Then along came the certified "B Corp." In 2006, three friends founded B Lab with the vision of making business a force for good. After successfully launching, growing, and then selling the basketball apparel brand AND1, Jay Cohen Gilbert was disheartened when the new owners quickly dismantled the values-based corporate responsibility efforts that had been baked into the company culture. In response, he sought to create a new movement of businesses for whom their social and environmental impact could be quantified and verified by an independent third party—B Lab.

In 2007, the first nineteen businesses were certified through a rigorous assessment of the good they do for their workers, their communities, and the environment. By 2021, there were over 4,400 certified companies spanning seventy-seven countries employing more than 370,000 workers. Rose Marcario, former CEO of one of the early certified B Corps, Patagonia, described its impact: "The B Corp movement is one of the most important of our lifetime, built on the simple fact that business impacts and serves more than just shareholders—it has an equal responsibility to the community and to the planet."[17] While only a small (but growing) number of global companies choose to pursue B Corp certification (there's a cost involved as well), it's an indicator of the increased desire to validate, measure, and promote the good that business can do. The advocacy work of B Lab has also led to a majority and growing number of states in the U.S. that now offer the "Benefit Corporation" legal structure (more on this in Chapter 2), which gives them the ability to codify their values by being held accountable to all stakeholders, not just shareholders.

The reality is that all businesses make a social impact, whether or not it's positive is another question. In sync with the assessment-focused B Corp movement were advancements in the standards used in measuring and reporting impact. Profit and purpose were combining to create the new double bottom-line; however, most businesses were only good at measuring profit. How does a business quantify its social impact? Measurement was becoming the new obsession as a wave of awakened investors wanted to put their money where their mission was. They called themselves impact investors.

The Global Impact Investing Network (GIIN) launched in 2009, giving structure to the growing movement that sought a social and environmental return on their investments, as well as a financial return. By 2021 the GIIN included more than 20,000 members devoted to expanding the impact investing industry. A 2020 GIIN survey found that the impact investing

---

17 Beverly Murray, "B(eing) Corp," R + M, accessed August 3, 2022, https://rmagency.com/being-b-corp/.

market size had reached $750 billion—more than $200 billion above the year prior. Importantly, more than 88 percent of impact investors reported their investments were meeting or surpassing their financial expectations.[18]

The focus of these investments often centered around the Sustainable Development Goals (SDGs) outlined by the United Nations, which first mentioned the concept of ESG (Environment, Social, and Governance) factors in their 2006 Principles for Responsible Investment report.[19] ESG, a specific approach to considering these factors in the lifecycle of an investment, has now gone mainstream. BlackRock's Larry Fink suggested in his 2021 letter that companies that don't already have robust ESG policies and practices may soon be required to do so by regulators.

A New Consciousness

The purpose train was gaining steam, and businesses large and small were now on board. For example, in 2013, Whole Foods founder John Mackey teamed up with marketing professor Raj Sisodia to release the book *Conscious Capitalism: The Heroic Spirit of Business*. While naysayers accused Mackey of using this as a smokescreen to avoid government regulation, it was yet another vote for stakeholder primacy, articulating four guiding principles:

- Higher Purpose: A business that adheres to the principles of conscious capitalism focuses on a purpose beyond pure profits.
- Stakeholder Orientation: A conscious business concentrates on the whole business ecosystem to create and optimize value for all of its stakeholders.
- Conscious Leadership: Conscious leaders emphasize a "we" rather than a "me" mentality to drive the business.
- Conscious Culture: A conscious culture is one where the policies of conscious capitalism permeate the enterprise, fostering a spirit of trust and cooperation among all stakeholders.[20]

Beyond the book, the non-profit organization Conscious Capitalism now boasts local chapters in more than two dozen U.S. cities and ten countries.[21]

18 Dean Hand, Hannah Dithrich, Sophia Sunderji, Noshin Nova, "2020 Annual Impact Investor Survey," Global Impact Investing Network, June 11, 2020, https://thegiin.org/research/publication/impinv-survey-2020#charts.
19 "About the PRI," Principles for Responsible Investment, accessed April 30, 2022, www.unpri.org/pri/about-the-pri.
20 "Conscious Capitalism Philosophy," Conscious Capitalism, accessed April 27, 2022, www.consciouscapitalism.org/philosophy.
21 Will Kenton, "Conscious Capitalism," Investopia, last modified November 8, 2021, www.investopedia.com/terms/c/conscious-capitalism.asp.

Further driving a stake into shareholder primacy was the Business Roundtable Proclamation in 2019. The Business Roundtable is the collective voice of the CEOs of America's leading companies, overseeing 20 million employees and $9 trillion in revenues[22]. Executives representing the likes of Apple, General Motors, and JP Morgan Chase work together to promote a thriving and equitable U.S. economy. In 2019, they released a "Statement on the Purpose of a Corporation" signed by 181 CEOs committed to leading their companies for the benefit of all stakeholders—customers, employees, suppliers, communities, and shareholders. Describing the Statement, the announcement noted:

> Since 1978, Business Roundtable has periodically issued Principles of Corporate Governance. Each version of the document issued since 1997 has endorsed principles of shareholder primacy—that corporations exist principally to serve shareholders. With today's announcement, the new Statement supersedes previous statements and outlines a modern standard for corporate responsibility.[23]

While some critics have argued the Business Roundtable Proclamation does not yet reflect corporate actions—especially those of large and complex multinational corporations—more and more companies are attempting to walk the talk. For example, in early 2022, Howard Schultz, the visionary who built the Starbucks brand from 11 stores to more than 28,000 in 77 markets over four decades, returned to the coffee giant as interim CEO following the retirement of Kevin Johnson. Faced with a growing unionization movement from dissatisfied frontline employees, Schultz made an announcement on his first day on the job: Starbucks would immediately suspend its $20 billion stock repurchasing program to be able to invest more into their workers and stores. Schultz stated:

> Our vision is to once again reimagine a first-of-a-kind for-purpose company in which the value we create for each of us as partners (employees), for each of us as customers, for our communities, for the planet, for shareholders—comes because our company is designed to share success with each of us and for the collective success of all our stakeholders.[24]

22 "About Us," Business Roundtable, accessed March 7, 2022, www.businessroundtable.org/about-us.
23 "Business Roundtable Redefines the Purpose of a Corporation to Promote 'An Economy That Serves All Americans'," Business Roundtable, August 19, 2019, www.businessroundtable.org/business-roundtable-redefines-the-purpose-of-a-corporation-to-promote-an-economy-that-serves-all-americans.
24 Tonya Garcia, "Starbucks Downgraded after Returning CEO Schultz Halts Share Buybacks, But Focus on Workers amid Unionizing Efforts Gets Support," MarketWatch, April 6, www.marketwatch.com/story/starbucks-downgraded-after-returning-ceo-schultz-halts-share-buybacks-but-focus-on-workers-amid-unionizing-efforts-gets-support-11649179512?link=MW_latest_news.

Clearly, a stakeholder focus is the future of commercial enterprise. Gone are the days of profit maximization followed by fix-it philanthropy, often seen as an attempt to undo the damage of unchecked capitalism. Toxic short-termism is giving way to a long-term strategy that benefits people and the planet, while delivering profit as well. As former Unilever CEO Paul Poleman states in his 2021 book *Net Positive*, the goal is "financial gain *because* of sustainability, not despite it—not profits with a side of purpose, but profits *through* purpose."[25] Companies are now betting on their values, hoping that purpose, in the long run, is profitable.

But what if it's not? Despite the advancements in corporate social responsibility, values-based leadership, and environmental and workforce regulations, commercial businesses are still, at their core, structured to run on profit. There is an inherent tension for the business that wants to run on purpose. Historically, there was a clear distinction between organizations that wanted to pursue a profit and organizations that wanted to pursue some form of social purpose. And the rules of the system were created to facilitate these competing priorities.

Are You For Profit, or Not?

When entrepreneurs are ready to formalize their business entity, they have to choose a legal structure. The structure chosen will dictate a number of important factors, including how the business is taxed, how it can raise money, how it is governed, and how transparent it must be about finances and operations. One of the first questions a mission-driven enterprise needs to navigate is the difference between for-profit and non-profit organizational structures. There are now mission-centric for-profit options that we'll discuss in the next chapter, but it's important to first understand how the rules of the game were historically set up, and why this can be limiting when your goal is to scale both profit and purpose.

For-Profit Business: Profit Over Purpose

Structurally speaking, the primary function of a for-profit business has been to make money. The business may improve society through the sale of products or services, by how it employs workers, and by how it interacts with the community, but the business entity itself is structured to make a financial profit. That well-earned profit can then be distributed to investors or shareholders who have risked their capital to support the business. Hence the concept of shareholder value.

The for-profit status of the business has implications on how it can raise funds, as well as the responsibility it has to the IRS for taxes. For-profit

---

25 Paul Poleman, *Net Positive: How Courageous Companies Thrive by Giving More Than They Take*, (Brighton, MA: Harvard Business Review Press, 2021), p. 2.

businesses can attract money from private investors (angel investors, private equity, venture capital) in exchange for equity or dividends. This gives entrepreneurs a potential path to quick growth to scale the venture, but comes with some risks we'll discuss later. For-profit businesses are also subject to taxes on income and property.

If you've determined you want to register as a for-profit entity in your state, you're not done with your decisions. There are a variety of for-profit structures that have implications related to how profits are taxed, the complexity of setup and ongoing administration, and liability protection for the owners. The typical options are: sole proprietorship, partnership, S-corp, C-corp, and LLC (limited liability company). The first three options are generally best for smaller, simpler operations, and utilize "pass-through" taxation—the taxable income from the business "passes through" to the personal tax returns of the owners. If and when you plan to operate on a larger scale with more complexity, and the possibility for more impact, a C-corp often becomes a better option. The largest publicly traded companies are C-corps. An LLC can be structured to be taxed as any of the previous entities, and offers liability protection to the owners in a way that proprietorships and partnerships do not.

Regardless of the for-profit business entity that is chosen, all options were created to help fulfill the primary purpose of the business—to profit. A lot of good can be achieved with immense profits, as you'll see in later chapters. But as much as a company prioritizes values, purpose, responsibility, and impact, there will always be some level of tension between serving shareholders and all stakeholders. The best businesses get good at the dance, but in the end, form dictates function.

Non-profit Organization: Purpose Over Profit

Non-profit organizations, on the other hand, exist to serve the public good. While they can certainly make a profit—think universities and hospitals—they cannot distribute the profit; rather, it is reinvested into the organization to further its mission. Non-profit organizations benefit from being exempt from paying taxes, and donors benefit because financial gifts to the non-profit are tax-deductible. Individuals, foundations, and corporations can find it attractive to fund non-profits both for the social impact and the tax benefits they provide, even though there is no additional financial return. Non-profits, also called NGOs (non-governmental organizations), are afforded these benefits because they are working to solve problems that governments have not been able to solve on their own. However, because non-profits often rely on donations, in part or in full, their funding sources are often inconsistent and can't reach the scale of business investments. And because non-profits are technically owned by the public, they are subject to public transparency in reporting their financial and operational details.

While there are more than thirty different types of non-profit organizations recognized by the IRS, many seek to meet the requirements of Section 501(c)

(3) in the U.S. Internal Revenue code. This allows non-profit organizations such as charities, churches, and foundations to receive favorable tax treatment as long as they do not deviate from their stated mission.

Not to be confused with non-profit organizations, "not-for-profit" organizations are a different type of entity. Not-for-profit organizations are considered "recreational," are not necessarily focused on the public good, are run by volunteers, and are focused on the specific goals of the owner and its members—such as a private club or society. Regardless, each of these structures was created to maximize and incentivize their benefit to society.

While the non-profit structure was designed to produce social impact, these organizations often struggle to address a social issue at scale because of the limitations of their structure. In his popular 2013 TED talk "The Way We Think About Charity is Dead Wrong," Dan Pollata outlined five inherent limitations that non-profit organizations face when trying to accomplish their ambitious missions:

- Low compensation of staff.
- Aversion to advertising and marketing.
- Inability to take risks for innovation.
- Short time horizon for growth.
- Not enough profit to attract capital investments.[26]

These limitations—or "discrimination" as Pollata states—prevent non-profits from using the levers available to commercial businesses to truly put a dent in global issues. So, if neither the for-profit nor the non-profit structures are ideal for combining profit and purpose, what are entrepreneurs to do?

Both/And

While corporate social responsibility was revolutionizing the commercial business world over the last few decades, a parallel movement was also taking place. Despite the lack of a system built with them in mind, trail-blazing entrepreneurs who desired to tackle the world's most pressing challenges began creating businesses with a *primary* mission of social change. Beyond simply being responsible corporate citizens while producing their products or services, these entrepreneurs intentionally built their enterprises to tackle a specific problem that government, business, or charity had failed to solve. They weren't capitalizing on a market opportunity, they were tackling a market gap. And they needed profit to fulfill their purpose. This was the mission of the social enterprise.

---

26 Dan Pallotta, "The Way We Think About Charity Is Dead Wrong," TED, February 2013, www.ted.com/talks/dan_pallotta_the_way_we_think_about_charity_is_dead_wrong?language=en.

2 For Purpose

Social Enterprises

If the Shoe Model Fits

For many years, if you asked the average person for an example of a social enterprise there was a good chance they would cite TOMS Shoes. Founded by Blake Mycoskie in 2006, the TOMS brand burst into popularity because of their innovative "one-for-one" business model—for every pair of shoes they sold, one pair would be donated to a child in need.

After hustling through Argentina for Season 2 of *The Amazing Race*, Mycoskie later returned to the country for vacation and learned of a shoe distribution program for barefoot children. After volunteering, he was motivated to further support the cause. Inspired by the *alpargata*—a comfortable, affordable slip-on shoe native to the Argentinian people— Mycoskie developed a business idea and launched his company. With the social mission as the "sole" purpose, he manufactured *alpargatas* for the North American market, and for every pair sold he donated one to a child in a developing country.[1]

The brand exploded. Mycoskie's winsome personality, genuine social consciousness, keen marketing sense, and timely celebrity support—in the emerging era of social media—all connected with a generation just waiting to support social causes with their purchasing power. Americans gladly shelled out $48–78 for a pair of simple canvas shoes as a stylish act of compassion. By 2013, TOMS had $250 million in annual sales and had donated 10 million pairs of shoes in its first seven years. In 2014, the company was valued at $625 million.[2]

TOMS Shoes (shortened from "Tomorrow's Shoes") made Blake Mycoskie the poster boy for the emerging field of social enterprise—an approach that uses a profitable business model to fuel its primary mission of social impact. In contrast to a commercial business that might value

---

1 Irene Anna Kim, "How Toms Went from a $625 Million Company to Being Taken Over by its Creditors," *Insider*, December 27, 2020, www.busi nessinsider.com/rise-and-fall-of-toms-shoes-blake-mycoskie-bain-capita l-2020-3.
2 Ibid.

DOI: 10.4324/9781003325987-3

corporate social responsibility in support or extension of their products or services, a social enterprise does not exist except for the social mission it is designed to achieve.

As TOMS expanded its product line to include sunglasses, coffee, back-packs, and more, other companies began to jump on the one-for-one bandwagon. Traditional businesses like Sketchers tried to get in the game with their "Bobs" brand (and an even better one-for-two model); however, many saw this attempt as disingenuously opportunistic. Currently successful companies like Warby Parker (eyeglasses), Bombas (socks), and Soapbox (soap) all model their social enterprises on the buy-one-give-one philosophy and retain a primary focus on their social mission.

After the initial success of TOMS, cracks started to appear in the company's foundation. After a TOMS-commissioned study on the impact of their shoe-donation program showed no evidence of life-changing impact—and, in fact, a slight increase in dependency on outside aid and a modest negative impact on local shoe markets—the critics became louder.[3] Around the same time, Mycoskie decided to give up some control of the company in order to raise money for more rapid growth. He sold 50 percent of TOMS to Bain Capital in 2014, with Bain's commitment to continue the one-for-one model. After the sale, Mycoskie's personal wealth was valued at $300 million.[4] In 2019, TOMS transitioned away from the one-for-one model they pioneered and instead committed to donating $1 for every $3 in revenue in the form of "impact grants." Eventually, TOMS faced a $300 million loan due in 2020 that they were not in a position to pay, and a group of creditors took over the company, ending Mycoskie's ownership.

There are many lessons to be learned from both the rise and fall of TOMS Shoes. What propelled their success? What contributed to their challenges? We think it's important to consider these key questions: How do you build a profitable social enterprise driven by a compelling mission? How do you finance commercial success but structure the business so as to retain control? How do you grow into a large-scale enterprise while ensuring long-term sustainability? We will address all these questions, but first, let's examine the origins of the social entrepreneurship movement that paved the way for companies like TOMS.

A New Way to Change the World

People we now call social entrepreneurs have been at work for generations, perhaps millennia, but only in the last few decades have we had the language,

---

3 Bruce Wydick, "The Impact of Toms Shoes," *Across Two Worlds* (blog), March 16, 2015, www.acrosstwoworlds.net/the-impact-of-toms-shoes-on-kids/.

4 Blake Mycoskie, "Blake Mycoskie Conceived the Idea for TOMS Shoes While Sitting on a Farm, Pondering Life, in Argentina," *Insider*, 9/21/2011, www.businessinsider.com/blake-mycoskie-argentina-toms-shoes-2011-09.

frameworks, and networks for the growing field. In 2003, *New York Times* writer David Bornstein published what would become the authoritative history of the social entrepreneurship movement with, *How to Change the World: Social Entrepreneurs and the Power of New Ideas.*[5] In it, he documents the revolutionary work of systems-changing innovators like Florence Nightingale, whose indomitable will advanced the field of nursing, and Fabio Rosa, whose relentless collaboration brought low-cost electrification to rural Brazil. Bornstein also tells the story of Ashoka and its founder, Bill Drayton, who is credited with coining the term "social entrepreneur."

Drayton founded Ashoka—"Innovators for the Public"—in 1980 after stints with McKinsey and Company and the Environmental Protection Agency. He recognized the power of entrepreneurs to advance social progress and Ashoka focused on identifying, supporting, and connecting these innovators, mostly working alone and in obscurity, across the globe. Ashoka now has more than 4,000 fellows in more than 95 countries, making it the largest worldwide network of social entrepreneurs. Ashoka fellows are transforming systems that impact issues like poverty, healthcare, education, human rights, and the environment.

Drayton sets a high bar for social entrepreneurs. In his view, a social entrepreneur isn't someone who simply launches a local venture with a social mission. A social entrepreneur is a dedicated visionary who implements a systems-changing idea that is innovative, sustainable, and scalable. This is best captured in his often-quoted fishing metaphor: "Social entrepreneurs are not content just to give a fish or teach how to fish. They will not rest until they have revolutionized the fishing industry."[6]

The social entrepreneur goes beyond direct service, beyond empowerment, and into the realm of changing a field or an industry. Bornstein describes six characteristics that are common in social entrepreneurs:

- Willingness to self-correct.
- Willingness to share credit.
- Willingness to break free from established structures.
- Willingness to cross disciplinary boundaries.
- Willingness to work quietly.
- Strong ethical impetus.

Embodying these characteristics, social entrepreneurs relentlessly pursue their mission and do whatever it takes to achieve it.

5 David Bornstein, *How to Change the World: Social Entrepreneurs and the Power of New Ideas*, 2nd edition (Oxford: Oxford University Press, 2007).
6 Kathleen Kelly Janus, "Planting the Seeds for Social Startup Success: 10 Things to Remember When Starting a Social Enterprise," Porchlight, February 7, 2018, www.porchlightbooks.com/blog/changethis/2018/planting-the-seeds-for-social-startup-success-10-things-to-remember-when-starting-a-social-enterprise.

Around the same time Drayton was launching Ashoka, a university professor in Bangladesh was piloting a program that provided small loans to the rural poor. Starting with just $27 of his own money, he supported 42 women with interest-bearing loans, believing in the inherent dignity and entrepreneurial potential of all people—even those too poor to approach a bank. By 1983, Muhammad Yunus had launched Grameen Bank and was serving more than 28,000 Bangledeshis, successfully launching the concept of "microcredit." Yunus was awarded the Nobel Peace Prize in 2006. The following year Grameen loaned $6.38 billion to 7.4 million borrowers. Others followed the Grameen lead, and the global rise of microcredit fueled the idea that business, or "social business" as Yunus called it, could be a powerful mechanism for social change.

Support Systems Emerge

Yet another social force was spawned in the 1980s when the growth equity firm General Atlantic launched Echoing Green (named after a William Blake poem about creating a better world). This organization set out with a vision to invest in emerging leaders, providing seed funding and leadership development to accelerate their impact. The Echoing Green community now includes nearly 1,000 systems-changing social entrepreneurs in more than 80 countries who have launched bold new organizations like Teach for America, CityYear, and the One Acre Fund. Cheryl Dorsey, a former Echoing Green fellow, assumed leadership in 2002 and has since elevated the organization to new levels of influence and impact, particularly on the issue of racial justice. In 2021, Echoing Green launched a $75 million Racial Equity Philanthropic Fund and plans to launch and scale 500 social enterprises by 2024.[7]

In the late 1990s, Hilde Schwab and her husband Klaus—founder and chairman of the World Economic Forum—observed this new model for social change that, "combines the mission, dedication, and compassion to serve the most vulnerable and marginalized populations of society with business principles and the best techniques from the private sector."[8] They founded the Schwab Foundation for Social Entrepreneurship in 1998 to identify and support individuals and grow the collective social entrepreneurship community. Since its launch, the Schwab Foundation calculates that it has directly improved more than 722 million lives through its community of social innovators.[9]

---

7 "Racial Equity Philanthropic Fund," Echoing Green, accessed April 1, 2022, https://echoinggreen.org/racial-equity-philanthropic-fund.
8 Hilde Schwab, "Our Story," Schwab Foundation for Social Entrepreneurship, accessed April 2, 2022, www.schwabfound.org/about.
9 "Our Impact," Schwab Foundation for Social Entrepreneurship, accessed April 2, 2022, www.schwabfound.org/what-is-the-impact.

A year after the Schwab Foundation began, eBay's first full-time employee and president, Jeff Skoll, created what would become the Skoll Foundation to invest in social entrepreneurs. The foundation now grants $80 million per year, and its current endowment of more than $1 billion makes it the world's largest foundation for social entrepreneurship. The Skoll Foundation has fueled, among other things, the Skoll Awards for Social Entrepreneurship and the Skoll Centre for Social Entrepreneurship at the University of Oxford, which hosts the annual Skoll World Forum.

Other universities got in the game as well, as higher education caught the vision for preparing a new generation of social entrepreneurs. Ashoka launched Ashoka U in 2008 to catalyze a movement of colleges and universities that could advance the field of social entrepreneurship and help create an "everyone a changemaker" world. Since its founding, Ashoka U has engaged more than 600 colleges and universities, granting 51 the designation of a "Changemaker Campus" after a rigorous vetting process. Ashoka U's influence has supported and inspired more than 4,000 educators and administrators working to leverage higher education for the public good, and more than 2 million students who have gained skills in social innovation.

To support the growing field of practitioners, a group of six men formed The National Gathering for Social Entrepreneurship in 1998, which would later become the Social Enterprise Alliance (SEA). Recognizing the growing interest in social entrepreneurship in the U.S., yet with little structure and connection, SEA developed a membership model to champion and advance the sector. SEA now has more than 500 members connected to 18 chapters in 38 states.

These organizations, and many others, have played an important role igniting and leading the field of social entrepreneurship. But as the energy and momentum grew, so did confusion about the definition of social entrepreneurship.

Defining a Field

So what exactly is social entrepreneurship? Greg Dees, the late Faculty Director at Duke University's Center for the Advancement of Social Entrepreneurship, penned a seminal paper in 1998 that sought to answer the many questions directed at this exciting new field. "Many associate social entrepreneurship exclusively with not-for-profit organizations starting for-profit or earned-income ventures," wrote Dees. "Others use it to describe anyone who starts a not-for-profit organization. Still others use it to refer to business owners who integrate social responsibility into their operations. What does social entrepreneurship really mean?"[10]

---

10 J. Gregory Dees, "The Meaning of 'Social Entrepreneurship,'" Duke University Fuqua Center, last modified 5/30/2001, https://centers.fuqua.duke.edu/case/wp-content/uploads/sites/7/2015/03/Article_Dees_MeaningofSocialEntrepreneurship_2001.pdf.

Dees came to the conclusion that while commercial entrepreneurs and social entrepreneurs share many of the same character traits, for social entrepreneurs, "the social mission is explicit and central." "Mission-related impact becomes the central criterion, not wealth creation," Dees asserted. Whatever the structure (for-profit or non-profit) or funding source (revenue or donations), social entrepreneurs look for the most effective method of serving their social missions. In summary, Dees argued that social entrepreneurs play the role of change agents in the social sector by:

- Adopting a mission to create and sustain social value (not just private value).
- Recognizing and relentlessly pursuing new opportunities to serve that mission.
- Engaging in a process of continuous innovation, adaptation, and learning.
- Acting boldly without being limited by resources currently in hand.
- Exhibiting heightened accountability to the constituencies served and for the outcomes created.[11]

In 2007, Sally Osberg (Skoll Foundation President) and Roger Martin (Skoll Foundation board member) sought to build on Dees's work with their now-influential article "Social Entrepreneurship: A Case for Definition," published in the *Stanford Social Innovation Review*.[12] They also distinguished the social entrepreneur by the value proposition of the venture, focused on delivering large-scale social impact:

> Unlike the entrepreneurial value proposition that assumes a market that can pay for the innovation, and may even provide substantial upside for investors," they wrote, "the social entrepreneur's value proposition targets an underserved, neglected, or highly disadvantaged population that lacks the financial means or political clout to achieve the transformative benefit on its own.[13]

Martin and Osberg then summarized their three-pronged definition for social entrepreneurship:

1   Identifying a stable but inherently unjust equilibrium that causes the exclusion, marginalization, or suffering of a segment of humanity that lacks the financial means or political clout to achieve any transformative benefit on its own.

---

11 Ibid.
12 Roger L. Martin & Sally Osberg, "Social Entrepreneurship: A Case for Definition," *Stanford Social Innovation Review*, Spring 2007, doi:10.48558/tsav-fg11, https://ssir.org/articles/entry/social_entrepreneurship_the_case_for_definition.
13 Ibid.

2   Identifying an opportunity in this unjust equilibrium, developing a social value proposition, and bringing to bear inspiration, creativity, direct action, courage, and fortitude, thereby challenging the stable state's hegemony.

3   Forging a new, stable equilibrium that releases trapped potential or alleviates the suffering of the targeted group, and through imitation and the creation of a stable ecosystem around the new equilibrium ensuring a better future for the targeted group and even society at large.[14]

The rigorous and focused definitions presented by Dees, Martin, and Osberg, along with the similarly high bar set by Drayton, have helped distinguish social entrepreneurship from the myriad efforts for social good in both the for-profit and non-profit spheres.

So what, then, is a social enterprise? It would follow that a social enterprise is the entity formed by social entrepreneurs to pursue their social mission. The Social Enterprise Alliance suggests that social enterprises can span the spectrum of for-profit and non-profit entities, and offers this definition: "Social enterprises are organizations that address a basic unmet need or solve a social or environmental problem through a market-driven approach."[15] Because of the enterprising, market-driven nature of these social ventures, many pursue a revenue-generating strategy and are formed as for-profit companies.

Early field-defining work by Virtue Ventures offered this definition: "A social enterprise is defined as any business venture created for a social purpose—mitigating/reducing a social problem or a market failure—and to generate social value while operating with the financial discipline, innovation and determination of a private sector business."[16] Whatever the form it takes (we'll talk about legal structures later), a social enterprise means business, both in terms of accomplishing the mission and sustaining itself financially.

Virtue Ventures adapted a useful model to help explain where a social enterprise falls on the spectrum between traditional non-profit and traditional for-profit ventures, which we have further adapted here (Figure 2.1).[17] The approach of commercial businesses described in Chapter 1 fall on the right side of the spectrum, while explicitly mission-driven organizations fall on the left. Social enterprises fall in the middle of this spectrum because they are both mission-driven and business-savvy, attempting to integrate social and

14   Ibid.
15   David Pérez, "We Can't Go Back to Normal! Let's Talk about Social Enterprises," Ruh Global IMPACT, July 5, 2021, www.ruhglobal.com/we-ca nt-go-back-to-normal-lets-talk-about-social-enterprises/.
16   "Definitions of Social Enterprise," Virtue Ventures, accessed April 3, 2022, www.4lenses.org/setypology/definition.
17   "Hybrid Spectrum," Virtue Ventures, accessed April 3, 2022, www.4lenses. org/setypology/hybrid_spectrum.

THE HYBRID BALANCING ACT	NONPROFIT (PHILANTHROPIC)	SOCIAL ENTERPRISE (HYBRID)	FOR-PROFIT (COMMERCIAL)
▶ Motives	Public / Stakeholders	Balanced	Profit / Shareholders
▶ Methods	Mission-driven	Balanced	Market-driven
▶ Mission	Social value	Balanced	Economic value
▶ Money	Reinvested internally	Balanced	Distributed externally

Adapted and modified from Virtue Ventures[42]

Figure 2.1 The purpose–profit spectrum.

commercial activities sustainably. We'll dive into the hybrid concept in more detail in Chapter 3.

Social Enterprise Business Models

Now that we have an understanding of where social enterprises lie on the spectrum of organizational types, let's dive into their varying forms. There's certainly no one-size-fits all model—creativity is the rule when building a strategy to achieve a social mission. Social enterprises can be constructed in many ways, and it helps to think in terms of *operation* (how you create value) and *organization* (how you structure your efforts).

Operational Models

In terms of operational models, a social enterprise must first define its "theory of change." A theory of change is simply an articulation of the intended impact of the social enterprise, and the mechanism by which it will make that impact. In other words, how are you going to do the good you want to do? How does your intervention lead to the desired outcome? For example, if your social enterprise seeks to reduce homelessness in your community, you should be able to explain how your inputs (such as funding and staffing) and activities (such as shelter services and job training) will logically lead to your expected shorter-term outcomes (housing and employment) and the ultimate long-term impact of your efforts (fewer homeless people in your community). Your theory of change is typically expressed in a framework called a "logic model." The Social Enterprise Alliance recognizes three general operational models for a social enterprise:

1 *Transformative products or services*: This approach attempts to create impact through the actual products and services offered by the enterprise.
2 *Opportunity employment*: This approach focuses on hiring people who face barriers to employment for any reason—income, education, ability, etc.

3   *Donate back*: This approach prioritizes the contribution of profits by the social enterprise to a partner or affiliate organization to address the mission.[18]

These three models represent just a few of many; for a deeper list of nine models, see the categories created by Virtue Ventures.[19]

Organizational Models

In terms of organizational models, social enterprises can employ any legal structure available in their state or country, yet often face a dilemma in building an entity to maximize mission impact. As we discussed in Chapter 1, traditional legal structures were not built with the social enterprise in mind. For-profits need to maximize value and return profit to shareholders; non-profits need to pursue a charitable purpose to maximize value for society. For-profits can access equity capital markets to raise money; non-profits can offer tax benefits to donors. If a for-profit sacrifices revenue for the sake of societal goals, it risks neglecting its fiduciary responsibilities. If a non-profit seeks revenue-generating activities disconnected from its charitable purposes, it risks losing its tax-exempt status. This is the dilemma many social entrepreneurs face.

Social entrepreneurs can find success using one structure or the other, but choosing between a for-profit and non-profit model often makes them feel like one hand is tied behind their back. Fortunately, new legal options have emerged in the last decade that attempt to bridge the divide by protecting companies that want to prioritize societal benefits, and we'll highlight those in Chapter 3. Figure 2.2 shows the legal structures that are available or can operate in most states in the U.S.

Social entrepreneurs can also get very creative in how they blend profit and purpose. You can register as a non-profit organization and implement an earned-income strategy relevant to your mission. Alternatively, your non-profit can create a separate for-profit partner that generates revenue for the mission. As

NON-PROFIT STRUCTURES	HYBRID STRUCTURES	FOR-PROFIT STRUCTURES
501(c)3, 501(c)4, etc.	L3C, Benefit Corporation	C-Corp, S-Corp, LLC, Sole Proprietorship

Figure 2.2 Spectrum of social enterprise legal structures.

18   Henah Velez, "What Is a Social Enterprise?" The Good Trade, accessed April 5, 2022, www.thegoodtrade.com/features/what-is-a-social-enterprise.
19   "Operational Models," Virtue Ventures, accessed April 3, 2022, www.4lenses. org/setypology/models.

we've noted, you can register as a for-profit business that achieves its mission through its products and services. Or the for-profit business can create a separate non-profit entity through which it funds the social mission. We'll dive more deeply into these types of hybrid structures in the next chapter.

So how do you determine what structure is right for you? In his insightful article in the *Stanford Social Innovation Review* titled "For Love or Lucre," Jim Fruchterman offers advice as a veteran social entrepreneur who has used all kinds of legal structures:

> The first thing to remember is that the legal structure is simply a tool for accomplishing your goals. Deciding structure first may lock you into a direction that won't get you where you want to go. It is important to take the time to explore your idea first; then answering the legal structure question will be easier.[20]

Fruchterman suggests considering four areas that can help illuminate your structural direction: motivation, market, capital, and control. What is your motivation for starting the venture? What market are you targeting? How do you plan to raise capital? What type of control do you want over the venture? Here are the key questions he suggests asking for each category:

1   Motivation:

- How fundamental is the social mission?
- What are your personal financial objectives for this venture?
- How do you define success?

2   Market:

- Who are your customers?
- Who or what is your competition?
- What is your value proposition?
- What is your market size and how profitable could you be serving that market?

3   Capital:

- How much money do you need to get your venture launched?
- How much money will you need to keep the business growing?
- Will you have assets you could borrow against?
- Will tax structure affect your business significantly?

20 Jim Fruchterman, "For Love or Lucre," *Stanford Social Innovation Review*, Spring 2011, doi:10.48558/0f4k-za71, https://ssir.org/articles/entry/for_love_or_lucre.

4   Control:

- How important are confidentiality and secrecy to you and your venture?
- Can you run and fund your venture yourself?
- Will you need to share control with investors?
- Will you want or need to share control with the public interest?

After reflecting on these questions, you will be in a much better position to determine what structure is best for you. Let's take a look at some examples of social enterprises that have chosen either a for-profit or non-profit approach to building their mission-driven organizations.

For-Profit Structures

A social enterprise can choose to register as a traditional for-profit company (such as C-corp, S-corp, sole proprietorship, or LLC) and use any operational model to achieve its mission, within the constraints of its chosen legal structure. The for-profit social enterprise has the advantages of being able to raise money through equity for faster growth, the legitimacy that comes from a known business structure, and time-tested best practices for organizational management. On the other hand, the for-profit social enterprise is reliant on its leadership to stick to the social mission, it can't receive tax-deductible contributions or grants, it has to pay income and property taxes, and it has a duty to act in the best (financial) interest of its shareholders. Let's take a look at a one example of a for-profit social enterprise.

Example: FRDM

FRDM is a for-profit technology company that uses their enterprise software platform to root out modern-day slavery in the supply chains of businesses. Attacking their social mission directly through their product, FRDM is a "social tech company" with a mission to "improve the world by improving supply chain transparency."

I (Jeremy) have known Justin Dillion since the late 1990s when his first band caught my attention while working at a radio station in college. As his music career progressed and he began touring around the world, Dillon became aware of the issue of human trafficking. Feeling compelled to somehow address it, Dillon used what he knew—music—to rally other artists in support of the cause. The result was a successful and eye-opening 2008 rockumentary that featured artists (like Moby, Matisyahu, Cold War Kids), dignitaries (like Madeleine Albright, Cornel West, Nikolas Kristof) and undercover footage to expose the plight of 25 million modern-day slaves. The musician-turned-abolitionist was pleased, but not satisfied.

Dillon went on to launch SlaveryFootprint.org in 2011—at the request of the Obama Administration—to pose an uncomfortable question to consumers based on their buying habits: "How many slaves work for you?" Millions of people in more than 200 countries have used the site to learn the disturbing truth about forced labor in supply chains. Building on that momentum, Dillon formed a non-profit organization called Made in a Free World to advocate for supply chain transparency and raise money to rescue children in slavery. But he wanted to dig even deeper to get at the root of the issue. As the late Desmond Tutu once said, "There comes a point when we need to stop just pulling people out of the river—we need to go upstream and find out why they are falling in."[21]

As he explains in his powerful book, *A Selfish Plan to Change the World*,[22] Dillon realized that going upstream meant using the force of the market itself to combat the multi-billion-dollar industry of modern-day slavery. So he started a business. If FRDM could fill the gaping hole in supply chain transparency, maybe he could work with businesses—some of the largest in the world—to create a new equilibrium that prevents people from falling into the constant stream of forced labor.

FRDM built the world's first product genome database that allows companies to input their spend data to understand and fix their risk factors, effectively "liberating supply chains with ground-breaking transparency technology." Companies like Virgin, Accenture, Boeing, SAP, and many others are on board in the modern-day fight against slavery simply by purchasing the FRDM software as a good business decision. For Dillon, business has been the most effective tool to achieve his mission.

Non-Profit Structures

A social enterprise may want the benefits of a non-profit entity to pursue its mission. It's important to remember that "non-profit" does *not* mean that the organization can't generate a large amount of profit, or receive significant funding. A non-profit model can be advantageous because it can receive tax-deductible donations and philanthropic grants, it is not taxed on mission-related income, it benefits from the reputation of a charitable organization, and it by nature prioritizes the social mission in its governance. That said, it's limited in access to capital, fundraising can be uncertain and inconsistent, and it doesn't have the same market tools for sustainability and scalability. Here's a good example.

---

21 "Desmond Tutu Mind-Blowing Quotes Will Make You Appreciate That He Was Not Just a Religious Leader," Sabasabaupdates.com, December 26, 2021, https://sabasabaupdates.com/2021/12/26/desmond-tutu-mind-blowing-quotes-will-make-you-appreciate-that-he-was-not-just-a-religious-leader/.
22 Justin Dillon, *A Selfish Plan to Change the World: Finding Big Purpose in Big Problems* (Nashville, TN: Thomas Nelson, 2017).

Example: Goodwill Industries

Because it's been around for 120 years, we can miss the brilliant concept behind the Goodwill Industries model. Instead of throwing away those unwanted items cluttering up your house—clothes, toys, electronics—you can simply drop them off at your friendly neighborhood Goodwill. They gladly accept the free inventory and subsequently sort, stock, and sell it for profit at their stores. The income supports their mission to, "help people overcome challenges to build skills, find jobs and grow their careers through the power of work." In 2020, Goodwill generated $5.8 billion in revenue, and only relied on $350 million in private donations.[23]

Founded in 1902 by Rev. Edgar J. Helms, a Methodist minister, the effort began by collecting used household goods and clothing in upscale neighborhoods in Boston. Helms then employed poor workers to fix up the donated items, which were sold or given away. He considered the model "a hand up, not a hand out." Helms described Goodwill as an "industrial program as well as a social service enterprise … a provider of employment, training and rehabilitation for people of limited employability, and a source of temporary assistance for individuals whose resources were depleted."[24]

The model has worked. There are now 165 Goodwill locations across the U.S., Canada, and twelve other countries. Each location is locally controlled and operated, formed as an independent non-profit with its own board of directors made up of community volunteers. In 2020, Goodwill stores in the U.S. provided 126,938 people with jobs and helped more than 1 million others build skills and find employment. In doing so, Goodwill diverted 3.3 billion pounds of usable goods from landfills.[25]

While social enterprises can find success using either the for-profit or non-profit models, neither were built with the idea of blending profit and purpose. Recently we have seen the rise of hybrid models that effectively and efficiently combine the two. They deserve a closer look.

23 William P. Barrett, "The World's Top 100 Charities," Forbes, last modified December 16, 2021, www.forbes.com/lists/top-charities/?sh=7105bd9e5f50.

24 "01 About Us," Goodwill, accessed April 3, 2022, www.goodwill.org/about-us/goodwills-history/.

25 "2020 Annual Report," Goodwill, accessed April 22, 2022, www.goodwill.org/annual-report/.

3 Combining Profit and Purpose
Hybrid Social Enterprises

Recent college graduates are well-schooled in the hybrid life. They've taken hybrid classes, attended hybrid events, and probably landed their first hybrid job—for which they drive to work (half the time) in their hybrid car. Even before the COVID-19 pandemic, the term "hybrid" was used to describe a blurring of boundaries, whether for educational formats, employment structures, musical genres, or biological species. It's no surprise that the ubiquitous term has also been ascribed to social enterprises that seek to blend profit and purpose. But what is the definition of a hybrid social enterprise? Is it simply one that seeks simultaneous social and financial objectives? Or is it one that is funded strategically by both donors and revenue? Or is a hybrid social enterprise one that uses a specific legal structure(s) to organize its double bottom-line efforts?

While teaching social entrepreneurship for the last decade, I (Jeremy) have seen little in the way of guidance for practitioners or students who wish to pursue a hybrid structure for their social enterprise. Other educators have noticed as well. In 2019, a group of prominent social entrepreneurship faculty and scholars (Mitra, Kikul, Gundry, and Orr) authored a paper entitled "The Rise of Hybrids: A Note for Social Entrepreneurship Educators."[1] It exposed "a hole in the literature with regard to the instruction and development of social entrepreneurs and others interested in hybrid organizing." We will address this gap, in part, in the following pages.

In a generic sense, all social enterprises—including the ones profiled in Chapter 2—can be considered hybrid because they attempt to combine both profit and purpose through their operation, regardless of their funding or legal structures. Figure 3.1 illustrates this reality, showing the balancing act any social enterprise undertakes.

Recognizing the growth of social ventures attempting the hybrid balance, the *Stanford Social Innovation Review* published an article in 2012 called "In Search of the Hybrid Ideal." The authors, representing researchers from

---

1 P. Mitra, J. Kickul, L. Gundry, and J. Orr, "The Rise of Hybrids: A Note for Social Entrepreneurship Educators." *International Review of Entrepreneurship*, 17 (2) (2019): article 1601, pp. 107–126.

DOI: 10.4324/9781003325987-4

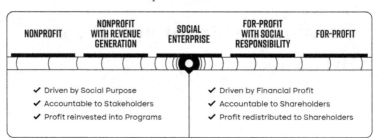

Figure 3.1 The hybrid balancing act.

Harvard Business School and Echoing Green, did the first large-scale, quantitative study of social entrepreneurs who were integrating aspects of non-profits and for-profits in their social enterprise. They defined hybrid organizations as: "enterprises that design their business models based on the alleviation of a particular social or environmental issue. They generate income and attract capital in ways that may be consistent with for-profit models, non-profit models, or both."[2]

Based on the study of more than 3,500 Echoing Green fellowship applications, they found significant growth in the number of ventures that combined earned revenue with donations. Almost 50 percent relied on this form of hybrid model in 2011—up from 37 percent in 2006. A review of recent Echoing Green data reveals a continuing trend. In 2020, 62 percent of applicants were incorporating earned revenue into their organizational models.[3] While this study did not reveal which specific legal structures these social enterprises chose, it is notable that revenue-generation has continued to grow as the preferred method of funding. It stands to reason that social entrepreneurs are also looking for the best vehicles with which to drive their mission-based, income-generating organizations. Let's consider some advantages and challenges of the general hybrid approach before diving into specific hybrid legal structures.

Advantages of Hybrid Social Enterprises

One of the key advantages of combining profit and purpose is mission integration. "In Search of the Hybrid Ideal," describes the ultimate goal:

> This hypothetical organization is fully integrated—everything it does produces both social value and commercial revenue. In the hybrid

2 Julie Battilana, Matthew Lee, John Walker, and Cheryl Dorsey, "In Search of the Hybrid Ideal," *Stanford Social Innovation Review*, Summer 2012, doi:10.48558/wf5m-8q69, https://ssir.org/articles/entry/in_search_of_the_hybrid_ideal.
3 Ben Beers, "State of Social Entrepreneurship 2020," Echoing Green, last modified March 30, 2020, https://echoinggreen.org/news/state-of-social-entrepreneurship-2020.

ideal, managers do not face a choice between mission and profit, because these aims are integrated in the same strategy. More important, the integration of social and commercial value creation enables a virtuous cycle of profit and reinvestment in the social mission that builds large-scale solutions to social problems.

Therein lies the value and potential of a hybrid approach—sustainability and scalability. No longer does a social entrepreneur have to tackle complex social challenges without the tools of the market. These tools serve as levers that ratchet up bigger and longer-term impact, and they do it more quickly and consistently. Revenue-generation as a core or supplemental strategy reduces reliance on donations, increases economic stability, and allows for growth and expansion in pursuit of the mission.

Not only does the move toward hybridization benefit the mission of the social enterprise, it also inspires other organizations on either end of the profit-purpose spectrum to find ways to blend the two. Traditional non-profits integrate financial value creation while traditional for-profits integrate social value creation. The hybridization movement has the power to move the needle toward greater impact across all organizational types.

Challenges for Hybrid Social Enterprises

Pursuing the hybrid ideal, however, is not without risks. The authors of "The Rise of Hybrids"[4] identify some of the challenges that typical hybrid social enterprises face. The first obvious danger is the conflict that can arise when trying to balance the motives, methods, mission, and money noted in Figure 3.1. "In their quest to incorporate incompatible logics and coalesce antagonistic practices, the stronger logic often tends to prevail and fight over the weaker logic," write the authors. "Thus, competing logics in hybrid social entrepreneurial ventures create stringent demands and operational tensions in the organization, where either the market logic wins over the social-welfare logic, or vice versa." Another challenge noted is the difficulty hiring staff who, based on their experience and education, tend to fall on either side of the hybrid framework with their expertise.

As a result of this tension, a significant challenge is "mission drift." Mission drift happens when competing priorities steer an enterprise off course from fulfilling its core objective. For a social enterprise, this often happens when the necessary pursuit of profit overtakes the reason for which it is making profit. It's also possible for a social enterprise to err on the side of its social mission and neglect generating the revenue it needs to survive. "Tensions and drift in mission tend to occur while intermingling paradoxical ideas of market dynamics with social purpose that is traditionally associated with non-profits or charities," write the authors of "In Search of

4 Mitra et al., "The Rise of Hybrids."

the Hybrid Ideal."[5] Even practitioners in the field of microfinance, a model built on the mission to empower the poor, have fallen prey to the lure of the billions that can be made from small loans.

In their 2015 article "Making Hybrids Work," Santos, Pache, and Birkholz note that the main difficulty is getting hybrids to align their profit-generating activities with their impact-generating activities.[6] "Despite the evidence of societal impact, research suggests that hybrids are fragile organizations that run the risk of internal tensions and mission drift due to holding incompatible goals, and they may find it difficult to achieve financial sustainability." And even when social enterprise leaders manage to avoid mission drift, they have difficulty finding a home within the system built for traditional organizations. There is hope, however. Progress has been made in the last decade in providing structural options to help a social enterprise balance profit and purpose. These options include Single-Entity Legal Structures and Combination Structures.

Single-Entity Legal Structures for Hybrid Social Enterprises

Social enterprises in many U.S. states can now choose single-entity for-profit business structures that were designed to support the pursuit of social goals and alleviate the aforementioned challenges. About a decade into the new millennium, states began adopting legislation for legal entities that promised to bridge the profit-purpose divide. Enter the L3C and the benefit corporation.

Low-Profit Limited Liability Company (L3C)

In 2008, Vermont was the first state to offer the option to incorporate as a low-profit limited liability company. The L3C combines the legal and tax flexibility of a traditional LLC with the social purpose of a non-profit organization. The L3C is by definition obligated to put its social mission first in the pursuit of "charitable or educational" objectives, but may not pursue political or legislative purposes. Despite the awkward inclusion of "low-profit" in the name, the L3C was designed to help for-profit companies—especially those with lower revenue—attract investments that support the mission.

The L3C, which is relatively simple to launch and flexible to manage, can access capital unavailable to a non-profit. The structure is designed to attract foundations or other institutions that want to invest in the social outcomes of the enterprise and have less expectation for a high return. One of the primary selling points of the L3C is its ability to receive program-related investments, or PRIs, from private foundations who are required to distribute 5

---

5 Battilana et al., "In Search of the Hybrid Ideal."
6 Filipe Santos, Anne-Claire Pache, and Christoph Birkholz, "Making Hybrids Work," *California Management Review*, April 2015.

percent of their assets each year. A PRI can come in the form of an equity investment, loan, or line of credit, as long as it aligns with one or more of the foundation's exempt purposes. Investing in an L3C gives the foundation a possible return on their (higher-risk) investment—something traditional grant-making does not provide. This could subsequently motivate other investors to participate as well. L3Cs also gain the reputational brand advantage of being both a legitimate business and a public benefit.

Marc Lane, a Chicago-based attorney, author, and pioneer of L3C legislation, summarized the benefits this way:

> An L3C can share risk and leverage co-investment, attracting traditional financial players to a social venture which would otherwise be unattractive to them. At the same time, it invites a flexible governance structure which can harmonize the disparate interests of non-profit, foundation and for-profit stakeholders.[7]

Currently 11 states allow for the creation of L3Cs, and as of 2020 there were 1,700 L3Cs nationwide. Most states had passed their L3C legislation by 2012, indicating that momentum may have stalled in the past decade.

More recently, a small number of states have adopted a variation of the L3C—the "benefit LLC"—which provides a similar structure as the L3C and requires public reporting on its impact. Delaware is the most recent of six states to pass benefit LLC legislation, which is significant because of its outsized influence in business creation. It's important to note that even if your state doesn't offer the option of an L3C or benefit LLC, you can incorporate elsewhere and do business in your home state.

Despite the benefits, some leaders in the field debate the necessity of L3Cs and benefit LLCs, given the general flexibility of the LLC structure to include purpose-driven objectives. In addition, the IRS has yet to officially confirm that all L3Cs qualify for PRIs, which can mean a time-consuming and costly process for foundations that want to verify that the IRS will sanction their investments.

Example: Verde L3C

Verde, one of the first L3Cs formed in Illinois in 2010, is an energy-efficiency company that helps businesses "find, implement and maintain energy-efficient solutions that make a measurable impact on the bottom line." By replacing outdated methods with more efficient and modern solutions, Verde pursues its

---

7 Marc Lane, "The Low-Profit Limited Liability Company (L3C)," The Law Offices of Marc J. Lane, February 25, 2010, www.google.com/url?sa=t&rct=j&q=&esrc=s&source=web&cd=&ved=2ahUKEwj6-ML-vZX7AhW-GD QIHXT7BYkQFnoECBIQAQ&url=https%3A%2F%2Fwww.marcjlane.com%2Fclientuploads%2FArticles%2FMarc-Lane-basic_l3c_primer.pdf&usg=AOvVa w0rxF0EKLJm2L1UXHRDKnZA.

environmental mission through its business operations—and it continues to grow in profitability. Birthed out of Chicago's startup incubator 1871, the L3C structure immediately resonated with Verde's leadership and they chose it, in part, to enhance their brand. They remain proud of their L3C designation, stating, "We stress protecting the environment and our mission over profit, but we still believe in profit as the solution, not the problem."[8]

Benefit Corporation

In 2010, Maryland was the first state to pass legislation for another kind of legal entity designed to balance purpose with profit—the benefit corporation, or public benefit corporation. This option is now available in 37 states and Puerto Rico, and about 4,000 businesses have registered.[9] Internationally, legislation has passed in Italy, Colombia, Ecuador, and Canada (British Columbia), with Australia, Argentina, and Chile considering it.[10]

A benefit corporation is designed to protect and further a company's social mission by reducing liability, increasing accountability, attracting talent, and providing access to capital. In terms of structure, a benefit corporation has more management and reporting requirements than an L3C, just as a C-corp is more involved than an LLC, but it also better serves the needs of larger purpose-driven corporations. A benefit corporation is organized and taxed much like an S-corp or a C-corp.

A benefit corporation provides a company the legal protection to prioritize its social purpose in addition to its financial purpose. Directors and officers are required by law to consider the effect of decisions on stakeholders—employees, suppliers, customers, the community, the environment—as well as shareholders. As a mission-driven for-profit business, the benefit corporation is attractive to impact investors who look for long-term accountability to the mission while also looking for a good return on investment. The structure is designed to keep the mission intact when raising money, during leadership changes, and even after an initial public offering (IPO).

As part of its requirement for transparency, a benefit corporation must release an annual report to inform the public about how it is meeting the general and specific public purposes for which it exists. This report also informs the company's directors as they seek to align day-to-day decisions with the mission. Benefit corporations are required to use one of many

8   "Here's What's Happening," Verde, accessed April 2, 2022, www.verde.exp ert/why-we-believe-in-being-an-l3c-company.
9   C. Kannel, M. Samali, "Startups: Should You Incorporate as a Public Benefit Corporation?", Venture Beat, accessed April 3, 2022, https://venturebeat.com/ 2017/04/30/startups-should-you-incorporate-as-a-public-benefit-corporation. "State by State Status of Legislation," Benefit Corporation, accessed April 3, 2022, https://benefitcorp.net/policymakers/state-by-state-status.
10 "International Legislation," Benefit Corporation, accessed April 3, 2022, http s://benefitcorp.net/international-legislation.

sanctioned third-party assessments to gauge their overall social or environmental performance. B Lab, the non-profit organization that certifies B Corps, provides a free version of the B Impact Assessment for benefit corporations to use for their reports.

Speaking of B Corps, it bears repeating that choosing to register your business using the legal structure of a benefit corporation is separate from becoming a Certified B Corporation (or B Corp), as described in Chapter 1. The B Corp certification is a third-party stamp of approval, much like certification for organic or fair-trade products, and is based on B Lab's impact assessment tool. A benefit corporation is the legal form that a company chooses to use when registering its business with its state or jurisdiction. A benefit corporation is not required to pursue B Corp certification, although a company may desire to do so. A certified B Corp, however, is asked to make a commitment to change its legal structure to a benefit corporation, or similar, if available in its jurisdiction, or to modify its existing Articles of Incorporation. A business of any size or legal structure in any state or country can pursue B Corp certification by meeting a certain score on the B Impact Assessment, which ranks a company based on its impact on its workers, community, and the environment.

Example: Patagonia

When it comes to environmentally focused businesses, outdoor apparel company Patagonia leads the pack. On the very first day the option became available in the state of California, Patagonia registered as a benefit corporation. For more than 40 years, the clothing leader has focused its efforts on environmental conservation and activism. Its mission states: "We're in business to save our home planet." As part of its registration as a benefit corporation, Patagonia defined six "benefit purposes" which it reports on annually:

- 1 percent for the planet (donations to environmental organizations).
- Build the best product with no unnecessary harm.
- Conduct operations causing no unnecessary harm.
- Share best practices with other companies.
- Transparency.
- Provide a supportive work environment.[11]

In late 2022, Patagonia founder Yvon Chouinard made big news when he went even further to fight climate change. Bothered that Forbes had listed him as a billionaire, the 83-year-old restructured the company to effectively give it away, and to ensure the mission would never die. "As of now, Earth is

---

11 "Annual Benefit Corporation Report," Patagonia Works, accessed April 8, 2022, www.patagonia.com/on/demandware.static/-/Library-Sites-PatagoniaShared/default/dwf14ad70c/PDF-US/PAT_2019_BCorp_Report.pdf.

our only shareholder," Patagonia announced. "ALL profits, in perpetuity, will go to our mission to 'save our home planet'."[12] The Chouinard family and a team of lawyers restructured the ownership of the company, creating a trust and a non-profit that together would determine control of the company, protection of the mission, and direction of the profits. Patagonia explains:

> Here's how it works: 100% of the company's voting stock transfers to the Patagonia Purpose Trust, created to protect the company's values; and 100% of the nonvoting stock had been given to the Holdfast Collective, a nonprofit dedicated to fighting the environmental crisis and defending nature. The funding will come from Patagonia: Each year, the money we make after reinvesting in the business will be distributed as a dividend to help fight the crisis.[13]

This is exactly the type of creative disruption that's needed—and it's the essence of the tandem hybrid vision that we'll discuss in Chapter 4.

Combination Structures for Hybrid Social Enterprises

As Patagonia recognized, despite all the options—including those designed for social enterprises —sometimes single structures are still limiting. Fortunately, existing options can be combined to create a hybrid structure that binds two organizations together to create something greater. While the best-of-both-worlds approach also has its unique complexities, it allows the social entrepreneur to maximize the benefits from each structure while avoiding the drawbacks. Need to raise capital to grow your operations? Do that through your for-profit entity. Want to accept donations and reduce your tax burden? Do that through your non-profit entity. This approach requires paying close attention to the legal requirements of each entity (and having a good lawyer), but combining legal structures can be a powerful approach. The options are only limited by your creativity, but here are two popular combinations.

Non-Profit with a For-Profit Subsidiary

Since the 2008 recession, and with the ongoing volatility of the market, non-profit organizations have, out of necessity, become more comfortable with generating revenue to fund their mission. One of the challenges of a revenue-generating non-profit is avoiding UBIT—unrelated business

---

12 Erin McCormick, "Patagonia's Billionaire Owner Gives Away Company to Fight Climate Crisis," *The Guardian*, September 15, 2022, www.theguardian.com/us-news/2022/sep/14/patagonias-billionaire-owner-gives-away-company-to-fight-climate-crisis-yvon-chouinard.
13 Yvon Chouinard, "Earth Is Now Our Only Shareholder," www.patagonia.com/ownership.

income tax. A non-profit needs to pay tax on any income that's not related to its public purpose. If it generates too much unrelated business income (UBI) or allows staff to spend too much time on unrelated purposes, it risks losing its tax-exempt status. Therefore, some non-profits have chosen to create a subsidiary for-profit entity to avoid this challenge. The L3C structure is an attractive option as a for-profit subsidiary of a non-profit parent.

The for-profit company is free to conduct its business, related or not, and donate money back (after taxes) to the non-profit. The donation isn't considered taxable income for the non-profit. Operating a for-profit allows better access to capital in a variety of forms, including investments and debt, which allows for faster growth for the business and in turn more income for the non-profit. The for-profit also has more freedom when hiring and compensating skilled employees, including the use of stock, without the need to disclose information to the public as a non-profit is required to do. Containing the for-profit activities in a subsidiary also reduces the liability for the non-profit parent should something go wrong with the business.

In terms of ownership, a non-profit can control the for-profit by holding a majority (or all) the stock, and therefore control the board of directors. This ensures the profit-generating function continues to fulfill the mission of the non-profit. This ownership capability applies only to non-profits that are designated as public charities, not to private foundations, as we will later show. Board leadership, however, cannot be shared between the non-profit and the for-profit, save for a few overlapping members. The best practice is to keep operations and boards separate, or at "arms-length," to avoid any perceived or actual conflict of interest in decision-making. Both boards are required to approve any transactions between the two entities.

Example: The Omidyar Network

In 1995, the 28-year-old Pierre Omidyar launched a website called AuctionWeb as a person-to-person purchasing portal for collectibles. By 1996, the site was hosting more than 800,000 auctions a day. Omidyar changed the name to eBay, and the company's IPO in 1998 made him a billionaire. In 2021, Forbes ranked him as the 24th-richest person in the world with an estimated net worth of 21.8 billion. Pierre and his wife Pam turned their attention to philanthropy, and in 1999 formed the Omidyar Family Foundation. Despite deploying thousands of grants through this non-profit structure, the Omidyars wanted to scale their philanthropy like they had scaled eBay's business platform to millions of entrepreneurs. They looked for a new structure to power their giving.

In 2004 they launched the Omidyar Network, a hybrid structure that includes a for-profit LLC and a foundation. This new dual entity enabled for-profit investing and non-profit grantmaking with their "impact first, tools second" approach. As noted on the Omidyar website: "This novel structure allowed us to support early-stage organizations that catalyzed economic and social change, and the autonomy to work flexibly across the returns continuum."[14] The Omidyar Network began investing in sector-specific organizations to address systems-level issues and eventually began spinning off separate entities as part of a larger collective called the Omidyar Group. Since inception, the Omidyar network has invested more than $1.64 billion in social change organizations, with $751 million in for-profit investments and $893 million in non-profit grants.

For-Profit with a Non-Profit Partner

On the flipside, a for-profit social enterprise may find it advantageous to form a non-profit partner. The for-profit does not own the non-profit (non-profits are "owned" by the public), but it can effectively control the non-profit with the right structure. If the management of social impact activities becomes too complicated within the for-profit structure, forming separate entities allows the business to focus on profit generation while the non-profit handles the social programs. This also expands the social enterprise's access to funding through donations and grants to the non-profit.

With the rapid expansion of corporate social responsibility programs, many businesses have considered forming separate entities to support their charitable and philanthropic efforts. This often comes in the form of a corporate foundation. While many of these traditional companies wouldn't fit our narrow definition of a social enterprise—having a social purpose as the primary reason for existing—they are steering their efforts toward greater social impact. And because of the amount of revenue they generate, the impact through their foundations can be very significant (we highlight some examples in Part III). Forward-thinking social entrepreneurs could choose to design their enterprise with this structure from the outset.

When deciding to register for a non-profit 501(c)3 designation, there are a few options based on the type of structure, funding, and control desired. Most organizations go the route of a public charity, which is an organization that runs programs and activities to carry out mission-oriented work. A second option is to register as a private foundation, which is typically formed to fund other charities that are doing the mission-oriented work. A third and less common form is a private operating foundation, which blends the previous two options to allow a private foundation to run its own charitable programs beyond grant-making.[15]

Public charities are meant to serve the public, so they need to receive a good amount of their support, at least 33 percent, from the general public

14 "Omidyar Network's Journey," Omidyar Network, accessed April 5, 2022, https://omidyar.com/omidyar-networks-journey.
15 Greg McRay, "Non-Profit Structure: Public Charity, Private Foundation, or Private Operating Foundation?", CEO's Blog (blog), Foundation Group, September 29, 2016, www.501c3.org/non-profit-structure-public-charity-priva te-foundation-private-operating-foundation.

rather than major donors like corporations or foundations. In addition, they can't have more than 50 percent of their board related by blood or marriage, or connected through business partnerships, and must ensure that no one on the board benefits from their insider position. A public charity structure may be the non-profit of choice for social enterprises that wants to run their own programs and have control over their social outcomes, while utilizing their for-profit parent to fund the operation. This requires the extra effort of setting up, governing, and reporting on two separate entities, but the synergy could be worth it.

Private foundations benefit from greater control and can be led and funded by a single person, a family, or a company. A company that forms a private foundation may want to use it to provide grants to other non-profits, to match the charitable giving of employees, or to set up a scholarship fund for employees' family members. The Google Foundation, for example, carries out the charitable, educational, or scientific purposes of Google, Inc. Such corporate foundations allow a business to build up philanthropic reserves or endowments during a season of profitability, and avoid the challenges that budget cycles present for direct corporate giving programs. The only requirement is that private foundations must distribute 5 percent of their assets each year. If a company is ready to take on the additional compliance obligations, has the capacity to manage grant-making activities, and will work to oversee the more complicated governance procedures, then a for-profit with a non-profit partner could be a compelling option.[16]

Example: Newman's Own

One of the more recognizable hybrid entities is Newman's Own, the for-profit salad dressing company famous for donating 100 percent of its profits to charity. In 1980, Hollywood actor Paul Newman and his friend A. E. Hotchner concocted a homemade salad dressing, put it in wine bottles, and gave it as Christmas gifts. The positive response led to the launch of the Newman's Own brand in 1982. That year the company brought in $300,000 in profit, and Newman said: "Let's give it all away to those who need it."[17] The brand expanded with pasta sauce, microwave popcorn, salsa, and lemonade, and in the first decade Newman's Own had given away $50 million to various non-profit organizations.

To more effectively manage his philanthropy, the Newman's Own Foundation was established in 2005 as a non-profit partner to the for-profit business, ensuring the company's giving would continue. It has. More than

16 Karen Wu, "Should Our Company Establish and Corporate Foundation?", Perlman and Perlman, August 29, 2019, www.perlmanandperlman.com/company-establish-corporate-foundation.
17 "History," Newman's Own Foundation, accessed April 2, 2022, https://newmansownfoundation.org/about-us/history.

$570 million has been contributed in the form of grants to non-profit organizations in all 50 states and 31 countries. Paul Newman's main mission was generosity—he didn't have a specific social cause he was trying to address. The foundation now focuses on encouraging philanthropy, helping children with life-limiting conditions, empowerment, and nutrition. The combination structure was best suited to his goals.

When Newman died in 2008, he gifted his ownership shares of the business to the foundation, making the foundation the sole owner of the company. The only problem was that the IRS does not allow a private foundation to own more than 20 percent of the voting shares of a business (known as "excess business holdings") without the penalty of an eventual 200 percent tax. During the five-year grace period before the penalty was enforced, Newman's Own advocated strongly for a change to the rules. Fortunately, the Philanthropic Enterprise Act was signed into law as part of the Bipartisan Budget Act of 2018. This grants a very narrow exception for a foundation to own, by gift or bequest, 100 percent of the voting stock of a company that distributes all its net operating income to the foundation.

Pros and Cons of Combining Structures

In his article, "For Love or Lucre," Jim Fruchterman succinctly summarizes the advantages and disadvantages of the multi-structure approach.[18]

Advantages:

- The non-profit and the for-profit entities each retain the advantages that are unique to those legal structures.
- Creating a subsidiary can protect the non-profit status of the parent by removing the unrelated income (if it becomes too large relative to the parent's size).
- The subsidiary shields the parent from liabilities arising from the subsidiary's activities.
- The for-profit subsidiary can be sold at the non-profit's discretion.

Disadvantages:

- Once assets are in the non-profit, they are locked into the non-profit sector and can't be transferred back to the for-profit.
- Shutting down the non-profit affiliate requires its net assets to be transferred to another non-profit.

18 Jim Fruchterman, "For Love or Lucre," *Stanford Social Innovation Review*, Spring 2011, doi:10.48558/0f4k-za71, https://ssir.org/articles/entry/for_love_or_lucre.

- Care needs to be taken that benefits flow from the for-profit to the non-profit, and not the reverse, and that charitable restrictions are respected.
- If the for-profit is the main source of funding for the non-profit, it can be difficult to diversify the funding base of the non-profit.
- Additional overhead for two organizations.

A Pharmaceutical Social Enterprise

When Scott Boyer wanted to address the global issue of undiagnosed and untreated epilepsy, he could have chosen any model. He could have created a non-profit that helped individuals with epilepsy mitigate the risks, stigma, and lack of access to medication in their communities. He could have formed a for-profit company that donated a percentage of profits to NGOs that address the issue. He could even have created a social enterprise that employed people with epilepsy to give them education, training, and income. But instead, from the beginning, Boyer wanted to design a structure that had the potential to impact the global epilepsy issue at scale. He decided to form two separate entities that together could be high-profit and high-purpose—OWP Pharmaceuticals and the ROW Foundation. This powerful combination is an example of what we call the "tandem hybrid."

4   The Next Level

Tandem Hybrid Social Enterprises

The "hybrid ideal" discussed in the previous chapter is not hypothetical. Scott Boyer and his team started a hybrid social enterprise in 2014. This chapter is an overview of their tandem hybrid model, illustrated by OWP Pharmaceuticals and the ROW Foundation.

The word tandem means, "A relationship between two persons or things involving cooperative action and mutual dependence." It is often associated with a tandem bicycle, which is a bike designed to be ridden in tandem by two or more persons. The frame, seats, and drivetrain are arranged to maximize the efforts of the riders. Two cyclists on a tandem bike can go faster than they could on separate bikes. "On conventional tandems," notes one description, "the front rider steers as well as pedals the bicycle and is known as the captain, pilot, or steersman; the rear rider only pedals and is known as the stoker, navigator or rear admiral. On most tandems the two sets of cranks are mechanically linked by a timing chain and turn at the same rate."[1]

You can't stretch a metaphor too far, but we can use the tandem bike as a picture for the tandem hybrid model. The two riders are the for-profit and non-profit entities. It's a little tricky to say which rider is which entity. One could argue that the rear rider, the stoker, is the head-down, pedaling power engine (business profit), and the front rider, the pilot, steers the bike (social vision). Or you could see the for-profit as the pilot who sets the course and provides a wind break for the non-profit. In this case, we consider the for-profit business, OWP, to be the front rider—taking on the headwinds of the market and driving the profit. The non-profit, ROW, is the back rider—pedaling hard and staying focused on the mission. Either way, the important aspect is that the two are structurally linked and working together in "mutual dependence."

---

1 "Tandem Bicycle," Wikipedia, last modified December 17, 2021, https://en. wikipedia.org/wiki/Tandem_bicycle.

DOI: 10.4324/9781003325987-5

Similar But Different

The tandem hybrid social enterprise is similar to, but different from, other social enterprises. In presenting this model, we aren't critiquing or disparaging other models. Traditional social enterprises can make a significant impact, as can socially responsible businesses and charitable organizations. Anything that moves people or businesses to address injustice or improve the lives of the disadvantaged is good. Many new approaches to social enterprises are being tried and found successful, as documented in the *Stanford Social Innovation Review* article:

> Rather than take a non-profit model and add a commercial revenue stream—or take a for-profit model and add a charity or service program—Hot Bread Kitchen's integrated hybrid model produces both social value and commercial revenue through a single, unified strategy. Hot Bread Kitchen exemplifies a larger trend among social innovators toward creating hybrid organizations that primarily pursue a social mission but rely significantly on commercial revenue to sustain operations.[2]

However, as another research paper shows,

> while expanding the social enterprise field to achieve greater benefits has significant appeal, it has also become clear that the field faces important challenges that impede its growth and hinder its ability to deliver more benefits ... Social enterprises now face these major obstacles: ill-fitting legal forms, obstacles to effective governance, problems in evaluating impact, weak supportive networks, difficulties in raising funding, and management tensions.[3]

How the tandem hybrid model addresses and overcomes these challenges will be explained in Part II. Here, we'll say a bit about each distinctive, then share how they shaped Scott's journey as a businessman and social entrepreneur. The tandem hybrid model is:

- Driven by a compelling social mission.
- Financed by commercial success.
- Structured to retain control.
- Scalable and sustainable for the long haul.

---

2 Battilana et al., "In Search of the Hybrid Ideal."
3 Alan J. Abramson and Kara C. Billings, "Challenges Facing Social Enterprises in the United States," Nonprofit Policy Forum, May 14, 2019, www.degruy ter.com/document/doi/10.1515/npf-2018-0046/html.

Driven by a Compelling Social Mission

Motive will determine what kind of organization you start. Historically, the majority of entrepreneurs want to make money for themselves, their families, their investors, and their employees. There's nothing wrong with that.

Money, and the security and power that comes with it, is the normal reason many people start businesses. But recent research shows that more people are doing so because they want to make a positive impact. Seventy-one percent of female entrepreneurs and 63 percent of male entrepreneurs start a business to make a difference in the world.[4]

Gregory Dees explains:

> Adopting a mission to create and sustain social value is what distinguishes social entrepreneurs from business entrepreneurs. For a social entrepreneur, the social mission is fundamental. This is a mission of social improvement that cannot be reduced to creating private benefits for individuals.[5]

We mentioned Scott's story in the Introduction, how after a successful career in the pharmaceutical business he was moved to personally address the social and medical injustice he saw in the world. "It became harder to overlook or rationalize that most disorders and diseases that could be easily treated by available and inexpensive medications went untreated," Scott says. "The cost to human life and human potential in these situations seemed staggering and inexcusable. I couldn't accept so many people around the world being left behind."

Scott's Story

I began to hear a "whisper" to do something about ROW; to find a way to equalize the graph when it came to medical care. This stirred my sense of justice from a medical and pharmaceutical perspective. I couldn't accept so many people around the world being left behind. It says a lot about us as humans if we've developed cures and treatments for diseases but consciously or unconsciously choose not to deliver them to all those in need. Their futures could be radically changed by a pill that costs a nickel or a dime! We had the medications, but we didn't have a way to distribute them.

---

4 "20 Entrepreneur Statistics You Need to Know (2022)," Apollo Technical, last modified December 2, 2021, www.apollotechnical.com/entrepreneur-statistics/.

5 J. Gregory Dees, "The Meaning of 'Social Entrepreneurship,'" Duke University Fuqua Center, last modified 5/30/2001, https://centers.fuqua.duke.edu/case/wp-content/uploads/sites/7/2015/03/Article_Dees_MeaningofSocialEntrepreneurship_2001.pdf.

I learned a lot about distribution, contracting, human resources, market access, and other aspects of the business. I got a better understanding of pharma operations from top to bottom rather than just from a marketing perspective. This knowledge gave me more confidence to start One World Pharmaceuticals (OWP), with the following social mission: "We envision a world where all people receive the best level of medical and pharmaceutical care regardless of who they are or where they live."

Financed by Commercial Success

The old axiom is still true: If there's no money, there's no mission. A social enterprise has to be profitable because it takes money to accomplish a mission. In the tandem hybrid model, the commercial entity funds the social entity. Donations and fundraising can be utilized, but they aren't the primary funding mechanisms.

If your mission is a fair-trade boutique, a food pantry, a homeless shelter, or an employment center for teens, that's great. A vision doesn't have to be global to be impactful. Many social enterprises have a local focus. You can use a non-profit enterprise or a for-profit enterprise to generate some or all of the funding. For a small-scale organization you don't need the hybrid model. A public charity will work for the non-profit entity and a traditional LLC, C-corp, or S-corp will work for the for-profit entity, if you have a separate one. They don't have to be linked.

To grow beyond the local community though, the tandem hybrid model has some unique advantages. But for it to work, the commercial business has to have products or services that can drive strong sales with a significant profit margin. A smaller-scale social enterprise can have a positive local impact, which might be all it intends, but it won't have much potential for a larger impact outside a local community without a powerful profit-engine to fuel expansion.

The business has to be innovative and stay innovative. If it doesn't come up with new ideas and products or continue to grow and evolve it will fade and there won't be enough money to fund the original mission. "Innovation requires having at least three things," according to Walter Isaacson, "a great idea, the engineering talent to execute it, and the business savvy to turn it into a successful product."[6]

The eight companies we look at in Part III are great examples of innovative organizations that have survived and thrived for decades. Although they aren't social enterprises, there are lessons for social entrepreneurs that apply to both the commercial and social parts of the tandem model.

6 Walter Isaacson, The Innovators: How a Group of Hackers, Geniuses, and Geeks Created the Digital Revolution (New York, Simon & Schuster, 2015), p. 215.

Scott's Story

I had a compelling social mission. I was, and still am, disturbed by a world in which those who have access to life-altering or life-saving medications withhold them from those in need simply because they don't have money or were born in the wrong country. I wanted to fight this medical and pharmaceutical injustice by making effective treatments available to all people at all times in all places. And I saw that such efforts needed to harness the financial muscle of business. Without the business "flywheel," we wouldn't be able to address social injustices globally. With my background, I decided to start a pharmaceutical company as my flywheel. But where to begin? Which medications for what conditions had the best chance of success? Whatever products we intended to sell had to be commercially profitable.

We determined our target would be epilepsy and (later) associated psychiatric disorders. One report estimated the U.S. market for epilepsy drugs at $1.3 billion in 2020, with the worldwide market reaching $5.8 billion by 2027. Epilepsy is a global problem that deserves a global solution. We would be part of that solution with our antiseizure drugs Roweepra (levetiracetam) and Subvenite (lamotrigine).

After being in business for a few years, we learned that our products needed to have a better profit potential and long-term sustainability. We had to find some exclusivity to compete in this market and we didn't have that with Roweepra and Subvenite. There was nothing unique about those medications, so we didn't stop there. The OWP development pipeline currently has six oral liquid drugs widely used in neuroscience. And we have filed patents for several of these oral liquid formulations.

Our goal is to be the premier branded oral liquid neuroscience pharmaceutical company focused on the neurology and psychiatry markets in the United States. Success in this niche market will allow OWP to flourish and fund the work of the ROW Foundation around the world.

Structured to Retain Control

If you plan to have impact through your social mission, you need to think about structure from the beginning. If you don't, it'll be very easy to lose control later. Your angel investors will push you to venture capitalists (VCs), and your VCs will push you to private equity, who will push you to venture debt, who will push you to structured debt. These are normal business transitions when it comes to capital, but they're not positive for mission-related social enterprises.

A startup needs money, and most go to VCs or private equity firms to get it. The VC might say, "I'll give you a half-million or more—for a chunk of the company." But if you start down that path, you will be owned, lock, stock, and barrel at some point by the VCs. VCs invest in people believing they're going to need more money. So every time they come back, the VC says, "Okay. I gave you X amount for 20 percent of the company. I'll give you another download, but it's for 40 percent of the company, and I want to change a few things."

Every time a VC or private equity firm gives more money, they take a bigger piece of the pie until they control the company. Along the way they often replace the leadership team, including the founder. There are many founders and CEOs who have been "retired" or fired by their financiers who want to take what is now "their" company in a different direction. The VCs have their own exit strategy—sell the company for as much as they can as fast as they can; it's not to perpetuate any social mission the founder had in mind.

To retain control, a founder or founders have to retain at least 51 percent of the equity or voting stock (or super-voting stock) in the company, either personally or in an organization he, she, or they control. A company can still go public and the founder can still maintain control by having a smaller float, maybe only 15 or 25 percent of the company.

Scott's Story

Being forced out by VCs is one way to lose control of a company. Being bought out is another, which makes sense if the motive for starting in the first place is strictly profit. Selling a successful company for a sizable sum is often the exit strategy of choice, but it can leave the social mission high and dry once the founders are out of the picture. The tandem hybrid model guards against these outcomes.

Our original plan was for my co-founder Bruce Duncan and I to donate the majority of our OWP stock to ROW so that the foundation owned a controlling share of the business. This would fund ROW's programs and they could keep the company from being sold out from under them. But this plan turned out not to work efficiently. The IRS doesn't allow a private foundation to have a controlling interest in a for-profit company, so foundations can't own more than 20 percent of the voting stock. We also discovered that for federal tax purposes, it's better that ROW does not hold an ownership interest in OWP.

In Chapter 7 I'll explain how we solved this dilemma, but the need to switch horses in the middle of the race shows why entrepreneurs need to have a Plan A, a Plan B, a Plan C, and a Plan D. You can't fall in love with Plan A. If it's not working, you've got to be brutally honest and make very tough business decisions incredibly fast. Such flexibility is key to being successful for the long haul.

Scalable and Sustainable for the Long Haul

Many social enterprises are small in scope and purpose. They're not created to be large-scale organizations, say $50 million and above in annual revenues. If you know from the outset your mission is national or international, your model needs to be scalable in order to generate the income needed to support the expanding philanthropic impact you want to have.

In his TED talk, "The Case for Letting Business Solve Social Problems", Michael Porter from Harvard asks and answers a key question:

> What's the fundamental problem we have in dealing with these social problems? If we cut all the complexity away, we have the problem of scale. We can't scale. We can make progress. We can show benefits. We can show results. We can make things better. We're helping. We're doing better. We're doing good. We can't scale. We can't make a large-scale impact on these problems. Why is that? Because we don't have the resources. And that's really clear now. And that's clearer now than it's been for decades. There's simply not enough money to deal with any of these problems at scale using the current model. There's not enough tax revenue, there's not enough philanthropic donations, to deal with these problems the way we're dealing with them now. ... So, if it's fundamentally a resource problem, where are the resources in society? How are those resources really created, the resources we're going to need to deal with all these societal challenges? Well then, I think the answer is very clear: They're in business. All wealth is actually created by business. Business creates wealth when it meets needs at a profit. That's how all wealth is created.[7]

To be able to scale, a business has to be creative, flexible, and innovative. We'll say more about this in Chapter 8.

Scott's Story

At the time of this writing, OWP is a small company with sales of less than $10 million. However, as our pipeline matures and medications make their way through the FDA, our sales will increase dramatically. OWP is the financial engine that funds much of the work of the ROW Foundation. That engine needs to be cared for and nurtured now and in the future.

We've already built the pharmaceutical infrastructure needed with our small-scale operations that will allow us to grow into a mid-sized company. This is no small feat as the pharma industry is very complex with

---

7 Michael Porter, "The Case for Letting Business Solve Social Problems," TEDGlobal, June 2013, www.ted.com/talks/michael_porter_why_business_can_be_good_at_solving_social_problems/transcript.

many medical, legal, and regulatory hurdles that need to be overcome before marketing products in the U.S. We've already completed this process for our initial products.

For the social entity of our model, we started the ROW Foundation in 2014 and secured our IRS designation as a 501(c)(3) private foundation in February 2015. Two months later we chose our first project. ROW would purchase EEG equipment for the Arabkir Pediatric Hospital in Yerevan, the capital of Armenia. The price tag: $24,000. While the original thinking had been for the foundation to provide epilepsy medications not normally available in low- and middle-income countries, we broadened the vision to include training professionals and providing equipment to diagnose and treat the disease—hence, an EEG machine. Our first shipment of Roweepra went to the same hospital.

Another choice we made that allows us to scale was to establish ROW as a funding foundation, not an operating foundation (we recently added ROW Global Health as a public charity, which we'll explain later). We fulfill our mission by supporting well-established organizations with proven programs. We aren't interested in reinventing the wheel; we just grease the ones that are effectively rolling so as to cover more territory. To date, ROW has expanded to work with more than 75 partners in 35 countries. We've made $21.7 million in grants and provided 176,589 prescription-months of medication as of the end of 2022.

Gregory Dees, quoted earlier in this chapter, also notes that, "Social entrepreneurs look for a long-term social return on investment. They want more than a quick hit; they want to create lasting improvements. They think about sustaining the impact."[8] When well-meaning people start non-profit organizations to do social good, they dedicate their time, energy, and resources to impact their areas of concern. But inconsistent cash flow can doom them to failure. This unpredictability of income undercuts the sustainability of non-profits, as Jim Schorr notes:

> Unless these organizations develop new models that enable social enterprises to deliver double bottom line results, or find permanent funding subsidies for their activities, their chances of long-term survival are not good. Most social purpose businesses lose money and require ongoing funding subsidies to support their operations. Unfortunately, these subsidies are not readily available.[9]

8 Dees, "The Meaning of 'Social Entrepreneurship.'"
9 Jim Schorr, "Social Enterprise 2.0: Moving Toward a Sustainable Model," Stanford Social Innovation Review, Summer 2006, https://community-wea lth.org/sites/clone.community-wealth.org/files/downloads/article-schorr.pdf.

The tandem hybrid model is the kind of new model Schorr calls for, one that delivers "double bottom line results." The ROW Foundation isn't solely dependent on grants and donations. It is funded by the profitability of OWP. This arrangement frees ROW from the time-and-cost-intensive effort to find, win over, and retain donors. This also means that 100 percent of any donations that do come in go to the projects designated by the donor.

Scott's Story

When I first thought of this organization, I was somewhat naive about a hybrid model of two organizations, one for-profit, one non-profit, working together. I was trying to figure out how to get one organization to do both. Then I heard about Tyndale House Publishing, which has both a non-profit foundation and a for-profit publishing company. I also came across some European pharmaceutical organizations that had very large non-profit foundations that owned the majority of the for-profit companies. These are industrial foundations and they aren't allowed in the U.S., but it got me thinking. I saw that we definitely needed two different organizations staffed by people with different skill sets.

OWP Pharma and the ROW Foundation have worked in concert to refine our hybrid model to make it as efficient as possible. We significantly revised our original arrangement with the help of attorney Ryan Oberly at Wagenmaker and Oberly. Their team of legal experts counseled us to change our initial design into a more elegant structure that will allow us to scale as we grow over time.

Sustainability and scalability are especially important to us. We need a sustainable way to help educate, diagnose, and treat people with epilepsy for the long run. We can't start a treatment plan and then tell patients we've run out of money and therefore run out of medication. We need a consistent revenue stream to support a sustainable solution, and we need it to be scalable because we're tackling a global issue.

Another way we improve sustainability and maximize growth is through product diversity. While OWP is centered on epilepsy and associated psychiatric disorders, we would eventually like to replicate our model for other diseases and conditions and encourage others to do so. One way we might do this would be to start separate divisions or holding companies for other markets. As Bruce says, "Right now we're focusing on neuroscience. Could we go into oncology or cardiovascular? Absolutely. I expect OWP to branch into other medical fields. And hopefully we will inspire entrepreneurs in other fields to adopt our model. It can work for almost any new business that has a clear vision and can create a reasonably strong cash flow."

In Part II we will take a deeper dive into the four distinctives of the tandem hybrid social enterprise.

ROW in Action

India Community Health Worker and Epilepsy Helpline

The *Lifeline Express* is a health clinic on a train that travels to rural villages in India to provide a range of healthcare services. Dr. Mamta Bhushan Singh (a New Delhi-based neurologist) launched a Mobile Epilepsy Clinic on the train in 2009. Ten times a year, Dr. Singh and a small group of volunteers known as "Epilepsy Educators" board the train and operate weekend clinics in new locations.

While the clinic has helped thousands of people to get diagnosed and on a path to treatment, a major limitation is that the clinic was a one-time event in a community. ROW launched a partnership in 2021 to significantly expand the scope of the Mobile Epilepsy Clinic to include long-term treatment and support for people with epilepsy, including:

- Launching a telehealth helpline that can be accessed remotely by patients. ROW identifies local doctors and trains them in the primary care of epilepsy so they can provide follow-up care to patients.
- Seeking an agreement with the Ministry of Health to equip a small group of Accredited Social Health Activists (ASHA) to support epilepsy care before and after the clinic has visited the community.
- Providing training to community health workers (CHWs) on how to support treatment plans and connect people to telehealth resources, as well as providing training and materials to address stigma around epilepsy at the community level.

Figure 4.1 Epilepsy educators and the Lifeline Express.

Part II

Building Tandem Hybrid Social Enterprises

Part II drills down into the nuts and bolts of the tandem hybrid social enterprise, with a chapter each on its four distinctives:

- Driven by a compelling social mission.
- Financed by commercial success.
- Structured to retain control.
- Scalable and sustainable for the long haul.

These chapters delve into initial vision, organizational structure, funding dos and don'ts, the roles of key stakeholders, ultimate size of the enterprise, the importance of innovation, the connection between scalability and sustainability, and how to retain control over the long haul. The principles are illustrated by the real-world struggles and successes of the tandem hybrid OWP Pharmaceuticals and the ROW Foundation.

DOI: 10.4324/9781003325987-6

5 Driven by a Compelling Social Mission

Startups, whether commercial businesses or social enterprises, have a high mortality rate. The stats vary based on a number of factors, but around 70 percent are gone within five years. The reasons for failure also vary, but the main ones are a lack of funding, a poor understanding of the market, a dearth of talent, and inadequate leadership. But the poor odds don't deter most entrepreneurs, commercial or social. There are more than 31 million entrepreneurs in the U.S. and a growing number of them are social entrepreneurs.[1]

What motivates entrepreneurs to tackle the high-risk challenge of starting something from scratch? Entrepreneur and author Larry Alton, writing in *Entrepreneur*, lists five motivations that drive people to choose entrepreneurship:

1 Money: You can deny it all you want, but the vast majority of entrepreneurs get into the game at least partially because of the potential to make lots and lots of money.
2 Flexibility: Some entrepreneurs venture out on their own because they're tired of the demands of traditional work.
3 Control: The desire for control drives many entrepreneurs who aspire to attain a leadership position.
4 Teamwork: Some people love working with others. They like the atmosphere of team-based creative problem solving, … and the thrill of succeeding together.
5 Legacy: Some entrepreneurs aren't in it for the money or the experience as much as they're in it for a lasting legacy.[2]

But according to research done by Cox Business:

> Freedom and passion, not money, is the main motivation. Cox Business found that more than half of small business owners start their own

1 "20 Entrepreneur Statistics You Need to Know (2021)," Apollo Technical, December 2, 2021, www.apollotechnical.com/entrepreneur-statistics/.
2 Larry Alton, "The 5 Motivations That Drive People to Choose Entrepreneurship," *Entrepreneur*, August 12, 2015, www.entrepreneur.com/article/249417.

DOI: 10.4324/9781003325987-7

businesses to be their own boss. They were also motivated by the idea of creating something from the ground up. Nearly two-thirds of respondents said they had started their own business for one of those two reasons. Money, on the other hand, is not as much of a factor for many small business owners: Just 8 percent of respondents said that was their main motivation.[3]

At the risk of being overly simplistic, we can say that two main reasons for starting a business of any kind are money (profit) and mission (passion).

Money

Whether it's the first reason or the last, money, and the security and power that come with it, are what make the commercial world go round. The greater the risk, the greater the potential for big rewards. You may start a business with the goal of selling it and cashing out. You might want to be a serial entrepreneur and repeat the process over and over. There's nothing wrong with going into business to make money, a lot of money. You want to provide for your family, give your children a good education, enjoy a comfortable lifestyle, be able to travel and afford the nicer things. That's what many entrepreneurs are after.

The key questions to ask yourself about money are: How much do you need? And, how much is enough? For many, the answer to both questions is "more!" They just think more is better, but that clearly isn't the case. There can be unintended consequences of too much money, to you, your children and grandchildren. History books and today's headlines are replete with examples of how undisciplined wealth has hindered or destroyed individuals and families. Among the saddest stories are those of children or grandchildren who were given too much, too early and it pushed them into poor choices, bad behavior, and in some instances an early grave.

In his book, *What Your Money Means*, Frank Hanna cautions against passing on too much wealth:

> Money can seriously damage those who receive it, particularly when those people are young and come into wealth before their characters have been formed. ... If we can provide the fundamentals to another person, that's great. But to do more—to give them non-essential wealth—may well be the worst thing we could do for them. All we're adding to their lives is danger.[4]

3 Shayna Waltower, "The Top Reason Most Entrepreneurs Start Businesses," *Business News Daily*, last modified February 9, 2022, www.businessnewsdaily.com/4652-entrepreneur-motivation-benefits.html.
4 Frank J. Hanna, *What Your Money Means (And How to Use It Well)*, Kindle edition (Dallas, TX: Crossroad, 2008), loc. 1224.

Scott's Story

If you can't put a limit on personal wealth, then starting a tandem hybrid enterprise is not for you. Personally, I don't want anyone in the C-suite at OWP who can't draw a line somewhere and say enough is enough. If they just want as much money as they can get, they should go work for Merck or Pfizer or Bristol. Even before OWP became profitable, my wife Ruth and I drafted a Founder's Pledge that puts a lifetime cap on what we will make from OWP. The idea of a Founder's Pledge is influenced by the Giving Pledge created in 2010 by Bill and Melinda Gates and Warren Buffett. Our Pledge was written in 2017 when OWP was still in the red. It says in part:

We believe in "wealth" as a proper reward for a life well invested, just as an abundant crop is the natural reward for a diligent farmer. But we are not interested in "riches" as hoarded resources, or zeros in a bank account, or a way to keep score. We have drawn a line between what wealth and riches mean to us and put a number on it. We pledge that everything we earn through our involvement and investment in OWP over that number will be given to charity. As the business does well, we will use our profits to assist others who have not had the incredible opportunities or undeserved blessings we have enjoyed. We hope our commitment will help the investors, employees, and beneficiaries of OWP Pharmaceuticals remember that we exist, not to enrich a few but to empower the many.

Mission

Any person or organization can explain WHAT they do," says Simon Sinek, "some can explain HOW they are different or better, ... but very few can clearly articulate WHY. The WHY is not about money or profit— those are results. The WHY is the thing that inspires us and inspires those around us.[5]

Many people today want more than money out of their working lives; they want meaning. This can be seen in the rise of social entrepreneurship. "Social entrepreneurship, once a niche area, is spreading its wings," notes an article in *Financial Times* in 2018. "Across the world, almost half as many people are creating ventures with a primarily social or environmental purpose as those with a solely commercial aim, according to the Global Entrepreneurship Monitor (GEM), a multi-country study."[6] The GEM report documents how this trend is being fueled by the younger generation:

---

5 Simon Sinek, "Inspire Your People," Simon Sinek, accessed April 5, 2022, http s://simonsinek.com/commit/.

6 Brian Groom, "A Third of Start-ups Aim for Social Good," *Financial Times*, June 14, 2018, www.ft.com/content/d8b6d9fa-4eb8-11e8-ac41-759eee1efb74.

[S]ocial entrepreneurship is taking root in both developing and developed nations—with more entrepreneurs focusing on doing good rather than solely making a profit. ... younger people between 18–34 years are more likely to start up social purpose organisations. "Social entrepreneurship is often associated with young change-makers who are idealistic in nature," says Niels Bosma (Assistant Professor with the Utrecht University School of Economics in the Netherlands). "There are more social entrepreneurs in this age bracket than commercial entrepreneurs in every global region, except for Latin America and the Caribbean. These findings indicate that in general, the younger generations may be more interested in making positive changes in their world through social entrepreneurship.[7]

Having a mission in life and business has to do with finding and following your passion and calling. While many people identify with certain social missions, not everyone will devote time, energy, or money to addressing those causes because they don't have a passion for the mission or sense of calling to get personally involved. Is there a cause you care passionately about that's motivating your entrepreneurial efforts? If so, ask yourself, "What do I need to do to make sure I accomplish my mission?" David Brooks presents a different perspective when he writes, "A vocation is not found by looking within and finding your passion. It is found by looking without and asking what life is asking of us. What problem is addressed by an activity you intrinsically enjoy?"[8]

One thing you need to do is secure funding, which we'll address in the next chapter. The tandem hybrid isn't about money *or* mission; it's about money *for* mission. The former has to be in service to the latter. But unless you are very clear in your vision and careful in how you structure your enterprise, the mission may be cast aside by those who give you money, whether they are friends and family or VCs and PEs. If you don't have a passion for the mission from the beginning, you won't fight for it with your investors when they apply exit pressures. If you don't maintain control of your company at all times, you won't be able to protect its mission from being deluded or destroyed.

Steve Jobs learned this lesson the hard way. He and Steve Wozniak started Apple in 1976, with Wozniak owning 34.6 percent of Apple and Jobs 65.4 percent after the departure of Ronald Wayne, who originally owned 10 percent. But by the time of Apple's IPO in December 1980, Jobs's share was down to 11 percent and Wozniak's to 8.7 percent. Both had sold stock to finance company expansion. So when Jobs's disagreements with the

---

7 "Entrepreneurs Worldwide Turn Their Focus Towards Doing Good," Global Entrepreneurship Monitor, accessed April 10, 2022, www.gemcon sortium.org/news/Entrepreneurs%20worldwide%20turn%20their%20focus% 20towards%20doing%20good.

8 David Brooks, *The Road to Character*, Kindle edition (New York: Random House, 2015), loc. 5091–5092.

board escalated to the breaking point in 1985, Steve was shown the door—and there was nothing he could do about it. He did get the last word, however, coming back to Apple in 1997 and leading the company to insane profitability until shortly before his death in 2011. That year it became the world's most valuable stock with a market cap just under $340 billion.

Finding Your Mission

Some social entrepreneurs find their mission; for others, the mission finds them. Whether you know the specific problem you want to tackle, or have a general sense of wanting to do good in the world, it's worth spending time to clarify the mission upon which your social enterprise will be built. It is, after all, the primary reason behind all the hours, dollars, and effort you will invest in your venture. There's no single right way to decide what social or environmental cause you will champion, but personal reflection is a good place to start. The following questions can help you explore, identify, and confirm your mission match.

What Do You Care about?

Forget about changing the world for a minute and think about yourself. What do you love? What do you hate? Because your life is so ordinary to you, it may be more difficult than you think to identify what makes your values and interests unique. It may help to ask yourself:

- What are my hobbies, and how do I spend my free time?
- What movies, shows, books, or news articles do I like to read/watch?
- What makes me so mad my blood starts to boil?
- What makes me so sad my heart hurts?
- What makes me so glad I shout with joy?
- What's right with the world?
- What's wrong with the world?
- Where have I seen injustice?

Your interests and emotions combine into what's often called "passion," a term commonly associated with intense excitement, romantic love, and, yes, the focused drive of an entrepreneur. The etymology of the word passion reveals a deeper meaning. The word comes from the Latin word *patior*, which means "to suffer." Someone who is passionate is willing to suffer for the purpose to which he or she is committed. This is why theologians refer to the death of Jesus as "the passion of the Christ." Passion in this richer sense means being willing to risk something—pain, reputation, status—because you believe so deeply in the cause.

This type of passionate suffering is often associated with entrepreneurs, who put their blood, sweat, and savings into creating something from nothing. It's especially the case with social entrepreneurs because of the added complexity of the seemingly intractable social problems they are trying to solve. As you consider the mission of your social enterprise, it's wise to choose an issue you care about enough that you're willing to make significant sacrifices.

What Experience Do You Have?

Sometimes an issue you care deeply about may stem from you or someone you care about having had personal experience with it. Poverty. Immigration. Domestic violence. No one on the planet is immune from trials, challenges, or suffering. Social entrepreneurs often commit to solving certain problems because the problems have crossed the threshold of their lives.

The most powerful example I (Jeremy) have seen first-hand is that of Brent and Kelly King, the parents of Chelsea King. Chelsea, 17, was jogging in a public San Diego park in 2010 when she was brutally assaulted and murdered by a repeat offender. The Kings channeled their grief into action and launched Chelsea's Light Foundation (and more recently Protect the Joy), which advocates for legislation to protect children from known violent predators. One of their first accomplishments was passing Chelsea's Law in California, signed by then-Governor Arnold Schwarzenegger, to help protect the state's 9.3 million children. Some of the most effective social entrepreneurs bring their lived experience to bear when building their organizations because they understand the challenge deeply and can communicate with credibility.

Even if you or someone you love hasn't been affected directly by a particular issue, you may have observed the problem with enough proximity to see and feel the pain that others are experiencing. Blake MyCoskie saw it in Argentina. Justin Dillon saw it in Uganda. Reverend Helms saw it in Boston. The next best thing to personal experience is empathy developed through relationships. And the best way to develop empathy is to get as close as you can—responsibly and ethically—to the people who are affected.

I chose to write my college honor's thesis on the topic of homelessness— a topic that I cared about but had never experienced. I had the opportunity to travel to Washington, DC and study homelessness; to observe it, to talk to lawmakers about it, and to serve alongside organizations that were addressing it. But the deepest and most significant learning came when I experienced it. With the guidance of the National Coalition for the Homeless, our group was introduced to trusted homeless individuals who shared their lives, experiences, and spaces with us. We ate at soup kitchens, tried to use bathrooms in restaurants, asked for money on the streets, and slept in alleys (and yes, there were rats). This experience, and the relationships built in the process, transformed my understanding of the challenge of homelessness.

Whatever your level of experience with your topic of interest, take a deeper dive into it. Take on the mindset of a researcher. Read books, blogs, and articles. Watch videos and documentaries. Interview experts, thought leaders, and practitioners. Volunteer or work with organizations that are addressing the issue. Observe—or if you can, immerse yourself in—the issue to get a first-hand view.

What Are You Good at?

Often a social entrepreneur's mission will grow out of, or be influenced by, his or her career. The late Bob Buford was an effective and influential social entrepreneur and life coach. He started or chaired such organizations as Buford Television, Leadership Network, The Peter F. Drucker Foundation for Nonprofit Management, and Halftime Institute. He writes:

> I seldom meet a social entrepreneur (SE) whose success hasn't grown out of his or her prior history. One reason for the tremendous impact of the latest class of SEs is that they're not leaving behind their business skill-sets when they cross over to the social sector. They see a social or spiritual opportunity and organize themselves in a businesslike way to address the challenge. What we are most effective at will be reflected in our life experiences. It's a key indicator of where and how we should be serving. That's why a potential SE who is considering a new venture should take a fearless inventory of what he or she brings to the party.[9]

The tangible skills you have developed throughout your life can help you identify how you might address a particular social challenge. Your formal education—college degree, certificate, training—has provided you with a bank of knowledge that's unique to you. Your informal education—on-the-job experience, family background, community network—has provided you with tools and strategies that can be deployed in the service of a cause you care about. While you can certainly grow and acquire new skills and knowledge along the way, it's often most effective to build on your proven abilities when launching a new venture.

One of the best ways to understand your unique talents is to use one of many personal assessment tools available. The field of positive psychology has been especially helpful in shifting the dialogue on work away from a deficit-based approach. That is, to find purpose and success in your endeavors, it's best to focus on your strengths and not your weaknesses. If you know the areas in which you are naturally wired to excel, you can be more efficient and effective. Don Clifton, dubbed the "father of strengths-based psychology," started with a simple question: "What would happen if we

---

9 Bob Buford, quoted in Merrill J. Oster and Mike Hamel, *Giving Back: Using Your Influence to Create Social Change* (Colorado Springs, CO: NavPress, 2003), p. 17.

studied what was right with people versus what's wrong with people?" The Clifton StrengthsFinder has now been used by nearly 27 million people, including 90 percent of Fortune 500 companies.[10] As a social entrepreneur, assessing your natural strengths, your knowledge and skills, and your personal experiences will help you determine what mission might be right for you.

What Does the World Need?

Once you have a solid grasp on what you care about, what you have experienced, and what you're good at, you can ask yourself: What does the world need? Where can I contribute? How can I apply my strengths, my skills, and my passion in an area where it's needed most? Successful (and unsuccessful) commercial entrepreneurs will tell you that timing is everything. You can have the best idea, with the best team, and the most resources, but your effort will not be successful if the world isn't ready for it. While social entrepreneurs aren't looking for market opportunities in the same way commercial entrepreneurs are, they still need to know what the world needs at this moment in time. The problem is that there are too many problems, too many opportunities when it comes to social challenges.

The blessing and curse of modern media is that it exposes us to all of the world's problems at once. The 24/7 news cycle bombards us with global crises at a pace we can't keep up with: political corruption, the climate crisis, global poverty, lack of access to healthcare, educational inequity, and more. Trying to assimilate the data and resulting emotions leads to what's known as "psychic numbing" and "compassion fatigue." This was especially true during a global pandemic when we couldn't comprehend the difference between 100,000, 500,000, or 1 million COVID deaths. You can't solve all of the world's problems—but you can start with one.

The advice that many social entrepreneurship educators give their students is to, "fall in love with the problem, not the solution." Like any entrepreneur, the first idea for a product or service usually isn't the one you end up with in the end. Market research, prototyping, and user feedback often leads to a pivot. For the social entrepreneur the same principle applies. If you're tied too tightly to your solution or intervention, you may miss the most effective means by which to address it. Instead, effective social entrepreneurs become students of the issue. They come to understand it inside and out, they've analyzed the system in which it exists, and they know what has been tried in the past—successfully and unsuccessfully.

An example that comes to mind in this regard is my (Mike's) friend, Chris Crane. Chris was a successful real estate entrepreneur in Southern California who built and sold a very successful commercial business. After some time off he took the position of CEO of Opportunity International. The organization

---

10 "The History of Clifton Strengths," Gallup, accessed March 30, 2022, www.ga
    llup.com/cliftonstrengths/en/253754/history-cliftonstrengths.aspx.

was founded in 1971 by two entrepreneurs whose vision was, "a world in which all people have the opportunity to achieve a life free from poverty, with dignity and purpose."

Here's how Chris recalls getting involved:

> About this time, the *Wall Street Journal* ran a front-page story on micro-finance featuring Grameen Bank and Professor Mohammad Yunus. Six years later, he won the Nobel Peace Prize for his work in this field. I was amazed that loans of $100, $200, or $400 to people living in poverty could help them significantly grow their small businesses. And even more amazing, 98 percent of the borrowers repaid the loans! That raised my interest in microfinance. Shortly after, in 2000, a fundraiser from a large Christian microfinance organization, Opportunity International, called on me. I made a donation and also offered to organize some fundraising events to introduce my friends to them. In the process I became friends with the CEO. I never suspected that two years later I would have his job.
>
> I was a for-profit businessperson who knew next to nothing about non-profits. But as I looked under the hood, I saw the similarities. This global non-profit ran like a business, orchestrating loans and setting up partnerships and lending alliances. They could use someone with my business acumen and experience. I was fifty years old in 2002 when I became president and CEO of this international ministry. I became a "social entrepreneur," someone who establishes or leads an enterprise with the aim of solving social problems or effecting social change.

Chris led Opportunity for seven years. During that time donations increased from $8 million to $51 million, a compound annual growth rate of 31 percent. Opportunity was now the world's largest faith-based microfinance organization, serving 1.5 million clients in twenty-eight countries. But based on years of international travel, Chris saw a new vision he wanted to pursue, low-cost education for the poor. He went on to co-found an organization called Edify that in its first eleven years has worked with edu-cational entrepreneurs in eleven countries, representing more than 10,700 low-fee schools and reaching more than 1 million students.

The moral of the story is, when you follow your passion, the direction may stay the same but your destination may change along the way.[11]

In the end, the goal is to find a need that you care about deeply, that is aligned with your skills and experiences, and that is significant and timely. Echoing Green produced a curriculum called "Work on Purpose" using insights gleaned from their social entrepreneurs. In it they suggest you have found purposeful work when you pair what's "right for you" and what's

11 Christopher A. Crane, *A Dream and a Coconut Tree: Transforming Education for the Poor* (Colorado Springs, CO: EMT Communications, 2019), pp. 32–32.

"good for the world." To do this, you use your head (skills and experience) and your heart (interests and passions) to find your hustle (the place where you're "in the zone"). German author and theologian Frederick Buechner, when writing about vocation, provided similar insight. He said you find your calling at the place, "where your deep gladness and the world's deep hunger meet."[12]

Scott's Story

The following is from my blog post on January 5, 2016: When I think about what motivated me to make wholesale changes in my life to launch OWP Pharmaceuticals and the ROW Foundation, the word compassion comes to mind. Imagine a friend or loved one suffering with epilepsy in the U.S. Now multiply their challenges ten times over and you begin to get a sense of what those with epilepsy in under-resourced areas go through physically, emotionally and socially. I want to help mitigate their suffering by leveling the field when it comes to treating epilepsy.

I am disturbed by a commercial world of "haves" with access to life-saving treatments, who withhold those treatments from the "have nots" simply because they don't have resources or were born in the wrong country. I want to fight this medical and pharmaceutical injustice that negatively impacts epilepsy patients by making effective treatments available to all people, at all times, in all places.

My strength is in the pharmaceutical industry; more specifically, in strategic planning and commercializing products. That's where I spent my career and where I can have the most impact. I'm not trying to reinvent myself; instead I'm focused on making the most of my experience and training in the service of a worthy cause. Creating and leading a for-profit pharmaceutical company is where my expertise lies, so that's where I spend the majority of my time. I chose to continue my vocation in pharma and for the most part let others do the work of the foundation, people who are passionate about the vision and have the skillset to organize and manage the charitable enterprise.

---

12 Frederick Buechner, "Vocation," accessed August 3, 2022, www.freder ickbuechner.com/quote-of-the-day/2017/7/18/vocation.

6   Financed by Commercial Success

An article in the *Harvard Business Review* points out what most social entrepreneurs already know—the major challenge that large social enterprises face is funding:

> Social enterprises are entrepreneurial organizations that innovate to solve problems. They include non-profit and for-profit ventures, and their returns blend social benefit and financial revenues. They come in many flavors, but they all face the same fundamental question: Can they generate enough revenue and attract enough investment to cover their costs and grow their activities? Some social enterprises can earn a profit that is sufficient to get the business funded by investors. ... But many, if not most, social enterprises cannot fund themselves entirely through sales or investment. ... Many social enterprises survive only through the largesse of government subsidies, charitable foundations, and a handful of high-net-worth individuals who will make donations or accept lower financial returns on their investments in social projects.[1]

The authors then highlight a solution:

> Some of the more forward-thinking foundations and social investors have realized that the current methods of financing social enterprises are inefficient, for the enterprises and themselves, and have started working to broaden the access to capital. Here are some of the mechanisms they're employing.[2]

They then delve into: Loan guarantees, quasi-equity debt, pooling, and social impact bonds. All these options involve investors and debt. What they don't entertain is the possibility of the commercial side of the enterprise

---

1 Antony Bugg-Levine, Bruce Kogut, Nalin Kulatilaka, "A New Approach to Funding Social Enterprises," *Harvard Business Review*, January–February 2012, https://hbr.org/2012/01/a-new-approach-to-funding-social-enterprises.
2 Ibid.

DOI: 10.4324/9781003325987-8

completely funding the social side, with enough momentum to ensure scalability and sustainability. This is what's different about the tandem hybrid. It isn't dependent on external resources like government largess, institutional investors, or wealthy individuals, but on the internally controlled financial engine of profitable products and services.

The tandem hybrid is designed *from the start* to be driven by the ongoing commercial success of the business entity. The profit funds the purpose. As the commercial activities find success in the market, the social impact accelerates through substantial funding to the non-profit. Where other hybrid models face tension between money and mission, the Tandem Hybrid finds synergy.

Mission Draft

As we mentioned in Chapter 3, one of the most significant dangers faced by typical hybrid social enterprises is mission drift. Focusing too much on profitability can steer an organization away from its social purpose. Focusing too much on mission can leave an organization without the funds to accomplish it. Because the tandem hybrid is financed by commercial success and retains both for-profit and non-profit structures, it achieves what we call "mission draft."

Sticking with the metaphor of cycling, but shifting from the tandem bike we used in Chapter 4, let's consider the world of competitive cycling. It is very familiar with the concept of drafting. When two cyclists ride together, one in front of the other, the lead rider takes on a bulk of the air resistance. The trailing cyclist follows in the low-pressure slipstream, which can result in an energy savings of about 30 percent. In a road race, drafting can make a significant difference in the overall performance of a cyclist (which is why it's not always allowed).

Financially speaking, a for-profit business can serve as a strong lead rider, taking on the headwinds of the market. This conserves the energy and effort that the non-profit would typically exert to secure funding, and allows it to be incredibly efficient in pursuit of the mission. Many non-profits and single-entity social enterprises need to pedal incredibly hard on terrain that their vehicle wasn't designed for. Rather than drifting, the non-profit can draft at the pace of the for-profit, accelerating its speed of impact. Profit maximization leads to mission maximization. This is the beauty of the tandem hybrid.

The commercial side can still access investment capital as needed from institutions and investors, but it isn't dependent on outside capital. And it never sells so much equity or ownership in the quest for growth that it loses control of the hybrid organization and its social mission. The non-profit side of the tandem hybrid can also generate funds in the form of grants, donations, and philanthropic investments. We'll illustrate throughout this chapter how OWP and the ROW Foundation have maximized their respective structures for collective benefit.

Startup Capital

Regardless of structure, all organizations need to create a funding strategy before they get to the starting line. And while the tandem hybrid is designed to be driven by the ongoing commercial success of the business entity, it obviously can't start there. When it comes to funding startups in general, research shows that entrepreneurs draw on a combination of the following sources: 77 percent use personal funds, 34 percent rely on loans, 16 percent borrow from family and friends, and 11 percent find other sources[3]. Loans can be secured from banks, impact investment firms, angel investors, venture capitalists, and private equity funds. Other fairly recent sources of startup capital include crowdfunding, pitch competitions, and fellowships. We'll consider the benefits of each of these funding sources available to business startups, and those available to nonprofits, because when it comes to funding, you can never have too many options.

Bootstrapping

Using personal funds to jumpstart a business is known as bootstrapping, which is defined as "relying entirely on one's efforts and resources."[4] This only works if you have some resources, which many younger entrepreneurs don't. Entrepreneurs can use personal assets like savings, home equity, retirement accounts, or personal debt in the form of credit cards, mortgage refinancing, or lines of credit. But just because these are options doesn't mean they are good ideas as they leave the borrower responsible. Entrepreneurs can also rely on cash flow from the business, although this can be a small stream at the outset.

In lieu of, or in addition to, cash, owners and early employees can invest sweat equity, taking less than they could make elsewhere because they believe in the mission or expect to be compensated later. Founders seldom are highly paid at the beginning of a venture, especially one linked to a social mission. If you don't have the capacity to reduce your income, you may not be in a good position to start a venture without the backing of others. But relying on others can impact your ability to stay the course with a social mission.

---

3 Allan Jay, "113 Entrepreneurship Statistics You Must Learn: 2021/2022 Market Share Analysis & Data," Finances Online, accessed January 30, 2021, https://financesonline.com/entrepreneurship-statistics/.

4 The Free Dictionary, www.thefreedictionary.com/pulling+up+by+bootstraps.

Bootstrapping is harder to do and usually takes more time than going to outsiders for an early capital infusion, but entrepreneurs who take this more arduous route maintain ownership and complete control of their business and the vision behind it. They don't have to explain their decisions to anyone or ask permission to follow their instincts. And they're often more frugal since it's their own money—or funds from people who are important to them—they're spending.

The upsides of bootstrapping for founders are maintaining control of the business and mission, choosing the direction they want to go without having to get permission from others, and reaping the rewards if things go well. The downsides may include slower growth, a longer path to profitability, and personally being on the hook if the venture fails. Investments and anything put up for collateral could be forfeit. This is a substantial gamble given the high failure rate of startups. It's even more risky if the commercial entity is conjoined with a social entity.

Family and Friends

People who know you can be a source of friendly capital because they believe in you or your mission. Unlike a bank loan, acquiring private money does not require filling out paperwork or waiting for the loan to go through. Obtaining financing from friends and family offers several advantages:

- Flexibility of a private loan: Unlike a standardized bank loan with inflexible terms, it is possible to work out a customized repayment plan.
- Credit history is not relevant: It may be nearly impossible to acquire a loan when the borrower has a history of credit problems or a previous bankruptcy.
- Lower interest rate: In most cases, the interest rate on money from family or friends will be much less than a standard bank loan.
- Collateral is unnecessary: Most friends and family will not usually require collateral to secure a private loan.[5]

Be careful, though. If the business doesn't pan out, it could cause stress or a breach in relationships. As the American proverb says, "Before borrowing money from a friend, decide which you need most."[6]

---

5 "Getting Money from Family and Friends for a Business," FindLaw, last modified June 20, 2016, www.findlaw.com/smallbusiness/starting-a-business/getting-money-from-family-and-friends-for-a-business.html.
6 Ascribed to Addison H. Hallock, The Big Apple, www.barrypopik.com/index.php/new_york_city/entry/before_borrowing_money_from_a_friend_decide_which_you_need_more.

Crowdfunding

This is a direct appeal to potential investors and customers. The goal is to get a "crowd" of hundreds or thousands of contributors each committing a small amount to help your product or service succeed. You choose the platform you want to use, the main ones being Indiegogo, GoFundMe, Kickstarter, Fundable, and Crowdfunder, and post what you're offering. You say how much money you want to raise and what people will get in return for pledging. This can be anything from perks and discounts to equity in your business. Your campaign runs for a set time, usually 30 to 60 days, and, depending on the host site, you receive what's been pledged if you reach your target goal.

Crowdfunding not only raises money, it raises awareness of your business at a grassroots level. It offers buy-in to your offering and builds customer loyalty at a small price. Success with this approach depends largely on having a broad demographic or large social following and a compelling product or mission. But it's a two-edged sword. If your campaign is successful you can leverage the support to impress larger investors in the viability of your business. But if you don't hit your goals, the failure could tarnish your reputation and dissuade potential investors.

Pitch Competitions

Like crowdfunding, pitch competitions are a fairly new avenue to startup capital. "A pitch competition is a contest where entrepreneurs present their business concept to a panel in the hope of winning a cash prize or investment capital," explains financial expert Chris Motola. "Pitch competitions all have specific parameters and rules, but no matter what, business owners will be up against any number of other entrepreneurs with their own business ideas. Even if you don't win, the pitch competition can be a way to introduce yourself to the elite world of venture capital and angel investment."[7] Motola goes on in this article to list the 20 best pitching competitions to enter in 2022, but other lists can also be found online.

Many colleges and universities offer pitch competitions through their entrepreneurship centers, and some allow non-attendees of the school to participate. One example is Rice University's annual business plan competition, dubbed the "world's largest and richest intercollegiate student startup competition,"[8] offering 40+ teams the chance to compete for $1.5 million in funding. Other community entrepreneurship organizations offer similar competitions, like the U.Pitch national event hosted by the non-profit

---

7 Chris Motola, "20 Entrepreneur Competitions To Pitch Your Startup Idea," Merchant Maverick, last modified December 3, 2021, www.merchantma verick.com/pitch-competitions/.

8 "Connecting startups to Capitol, Networks and Success," Rice Alliance, http s://alliance.rice.edu.

Future Founders. These competitions offer cash prizes in addition to mentoring, networking, visibility, and access to other useful resources. Many competitions are also geared specifically for social ventures, such as the global Hult Prize that offers $1 million in startup funding, and the Global Social Venture Challenge hosted by UC Berkeley's Haas School of Business, which offers $80,000 in prize money. These, and many others, target social entrepreneurs who are attempting to tackle the world's most pressing challenges with their business ideas.

Pitch competitions are just that, competitions. Think *Shark Tank* for a high-profile, winner-take-all example, except most don't ask for an equity stake, they just give prize money. Some have an entry fee but even the free ones come with time and opportunity costs in that you have to prepare and perform a presentation.

Incubators, Accelerators, Fellowships

These programs are designed to help launch and grow early-stage enterprises and invest in their founders with financial support, mentoring, and networking. They usually have stringent application requirements and are limited in the number of entrepreneurs they accept. As explained by Acumen Academy:

> Typically, for-profit accelerator programs provide funding in exchange for equity in the company, usually around 5%–10%. The Gust Global Accelerator Report 2016 found that 35.5% accelerators surveyed were non-profit, many of which support specific fields—such as healthcare or education—or serve a specific demographic—such as women entrepreneurs—and may not take equity in exchange for their support.[9]

Being selected can "boost your enterprise's credibility and exposure. ... (and) provide an excellent opportunity to get connected with the right investor networks if you plan to pursue more equity investment." The major downside: "Participating in these programs can be very time consuming. They can also be distracting if program goals are not aligned with the priorities of your stage of business and your organizational values and goals."[10]

Angel Investors

The first angel investors were wealthy individuals who financially supported Broadway theatrical productions. Today, the term applies to high-net-worth investors who fund startups with their own money. As Investopia explains:

9   "The Ultimate Introductory Guide to Funding Your Social Enterprise," Acumen Academy, July 27, 2019, https://acumenacademy.org/blog/impact-capital-funding-your-social-enterprise.

10   Ibid.

Angel investors provide more favorable terms compared to other lenders, since they usually invest in the entrepreneur starting the business rather than the viability of the business. Angel investors are focused on helping startups take their first steps, rather than the possible profit they may get from the business. Essentially, angel investors are the opposite of venture capitalists.[11]

Angels are often successful entrepreneurs who want to invest in similar businesses. They can get involved with a startup early on and take more risks than institutional investors. In addition to cash, they can bring access to networks of contacts with additional resources or business expertise. Angels often ask for equity in return for investment and plan to sell their stake at some point, but the terms can be more favorable than with venture capitalists or private equity firms.

Family Offices

Family offices are private wealth management firms that work with high-net-worth individuals and families. There are single-family offices that just serve one individual or family, and multi-family offices that work a few families. Many clients have family-owned companies with buyout or succession plans that call for the establishment of a trust or private foundation to handle the proceeds. There may be guidelines or restrictions on how the assets can be invested, and these could align with a non-profit's mission.

Family offices offer a great opportunity for social enterprises because they are often mission-oriented and they care as much about the mission as the money. This is where OWP received most of its capital in the early days.

Impact Investment Firms

Impact investors look for "companies that promote ethical and socially responsible consciousness such as environmental sustainability, social justice, and corporate ethics. Impact investing goes a step further by actively seeking investments that can create a significant, positive impact."[12] According to one business overview:

> The bulk of impact investing is done by institutional investors, including hedge funds, private foundations, banks, pension funds, and other fund managers. However, a range of socially conscious financial service

---

11 Akhilesh Ganti, "Angel Investor," Investopia, last modified March 22, 2022, www.investopedia.com/terms/a/angelinvestor.asp.

12 J.B. Maverick, "The Top 5 Impact Investing Firms," Investopia, last modified January 19, 2022, www.investopedia.com/articles/active-trading/090115/top-5-impact-investing-firms.asp.

companies, web-based investment platforms, and investor networks now offer individuals an opportunity to participate, too. ... Like any other type of investment class, impact investments provide investors with a range of possibilities when it comes to returns. But the most important thing is that these investments offer both a financial return and are in line with the investor's conscience.[13]

Impact investors sometimes use what's known as "patient capital." Patient capital "combines aspects of venture capital and philanthropy," says research scholar David Maurrasse:

Like venture capitalists, providers of patient capital commit to a lengthy period of support for their investees, and they have a higher tolerance than traditional investors for the risk of capital losses. Like philanthropists, patient capitalists have the aim of increasing societal value, sometimes known as a social return, when disbursing funds. The attributes of patient capital therefore make it an investment instrument that is naturally aligned with the missions of non-profits.[14]

Venture Capital

Whereas angel investors are individuals, venture capital (VC) is invested by companies that pool money from a group of investors or "limited partners." Business journalist Andrew Blackman highlights some of the differences between angels and VCs:

Whereas the average angel investor invests $520,000, the average venture capital deal ranges from $2.6 million for a brand new start-up to $10.3 million for a later-stage company. Also, while the expected time frame and returns are similar—a 10 times return over five to seven years is a good rule of thumb—the venture capital firm is on a much stricter schedule.[15]

VCs often step in when a new business has some operating history and initial funding but before it's large enough to secure sizable loans or go public. Because of the high risk involved at this stage, VCs want a high

---

13 James Chen, "Impact Investing," *Investopedia*, last modified June 13, 2021, www.investopedia.com/terms/i/impact-investing.asp.

14 David Maurrasse, "Patient Capital: Financing Nonprofits," Columbia Climate School, February 15, 2017, https://news.climate.columbia.edu/2017/02/15/patient-capital-financing-nonprofits/.

15 Andrew Blackman, "How to Raise Money from Venture Capitalists," Envato Tuts+, March 11, 2014, https://business.tutsplus.com/tutorials/how-to-raise-money-from-venture-capitalists--cms-19799.

return on investment and make no secret of how they operate, as Bharat Kanodia, Founder of Veristrat, explains:

> Venture capital firms are not in the business of running companies long-term. Their business model is to invest in numerous compa-nies, double down on companies that do well, and sell them for a big payday. The only way this model works is when their portfolio companies are successful in raising capital at higher valuations in each subsequent funding round. For VCs, the valuation itself is not a significant factor; the difference between investing $200,000 for 10% or $500,000 for 50% is negligible. A better benchmark is how fast they can increase the valuation such that they can double their investment.[16]

Private Equity

Private equity (PE) funds are similar to venture capital funds in that they look to get a high ROI within a set period of time. But they tend to play for bigger stakes, which makes them unlikely to invest in startups. Black-man, who noted the distinction between angels and VCs, also describes how VC firms differ from PE firms:

> But whereas venture capital is focused on early-stage companies with high growth potential, private equity firms invest in a much wider range of companies. Often they're mature firms that have been trading for a long time, but need access to funds either to fuel growth or to recover from financial difficulties. ... most private equity deals are for between $500 million and $5 billion. Deals below $100 million are rare.[17]

For this kind of capital PEs usually want a majority stake in the company and controlling interest to direct it as they see fit, which means to their capital advantage. They owe no allegiance to the founding vision or social mission of the enterprise.

Banks

The longer you can go without borrowing capital, the better positioned you'll be when you do need outside funding to continue growing. If you do decide to get a loan at some point, there are many sources. Banks or

---

16 Bharat Kanodia, "5 Factors VCs Look at When Investing," Inc., accessed February 9, 2022, www.inc.com/bharat-kanodia/5-factors-vcs-look-at-when-investing.html.

17 Andrew Blackman, "The Pros and Cons of Having Private Equity Firms Invest in Your Business," *Envato Tuts+*, March 18, 2014, https://business.tutsplus.com/tutorials/the-pros-and-cons-of-having-private-equity-firms-invest-in-your-busi ness–cms-19887.

credit unions are the best because their interest rates are lower and they aren't looking for equity, ownership, or control. Such loans may be hard to get, however, if you don't have sufficient collateral and cash flow. You have to convince the loan officer that you're a safe investment with positive growth potential that will allow you to repay the loan. This usually requires presenting a sound business plan and financial proformas.

In the U.S., the Small Business Administration (SBA) has programs to back loans made by banks to qualifying small businesses. These are usually low-interest, long-term loans ranging from general purpose loans (working capital, real estate) to special loans tied to business ownership (minority or gender specific loans), or special circumstances (natural or economic disasters, export activity). The six types of SBA loans are:

- SBA 7(a) Loans: Working capital up to $5 million
- SBA CDC/504 Loans: For purchasing owner-occupied commercial real estate
- SBA CAPLines: A line of credit that can be used again
- SBA Export Loans: Financing for exporters to bolster their export activity
- SBA Microloans: Working capital loans of up to $50,000
- SBA Disaster Loans: Loans for businesses that have been impacted by a declared natural or economic disaster.[18]

Because the government is involved, the application process can be long and complicated. And if you default, the bank will still come after you for what you owe, followed by Uncle Sam.

Scott's Story

Bruce and I began OWP with a half million dollars of our own money. We watered it with long hours of free labor (sweat equity). We put together a business plan and went looking for investors. We quickly discovered our hybrid model wherein the ROW Foundation received a big chunk of company profits didn't interest venture capitalists. We tried to get investors who wanted to make money but also wanted to have a positive social impact in the world. If you know VCs, you know this mindset isn't very common.

We tapped into family, friends, and angel investors with a like-minded desire to address injustice. In 2017, I was invited to the Lion's Den in Alabama, a Christian version of Shark Tank. As a result, OWP got almost a million dollars in new investments from family offices and like-minded investors. We learned quickly to be very cautious with VC's. Even if they're a minority stakeholder, they may have majority rights based on

---

18 Tom Thunstrom, "SBA Loans: Types, Rates & Requirements," Fit Small Business, January 18, 2022, https://fitsmallbusiness.com/types-of-sba-loans/.

the terms of your agreement. They can force decisions that are in their short-term interest but not in the best long-term interest of the company.

The easy thing is to lean into the investors who can make your life a lot smoother. But in the end they have so much invested that they can push you around. They want to make money and they can micromanage you. They can even pull you under. There is good or friendly money and there is definitely unfriendly money, too. This almost happened to us and without the help of a financial mentor it could have been disastrous for OWP as well as the ROW Foundation. With the counsel of this key person we were able to negotiate an opportunity for OWP to buy out this PE for a 25 percent IRR (internal rate of return), which we were able to do in 2018.

Non-Profit Funding Sources

While the tandem hybrid is designed to run on fuel from the for-profit business, the unique dual structure allows it to attract funding through its non-profit entity as well. This allows for a diversified resource stream that can infuse even more capital directly toward the mission. Typical sources for non-profit funding are donations, grants, and philanthropic investments. Donations are usually cash gifts that come from supportive individuals or organizations (including corporations and their related foundations) that want to support your mission with their generosity. These gifts are tax-deductible for the donor, can be one-time or recurring, and do not need to be repaid.

Donors can give directly, although an increasing number are choosing to set up donor-advised funds (DAFs). DAFs allow donors to contribute money to a fund that they establish but is held and managed by a sponsoring organization, typically a foundation or the non-profit arm of a financial institution. Donors can request that contributions be made to their preferred charitable organizations at the time of their choosing.

Grants are sums of money also given from an organization to a nonprofit, though they typically come with more structure, requirements, and are directed toward a specific purpose. The grant process typically involves a well-defined application, clear budget, and detailed report(s) that assure the granting organization that the money achieved the desired result. Grants can come from foundations, government agencies, aid organizations, and other non-profits. If you have the capacity to manage the process, grants can be a significant source of funding that for-profit businesses cannot access. The non-profit side of a tandem hybrid social enterprise provides the advantages of a charity without creating a dependency on charitable giving, as OWP and the ROW Foundation illustrate.

Scott's Story

Just as OWP has had to adjust to changing circumstances, ROW has had to evolve to effectively pursue its mission, as its first president, Dr. Paul Regan, explains:

> As a 501(c)(3) private foundation, ROW can accept charitable contributions, but there are some limitations. Private foundations are often associated with a single funding source. As such, they aren't subject to all the same regulations as other charities, and they don't do a lot of fundraising among the general public. Consequently, they don't attract many outside donors, even if they believe in the foundation's mission.
>
> But there's another type of 501(c)(3) called a public charity, which is the most common form of non-profit organization. Public charities have a more advantageous tax status with the IRS, as well as some other benefits. Based on advice from non-profit attorneys and advisors, we created a public charity in 2021—ROW Global Health—to work alongside the ROW Foundation. People and entities who want to give to a public charity can give to ROW's public charity. ROW Global Health started receiving donations from donor-advised funds (DAFs) immediately after it was established. Those who want to fund our work through a private foundation can give to ROW's private foundation. These two options will increase our funding, expand the work we can do around the world, and increase the speed at which we can reach the under-resourced with neuroscience disorders in low- and middle-income countries.
>
> There is no legal connection between the private foundation and public charity, but Scott is the founder of both organizations and the chairman of the public charity. And all the monies raised by either goes to the same cause.

The tandem hybrid model is designed for its commercial engine (money) to be in the service of its social purpose (mission). This arrangement is not an appealing investment for traditional VCs and PEs who are after high profits and quick exits. For this reason, startup funding usually comes from the founders, family and friends, angel investors, family offices, and some of the other sources described above.

When you grow past the startup phase and have to scale the commercial business to the next level you may need outside capital—and lots of it depending on your business. You may now have proof of concept and enough sales to interest some institutions and investors who can provide the needed capital, networks, and expertise to help expand your business. But such benefits come with a steep price tag. You don't want to become dependent on outside money or give up too much control to get it. The next chapter will address how to structure the tandem enterprise from the outset to retain control as you scale toward becoming a medium-to-large-cap organization.

7 Structured to Retain Control

Just like location is vitally important in real estate, structure is vitally important to the tandem hybrid model. And it's far easier to begin with the right structure than to make adjustments later, although some mid-course corrections can be part of an organization's life cycle. You want to have the for-profit and non-profit entities connected in a way that maximizes the benefits of being synchronized and minimizes the possibility of being separated down the road.

Your "intent at inception" is also critically important. You don't take on the additional complexity and hard work a social enterprise requires as an afterthought. If your intent in starting a business is just to make money, you don't need a tandem bike, which we described in Chapter 4 as a metaphor for the tandem hybrid. Get yourself a carbon road bike built for speed and take off! The more aerodynamic your equipment and the faster you pedal, the more prize money you earn. But if your intent is to use a for-profit business to drive a social mission, you need an efficient way to connect the two. The internal structure of the entities may vary. The for-profit entity could be a partnership, S-corp, C-corp, LLC, L3C or benefit corporation. The non-profit entity could be any of the charitable organizations recognized by the IRS, the most preferred being one with a 501(c)(3) designation. What they are isn't as important as how they are connected in the tandem hybrid model.

One Approach

When it comes to OWP Pharmaceuticals and the ROW Foundation, the former is a C-corp and the latter is a 501(c)(3) private foundation. (ROW Global Health was established in 2021 as a public charity to work alongside the ROW Foundation and both organizations fund the same programs.) The for-profit and non-profit entities are linked in a unique way that guarantees they will always stay joined together.

DOI: 10.4324/9781003325987-9

Scott's Story

In Chapter 4, I explained how our initial plan was for my co-founder Bruce Duncan and I to give enough stock to ROW so that it had a generous revenue stream and a controlling interest in OWP. This was a very straightforward arrangement. Then we learned the IRS doesn't allow a non-profit to have a controlling interest in a for-profit. Bruce worked with our attorneys to come up with an elegant solution. I'll let him explain the details:

> There are two items the structure has to address. One is control and the other is making sure ROW has an ironclad claim on profits. The tricky part was coming up with a vehicle that allows ROW the security of getting cash year in and year out, but allows OWP to control the underlying assets. Here's the way we handled it.
>
> OWP has patents and other intellectual property that are key to generating economic growth and building enterprise value. We put them in an LLC we call an IP Holding Company. The LLC is jointly owned by OWP and ROW. Legally, it's an LLC but you can think of it as a partnership. It owns OWP's intellectual property and OWP pays it licensing fees and royalties on sales. We assigned ROW a 40 percent ownership of the holding company so it gets 40 percent of the income in perpetuity. This percentage could go up in the future as OWP continues to grow and mature as a business. This gives ROW a legally enforceable claim on the revenue. We've put in the operating agreement that any primary assets of the holding company can't be sold, exchanged, or released without the unanimous vote of the shareholders. So while ROW doesn't have significant say over the use of these assets, it has veto power and can prevent them from being sold or exchanged or given away.
>
> Here's a hypothetical example of what the cashflow could look like: OWP pays the holding company 12 percent of net revenue royalty on all lamotrigine product sales. Twelve percent is a normal royalty rate for use of a patent in the pharma industry. If our net revenues in a given year are $20 million, OWP will pay a royalty of $2.4 million (12% of $20 million), of which $960,000 (40%) would go to ROW. Royalties will be paid regardless of whether OWP is profitable since they are based on revenue, not profit. The 60 percent share OWP has could be used to help the company come out with new products. In addition, OWP will continue to make gifts of product to ROW and continue to make its maximum cash contribution to ROW annually, which is 10 percent of pretax profits. The 40 percent from the holding company, plus the 10 percent from OWP pretax profits, equals 50 percent of profits going to ROW, an unheard-of percentage in corporate giving!
>
> In the future we will set up separate holding companies to own the intellectual-property-related assets of different products. ROW will be a partner with a percentage of ownership and royalties. This gives us the

> flexibility to sell a product if the partners—OWP and ROW—decide it's in our best interest to do so without compromising our other arrangements. We've already had interest in a few of our products but we haven't had an offer that's appealing enough to accept, but if that changes in the future we will need ROW's agreement to make it happen.

Other Options

There is a caveat, however. This approach only works if your business owns valuable patents, trademarks, proprietary software, or other intellectual property to put into the holding company. There are other ways for founder-owners to maintain control of a business and connect it to a specific non-profit. We will see several examples in the history chapters in Part III. They include:

Private Company

Private companies stay privately owned and don't have to answer to shareholders and may not have an independent board. They can issue stock and have shareholders, but they don't trade on public exchanges. They can be sole proprietorships, LLCs, L3Cs, S-corps, C-corps, or benefit corporations. Many companies stay private to maintain family ownership over multiple generations. But staying private can be difficult for companies that want to grow large because it's more difficult for them to raise capital. They may have access to some equity funding and bank loans, but they can't raise large sums of cash through an IPO or bond offerings.

Still, the vast majority of companies are privately owned, including some of the largest companies in America, and the world. The *Forbes* list of privately held companies features well-known names like Koch Industries (2021 revenues, $115 billion), Mars (2021 revenues, $40 billion), Fidelity Investments (2021 revenues, $21 billion), as well as little-know companies like Reyes Holdings, (2021 revenues, $30 billion), and Southern Glazer's Wine & Spirits (2021 revenues, $21 billion). There are 225 companies with more than $2 billion in annual revenues that made the 2021 list.[1]

OWP is one example of a private company. Another is Mars Inc. (Chapter 9), one of the most successful private companies in the world.

Public Company—with Controlling Ownership

Entrepreneurs or founders can start private companies and take them public at some point. But if they want to guarantee the commercial business will continue to support their social mission, they need to own at least 51

---

1 "America's Largest Private Companies, 2021 Rankings," Forbes, accessed March 6, 2022, www.forbes.com/largest-private-companies/list/#tab:rank.

percent of voting stock at all times. They should only give or sell stock—or bequeath it when the time comes—to those who are as committed to the original vision as they are, perhaps family members or co-founders. If they dilute their controlling interest, either to acquire investment capital or during an IPO, they will have lost control of their mission.

The chances of founders retaining control of their companies after going public is slim. Research shows that, "While it may be painful to consider handing over the reins of your company to someone else, founders should be prepared for the possibility. One study of startups found that after three years, 50 percent of founders were no longer the CEO, and less than 25 percent were the CEO during the company's IPO. Sometimes it comes down to simple math. "Ultimately, many founders choose to receive outside investment based on the logic that they would rather have 20 percent of $1 billion than 100 percent of $100 million."[2]

The Upjohn Company (Chapter 12) was a public company controlled by the founding family for most of its existence.

Industrial Foundation

An industrial foundation—or Nordic foundation, as they're sometimes called—is a tax-exempt or charitable foundation that owns or controls one or more conventional business firms," explains journalist Scott McCulloch. They aren't legal in the U.S.:

> The difference with a US foundation is that a Nordic foundation has a company purpose—the preservation and development of the business. The US reformed its tax laws in 1969 to effectively prevent private foundations from having control of businesses. It sought to remedy perceived abuses that private foundations' charitable organizations served the interests of the rich rather their charities.[3]

McCulloch goes on to quote Steen Thomsen, professor at the Center for Corporate Governance at Copenhagen Business School:

> You get these founders who love their company and who regard it as their contribution to humanity, and they really want to see it preserved. Many companies crumble when the founder dies. Industrial foundations create a structure where the owner donates the company to a foundation charged with running the company as best they can.

2 Rand Hawk, "Founder Control," IPOHub, October 14, 2019, www.ipohub. org/founder-control-overview/.
3 Scott McCulloch, "Industrial Foundations: The Imperfect Solution to Long-Term Prosperity?" *Campden FB*, August 1, 2018, www.campdenfb.com/a rticle/industrial-foundations-imperfect-solution-long-term-prosperity.

It's harder in the U.S. to create tandem hybrid social enterprises like OWP/ROW because of the IRS Tax Code. In European countries like Denmark, companies are encouraged to create hybrid models like Novo Nordisk Pharmaceuticals and Lundbeck Pharmaceuticals. If these companies were not majority owned by their respective foundations deeply rooted in the country, it's very likely they would have been acquired by international conglomerates and moved out of Denmark, along with their jobs. According to McCulloch, the companies controlled by Danish foundations make up two-thirds of the total market capitalization of the Copenhagen Stock Exchange[4].

The Lundbeck Foundation and the Novo Nordisk Foundation (Chapter 11) are industrial foundations with controlling interest in their various business entities.

Outside Organization

While industrial foundations aren't legal in the U.S., it is possible for outside organizations to have a controlling interest in a business. Several types of organization could work for this, such as trusts or limited partnerships. Some non-profits can do many of the same activities that for-profit companies can, including own stock, with the rights and responsibilities inherent in ownership. Non-profits just have to follow the IRS rules and federal and state regulations for the type of entities they are. Legal and tax experts are required to set up the appropriate relationship between business entities and non-profit entities should you decide to go this route.

The Tyson Limited Partnership (TLP)—a private foundation, not a charitable institution—owns about 71 percent of Tyson Foods' outstanding voting stock. Its FORM 10-K filing notes, "As a result of these holdings, positions and directorships, the partners in the TLP have the ability to exert substantial influence or actual control over our management and affairs and over substantially all matters requiring action by our stockholders."[5] In the case of Hormel Foods, the Hormel Foundation owns 48 percent of Hormel stock and has as one of its three goals, "to preserve the independence of the Hormel Foods Corporation." The foundation is a 509(a)(3) supporting organization. As such, it is operated for the benefit of the charitable or educational organizations represented on its board.

Hormel Foods and Tyson Foods (Chapter 10) both have outside organizations that hold controlling interest in their companies.

Capital Weakness

One of the biggest points of structural weakness in the tandem hybrid model can be how it acquires capital. In Chapter 6 we explored the various

4 Ibid.
5 "United States Securities and Exchange Commission FORM 10-K," Tyson Foods, fiscal 2020, accessed April 4, 2022, www.annualreports.com/HostedData/AnnualReports/PDF/NYSE_TSN_2020.pdf.

sources of startup capital, such as personal funds, investment from family and friends, loans, crowdfunding, pitch competitions, etc. But at some point, more capital may be needed to scale up the enterprise, as we'll look at in the next chapter. This is often where VCs and Private Equity Firms enter the picture. We've warned about the dangers of going to VCs and Private Equity Firms because they want too much control in exchange for their capital. Their agenda isn't your agenda and if things don't go well you could lose the organization you've envisioned and built just as it's picking up speed.

The stats are slightly different from those cited under "Public company," but a 2018 working paper, "Do Founders Control Start-Up Firms that Go Public?" reports:

> Using a sample of over 18,000 VC- backed firms, we show that founders generally do not reacquire control via IPO. In almost 60% of firms that go public, the founder is no longer CEO at IPO. ... As of initial VC financing, the likelihood that a founder takes her firm public and retains the CEO position and voting control for three years is about 0.4%.[6]

You should weigh the costs and know the risks before making a deal with investors. *Forbes* asked a panel of Young Entrepreneur Council members why they would *not* seek VCs and Private Equity Firms as investors and their reasons included:

- Investors may have differing visions.
- You won't be able to take as many risks.
- You'll have to give up control and management.
- Your culture will change.
- You can't make business decisions alone.
- Investors may decide to pull their funding.[7]

If you've already given up too much to VCs and want to regain some of what you've ceded, you can learn from founders who have done just that. Their advice, as shared with Kimberly Weisul, editor-at-large at INC.com, includes:

> *Redo your math*: First, you'll have to figure out if your investors are willing to sell back their stake to you—and at what price. Good news: You might not have to pay them as much as you think. "You have to stop thinking about venture math" and the headline-grabbing valuations that VCs like to brag about, says Bryce Roberts, founder of

6 Brian Broughman and Jesse M. Fried, "Do Founders Control Start-Up Firms that Go Public?" ECGI, May 2018, https://ecgi.global/sites/default/files/working_papers/documents/finalfriedbroughman.pdf.

7 Expert Panel, "10 Good Reasons Not to Seek Investors for Your Business," Forbes, December 22, 2021, www.forbes.com/sites/theyec/2021/12/22/10-good-reasons-not-to-seek-investors-for-your-business/?sh=5a4a4c2f20fc.

alternative-investment fund Indie.vc. Instead, research the financial terms of recent M&A deals in your industry.

Research your VC: If you're not planning to go public, sell, or raise more money, your investors may consider you a "zombie company," meaning they might be eager to get rid of you, especially if they've profited from other companies in their portfolios. So do your research: Are your VCs still counting on your company to hit it big? Or have they already paid back their own limited partners?[8]

The ultimate danger of losing control is getting fired from your own company. According to entrepreneur Tero Isokauppila, "nearly 50% of founders get kicked out of the companies they founded or are removed as CEO within 18 months following a funding event." He offers steps founders can take to keep from losing their companies:

> Don't sleep on shares, board seats, and blocking rights. There are many classes of shares, and investors usually require a higher class. This means the investors' shares are worth more than the founders might be. But a lot of entrepreneurs don't realize that their shares are worth less. They'll look at the percentages and see that they own 80% and the investor owns 20%, which looks good. Well, not if the shares are worth different amounts.
>
> If you control the board and the majority of the shares you aren't always home free. Investors may still have special rules hidden within the stockholder's agreement. The most aggressive of these is private equity because if you don't hit a certain number, the valuation goes down. And, if you don't hit your numbers, they can fire you or get more money back. ... Even if investors only own 10% of the business, they could have you in their pockets.
>
> To keep control of your own company, it really comes down to this: make sure you're confident in your ability to understand legalese (or get an advisor who does), ensure your business has legs, and don't agree to unfavorable terms out of desperation. Because it's almost impossible to fix those mistakes once they're made.[9]

In Sync

Keeping the two entities in the tandem hybrid legally linked is important, and so is keeping them in sync with one another. The authors of the paper "Making Hybrids Work: Aligning Business Models and Organizational

---

8 Kimberly Weisul, "The Best (and Only) Way to Get Rid of Your Investors," Inc., accessed February 17, 2022, www.inc.com/magazine/201902/kimberly-weisul/buy-out-vc-investors-take-back-company.html.

9 Tero Isokauppila, "Tips to Avoid Getting Fired from the Company You Started, (from a Founder)," Minutes, accessed February 17, 2022, https://minutes.co/5-tips-to-avoid-getting-fired-from-the-company-you-started-from-a-founder/.

Design for Social Enterprises" get into the nuts and bolts of creating and maintaining synergy between the entities. They distinguish among four types of hybrid organizations, which they call Market Hybrids, Blending Hybrids, Bridging Hybrids, and Coupling Hybrids. They address the strengths and vulnerabilities of each and offer concrete management advice suited to the different structures. For example, OWP is a Coupling Hybrid in their scheme:

> To make Coupling Hybrids work, we recommend establishing structural differentiation so that the organization develops an internal capacity to perform both the commercial and the impact operations with the highest level of expertise. In some cases, this may happen through the development of a separate legal entity. … the impact activity should always remain under the control of the hybrid (instead of being outsourced to partners) because the Coupling Hybrid should not lose control over the relationship with its beneficiaries. If this happens, the focus on the social mission is seriously jeopardized and, over time, its hybrid nature may disappear and its potential for impact could be diminished.
>
> Structural differentiation will require Coupling Hybrids to recruit differentiated staff, i.e., different groups of organizational members with expertise in commercial and social impact operations, respectively. To ensure the coordination between these structurally differentiated groups of organizational members, it will be important for these organizations to create coordination mechanisms and processes that can prevent the emergence of tensions between potentially conflicting demands from customers and beneficiaries. To avoid mission drift and ensure the highest level of performance on both activities, performance management systems should rely on the monitoring of both operational (commercial) KPIs (key performance indicator) as well as impact KPIs.[10]

Downloading and studying "Making Hybrids Work" can help social entrepreneurs understand the nuances of different hybrid social enterprises and better manage the version they find themselves leading.

Scott's Story

The people doing the work of the ROW Foundation are non-profit born and bred. They have the right temperament and personality, they know the rules and regulations of the non-profit world, and they can execute programming effectively. The people on the for-profit side, OWP

---

10 Filipe Santos, Anne-Claire Pache, and Christoph Birkholz, "Making Hybrids Work: Aligning Business Models and Organizational Design for Social Enterprises," *California Management Review*, May 2015, www.researchgate.net/p ublication/277965692_Making_Hybrids_Work.

Pharmaceuticals, are either experienced pharma people or they're fresh out of college and we train them on pharmaceutical selling and management. Workwise, the two groups really don't mix. But office-wise we do, and I think that's very important.

Just recently I watched a new OWP employee help unload two pallets of medication headed for Poland, Ukraine, and other countries. It's OWP product going through ROW to meet a crisis situation. It's so good for OWP staff to see what we're really all about. All staff get regular email updates and attend monthly town hall meetings that rotate being hosted by OWP and ROW. They hear from our partners in different countries via Teams or Zoom about the lives being changed and are able to ask them questions about our projects. This builds alignment between the two organizations. Otherwise, people would lose the sense that OWP contributes to ROW and ROW contributes to the mission of OWP.

This close association is easy to do now with a smaller number of staff, but we plan to keep the same office arrangement even when we get into the hundreds of staff required by a large-scale hybrid organization.

The two organizations have separate boards, but they work together. "On the OWP board, we always focus on our greater purpose as the income generator for ROW," says board member Jim Milligan:

> ROW is our primary stakeholder and the two organizations share a common mission. The legal entities are different but there's so much connectivity between how ROW wants to fulfill its mission and how OWP wants to fund it that I can't foresee anything OWP would initiate that would be contrary to ROW's goals.

"I agree completely," says fellow board member Carol Gavin:

> I don't envision any conflict just by virtue of the people who are involved with the three entities, OWP, the ROW Foundation, and now ROW Global. Scott and Bruce and Paul are the connecting tissue among the organizations and boards. I haven't seen any tension because of their common vision, which is to see a world where everybody gets the same kind of healthcare and access to medications for neurological disorders.

Passing the Baton

At some point, founders and owners step out of leadership roles, either through planned succession, retirement, ill-health, or death. While this is a stark reality, most companies aren't prepared for it. As the humorist Ashleigh Brilliant quipped, "One possible reason why things aren't going according to plan is that there never was a plan." Deloitte's *Business Succession Planning* points out:

> According to the National Association of Corporate Directors, fewer than one in four private company boards say they have a formal succession plan in place. There isn't a good reason to justify the common oversight of not planning for business succession. Some business leaders are too caught up in the challenges of the present. Some have a subconscious aversion to the reality that they won't be around forever, or assume succession will work itself out naturally. Others are aware of the task's true complexity and find it overwhelming. Ultimately, however, the reasons people avoid succession planning aren't as important as the reasons they should embrace it. For a business, working without a succession plan can invite disruption, uncertainty, and conflict, and endangers future competitiveness.[11]

A well planned and orderly transition of leadership is essential for a tandem hybrid so that its mission continues to be funded by its business. A smooth passing of the baton allows for:

- Survival and growth of the business or its assets.
- Preservation of harmony when the business is family (or privately)—owned.
- Reduction or elimination of estate and income taxes.
- Facilitation of retirement for the current leadership generation.
- Ability to retain control of the process instead of having someone else make decisions.[12]

The steps to be taken for a smooth transition will depend on the type of organization. For a C-corp like OWP, "becoming aware of the rules surrounding business succession is even more important due to pitfalls resulting from the corporation's separate entity status," notes an internal Transamerica guide:

> When succession planning is put into place for a C corporation, there are many factors to consider such as the tax consequences of the type of buy-sell agreement selected, as well as family attribution, alternative minimum tax, and basis consequences.[13]

11 "Business Succession Planning Cultivating Enduring Value," Deloitte, accessed March 16, 2022, www2.deloitte.com/content/dam/Deloitte/us/Documents/deloitte-private/us-dges-business-succession-planning-collection.pdf.

12 Ibid.

13 "Business Succession Planning with C Corporations," Transamerica Life Insurance Company, accessed March 16, 2022, http://static1.squarespace.com/static/52a53e3de4b0d9959707caee/t/52e5f673e4b063fbaac12bb8/1390802547324/transamerica-business-succession-planning-with-c-corporations-producer-guide.pdf.

Succession planning can take several years to craft and implement. In the meantime, companies should have key man insurance on the founder(s) and top leaders in case the unimaginable happens. Designated replacements could also be in the wings like understudies in Broadway plays. Founders who hold the majority of stock may want to have a trust or other organization set up to receive the stock should they become disabled or die that are chartered to keep the social enterprise true to its original vision.

For example, a founder can set up a living trust and give her chosen successor legal authority to handle all tasks related to running the business. The successor may or may not have a financial interest in the company and may or may not be a family member. She can choose someone she trusts to be committed to the vision and values of the company and the social enterprise it is a part of.

What about family when it comes to succession? Some large-cap companies are family affairs while most are not. The tandem hybrid model is neutral on the subject. If family members have the capacity to run a multimillion or billion-dollar enterprise, that's great. Continuity of leadership has many advantages. But if they don't, they shouldn't be put in leadership roles just because of their last names.

Scott's Story

I don't intend to pass this company on to my two children, one of whom works for OWP, while the other doesn't. I gave each of them 1 percent of OWP stock and that's it. It's a nice bonus for them, especially with the size OWP will be one day, but it's not enough that they can stay home and live off that income. There are way too many examples of children and grandchildren who are negatively impacted by not having to work for a living. That won't be my kids.

My exit strategy may involve going public and selling some of my stock; I'm not sure yet. Several of the large companies I've studied, including many in Part III of this book, are public companies. OWP could go public with a low-float public offering where we limit the amount of stock sold. This would help with our investors and with current and future employees who receive restricted stock options, which are important to get high quality people. The bulk of the stock I keep would eventually go to ROW and perhaps to creating an OWP Investment Fund to help tandem hybrid social enterprises get set up and rolling.

I didn't start this social enterprise with the intention of getting wealthy beyond where I was when I came into this. I had a successful career at Abbott and Bristol Myers Squibb, and got pensions from each for retirement. I built this with the idea of treating "the least of these" around the world, who don't have access to the medications we in America take for granted. That mission still motivates me every day. I'm physically and mentally healthy, with a high energy level, and don't plan on retiring any time soon.

"As the majority shareholder, Scott can pretty much do what he wants," says OWP board member Kurt Florian, "including replace the board. He's very cognizant of his skills, but he also understands the value of board members with complimentary skillsets. He recognizes that he's gotten OWP to where it is and there's a need for other people to be involved who can help take it to the next level. One or our key future tasks will be helping with succession planning. Any successor to Scott is going to be determined in greater part by him, but he'll expect the board to be heavily involved in identifying and reviewing potential candidates. We'll need somebody who understands and is dedicated to our mission."

Retaining control of a tandem hybrid social enterprise is key to keeping it on target as far as its vision and mission. That's the *focus*. The *impact* it has on the target depends on its size and sustainability, which we'll consider next.

8 Scalable and Sustainable for the Long Haul

The tandem hybrid model is calibrated for organizations that intend to grow large from their inception and to be around for generations. Even if they start small to prove the business concept or because of limited resources, they are determined to grow large enough to have a national and probably international impact with a world-changing mission.

It's absolutely essential that the founders have a clear picture of what they're trying to accomplish with their social enterprise from the outset (see Chapter 5). An organization this size requires huge amounts of capital and the "usual suspects" who fund such enterprises aren't supportive of the hybrid model. And outside capital can't be accepted at the expense of losing control of the business, which ultimately has to be successful enough on its own to drive accelerated growth (see Chapter 6). The commercial and social entities involved in the tandem hybrid have to be connected in such a way as to support and protect the mission over time (see Chapter 7). Which brings us to scaling up the organization in ways that sustain it for generations. We will consider three components of this here: understanding the difference between scaling and growing, creating a unified corporate culture, and building a team of committed stakeholders.

Scott's Story

From the outset we knew that OWP and ROW would be national and international in their reach. Given the high cost and complexity of doing pharma, our for-profit business had to target the entire U.S. from a sales standpoint. We couldn't start small with Illinois or a few states; we had to be large scale to begin with. The U.S. is by far the largest and most competitive pharmaceutical market in the world. We had to generate enough profits to support our charitable foundation, which had a global mission.

Our social mission was helping people in under-resourced areas of the world. Potentially that's millions of people in low- and middle-income countries where the treatment gap for epilepsy and psychiatric disorders

DOI: 10.4324/9781003325987-10

is enormous. And we couldn't just do a one-time intervention. Epilepsy is a lifetime condition, so when we partner with healthcare organizations to provide antiseizure drugs, it's a long-term commitment. We don't want to start people on a treatment plan that can't be sustained.

In 2021 we were looking at a private equity deal, but as we got into what's called a security agreement, it ended up being 92 pages long, and we weren't even done! Bruce and I said, "This is getting absurd. This is not good. It's bad money because it comes with too many hooks." We were able to close a more favorable private equity deal for $8 million and secure a bank loan for $4.5 million. The best thing we have going for us is we're not burning cash. We're making enough to pay our expenses and don't owe anything more than 30 days out. If you're burning cash to scale up, you are vulnerable because if you're going to run out of money in six months, you have to close a deal or you could disappear.

Scaling versus Growing

Business experts Robert Sutton and Huggy Rao explain the difference between growing and scaling to Leigh Buchanan, editor-at-large for Inc. Magazine:

> In their book, Sutton and Rao argue that scaling isn't just about getting bigger. It is also about getting better. It's about spreading exceptional ideas, systems, or business models, and then persuading—ideally inspiring—others to make them their own. "The question we started with is, 'How do you spread something good from the few to the many, or from those with to those without?'" says Sutton. "It starts with, 'You've got something good.' The way you know you've succeeded is to ask yourself, 'If I stopped putting energy into this, would it continue to go well?'"[1]

The distinction is further spelled out by investment advisor Kelly Ford Buckley:

> Building a successful company isn't just about growth—it's about scale. Growth means adding resources at the same rate that you're adding revenue. For example, a company that gains a customer, hires more people to service them, and adds revenue at the same rate it is adding more cost. This is typical in many professional services-driven business models. While the company is technically growing, they're not scaling. Scale is about adding revenue at a rapid rate while adding resources at an incremental rate.

1 Leigh Buchanan, "How to Grow Without Losing What Makes You Great." *Inc.*, accessed Feb. 10, 2022, www.inc.com/magazine/201403/leigh-buchanan/how-to-scale-your-company.html.

Scaling growth is about creating business models and designing your organization in a way that easily scales in order to generate consistent revenue growth and avoid stall-points without adding a ton of extra cost and/or resources along the way. Here are five strategies for consideration as you think about scaling your early or growth-stage business:

Strategy #1:Boost Renewals
Strategy #2:Hire Good Product-Minded People
Strategy #3:Package Value-Added Services for Repeatable Selling & Delivery
Strategy #4:Combine Ownership of Product Management with Services Delivery
Strategy #5:Fire the Sales & Marketing Engine on Multiple Cylinders[2]

There is abundant material online and in print on how to scale up commercial businesses. We've listed a few resources in the endnotes for starters.[3] Scaling up a social enterprise is similar in some ways and different in others. A few differences are highlighted in "The Complete Guide to Growing and Scaling Your Social Enterprise," including the following:

Social enterprises are harder to start than for-profit organizations. They are likely to pay a little less than giant corporations with unlimited resources, and because of mission alignment as an additional screen, your pool of talent is smaller than most. Finding and developing the right people is hard enough, and like all things social enterprise, creating a model that is also focused on impact can actually make it more challenging to get to true scale and impact.[4]

A business scales to maximize profits; a social enterprise scales to expand impact. A business scales by developing new products and entering new markets; a social enterprise scales by leveraging new resources. A business

2 Kelly Ford Buckley, "You're Growing, But Are You Scaling? 5 Strategies to Help You Scale Growth," *Edison Partners*, March 22, 2017, www.edisonpartners.com/blog/5-strategies-scaling-growth.
3 Patrick Whatman, "Growth vs Scaling: What's the Difference and Why Does it Matter?" *Spend Journal*, June 8, 2021, https://blog.spendesk.com/en/growth-vs-scaling; "10 Ways to Scale a Business from Startup to a Huge Company, According to These Titans," Entrepreneur, June 11, 2019, www.entrepreneur.com/slideshow/334818; Lauren Landry, "Tips For Scaling Your Business," *Harvard Business School Online Business Insights Blog*, March 7, 2019, https://online.hbs.edu/blog/post/how-to-scale-a-business; "Guide: How To Scale Your Business in 2020," Studio, www.growwithstudio.com/how-to-scale-your-business.
4 "The Complete Guide to Growing and Scaling Your Social Enterprise," Movingworlds, accessed April 4, 2022, https://movingworlds.org/social-entrepreneurship-guide.

can scale through mergers and acquisitions; a social enterprise can scale through strategic partnerships.

Scott's Story

We wanted our hybrid model to be sustainable, to be able to evolve with the marketplace and last for generations. The longevity piece of the puzzle is difficult because the for-profit company has to continue to innovate or it will fail, like Sears, Kodak, Xerox, and other mega companies that were once leaders in their respective industries and are now just a shell of their original self or not in existence at all. The non-profit organization needs to evolve as well. It should look for more than just one source of funding and spend more time thinking outside the box.

At the outset we established ROW as a funding foundation, not an operating foundation that runs its own programs. It fulfills its mission by supporting well-established organizations that have proven track records. Around the world and at home, ROW is cultivating relationships with leading epileptologists, neurologists, and psychiatrists. For us, working smarter means partnering with others by pooling resources and expertise to reach common goals. We aren't interested in reinventing the wheel; we just grease the ones that are effectively rolling so as to cover more territory. We aren't interested in credit or control in these relationships. We have no problem playing a supporting role because we don't see ourselves having competitors, only comrades in a common cause: to improve the lives of those struggling with epilepsy and associated psychiatric disorders as efficiently and economically as possible.

Another way we've scaled up ROW is by starting a public charity alongside our private foundation. We've hired a fundraiser to help us with donor-advised funds (DAFs), which we couldn't do as a private foundation. We want to grow ROW beyond what OWP can provide. The business gives us a great base, but we don't want it to be our ceiling. In the near future we also want to develop more innovative ways to share our mission and reach potential donors. We'd like to see a phone app people could use to learn about specific projects anywhere in the world and target their donations.

In the tandem hybrid, the for-profit and non-profit entities are joined together—think tandem bike—and the leadership must establish a unified culture that incorporates the strengths of each and synchronizes their efforts. Both entities need to grow and scale at the same rate. If the non-profit tries to grow and expand its programs, but the business isn't increasing revenues at the same rate to provide sufficient funding, the impact will stall. If the business flourishes and the non-profit can't grow their programs or staff to handle the available resources, the impact will also plateau. Good communication, planning, and forecasting between both entities is essential.

Unified Culture

A corporate culture is the complement of vision and values, beliefs and behaviors, benchmarks, and goals, that determine how an organization operates. It's a company's personality, expressly stated and organically implied. It starts with the founder and is shaped over time by the people who are hired. It is influenced by external factors such as country of origin, economic trends in its market, company size, products, competitors, etc. Just as there are general types of personalities, there are general types of corporate cultures with their characteristic strengths and weaknesses.

Successful companies have strong, value-based cultures. Their leaders live the culture and set the example. Internal structures and policies reinforce the culture and hold the organization together like the bones in a body. This doesn't mean the culture is rigid and inflexible. It has to evolve as the organization grows. Some changes will be strategic and come from the top down while others will be organic and come from the bottom up.

Corporate culture will be evident to the outside world through a company's products, services, marketing, and branding. Everyone has heard about the culture at Apple, Amazon, Google, and Facebook and how it shapes the products and services for which these companies are known worldwide. In each instance, it started with their founders. Molly Graham, who helped shape the corporate culture at Facebook, says:

> 80% of your company's culture will be defined by its core leaders. These are the people who sat down and said this is such a good idea that I want to devote my entire life to it. Companies tend to reflect everything about them—their personality, strengths, weaknesses. So when you start defining culture in an intentional way, first look at yourselves. If you're not a founder, look at your CEO and the people who were there at the very beginning.[5]

The leadership component is even more critical in tandem hybrid social enterprises where the founders face the special challenge of building a unified culture shared by a commercial business and a charitable entity. "To keep the mission on course while still making enough money to sustain their operations, the leaders of hybrids must make deliberate cultural decisions," notes the study "In Search of the Hybrid Ideal":

---

5 "80% of Your Culture is Your Founder," First Round Review, accessed March 24, 2022, https://review.firstround.com/80-of-Your-Culture-is-Your-Founder.

First, they must identify and communicate organizational values that strike a healthy balance between commitment to both social mission and effective operations. Equally important is the selection, development, and management of employees who are capable of recognizing and pursuing social and economic value. ... hybrids face the additional challenge of designing compensation systems, tasks, and governance policies that reinforce an organizational culture committed to both social mission and effective operations.[6]

As the enterprise grows, the founder can no longer interact with everyone personally. He or she can't interview every new hire or oversee every promotion. The founder must create and reinforce a culture, but others have to implement it on a daily basis. That's why early hires are so important. They must have the same commitment to the vision; the same willingness to sacrifice and go the extra mile to make the enterprise successful. "Smart decisions lead to success, and those decisions are made by the people you hire," says Andrew Filev, founder of Wrike:

It all starts with recruiting, so building the right team should be a key focus area for you. ... Once you've built a good foundational team codify and reinforce your culture. It's a difficult and disruptive process to change the culture in a large and established business. During the scaling process, your culture is more malleable. You can lose it with the influx of new hires, investors, and priorities, or you can improve it with the right focus and tools. It's key to set up feedback loops that identify challenges and successes like employee satisfaction surveys, 360s, and ask-me-anything forums. Listen to that feedback, lead by example, and demand no less from your executive team.[7]

Committed Stakeholders

No matter how grand and noble a vision, it has to be converted from idea to reality by people. A large-scale social enterprise will eventually require hundreds, if not thousands, of people to carry out the mission long term. Some will be in the center of the action; others will be on the periphery. Those who have a vested interest in an enterprise can be referred to as stakeholders. Equity stakeholder are owners, partners, stockholders, and investors. Non-equity stakeholders could be employees, customers, contractors, coaches, consultants, and

---

6 Julie Battilana, Matthew Lee, John Walker, and Cheryl Dorsey, "In Search of the Hybrid Ideal," *Stanford Social Innovation Review*, Summer 2012, doi:10.48558/ wf5m-8q69, https://ssir.org/articles/entry/in_search_of_the_hybrid_ideal.

7 Andrew Filev, "3 Keys to Successfully Scale Your Organization from Small Biz to Big Time," *Forbes*, August 5, 2021, www.forbes.com/sites/andrewfilev/ 2021/08/05/3-keys-to-successfully-scale-your-organization-from-small-biz-to-big-time/?sh=3d4ea4d442ac.

the local community. The social entity part of a tandem hybrid is the biggest stakeholder in the business entity, just as the ROW Foundation is the biggest stakeholder in OWP Pharmaceuticals, and vice versa. Subsequently, stakeholders in the social entity automatically become stakeholders in the business entity, and stakeholders in the business entity automatically become stakeholders in the social entity.

To a greater or lesser degree, all stakeholders play a part in an enterprise's success and sustainability. As on any professional team, there are franchise players and support staff. Here's the lineup:

Owners and Partners

Tandem hybrids are started by social entrepreneurs who invest their time, talents, and treasures to solve social problems or address social injustices. They "own" the mission and the organizations they create to pursue it. As we say in the Introduction, "They are the driven, creative individuals who question the status quo, exploit new opportunities, refuse to give up, and remake the world for the better."[8]

Sometimes organizations are started by more than one person. When it comes to partnerships, the two or more people need to agree on the mission and the means to accomplish it. But being yoked together in a business venture doesn't mean equal ownership. One partner may have more money or expertise in the field where the business operates. The danger of a straight 50/50 partnership is that there's nobody to break the tie when it comes to decisions or disagreements. A written contract that spells out the relationship between partners is important. It should address what happens if one partner wants out for whatever reason. It should clearly state the financial terms of separation. The business might not be able to repay a partner's initial investment and the party leaving might have to forfeit his or her investment or have repayment deferred until the company becomes profitable.

Board

A board is not that important in the early stages of a startup when the founder is the driving force. But for the company to grow and scale, a strong, independent board becomes vital. You'll want smart, experienced businesspeople who believe in your mission and your approach to accomplishing it. They have to be committed to the long-term vision and not simply looking to build the company for a quick and profitable exit.

Carol Gavin brings a strong governance background to the boards of OWP and the ROW Foundation. "I was involved with the boards of two

8 David Bornstein, "How to Change the World," David Bornstein blog, accessed March 3, 2022, https://davidbornstein.wordpress.com/books/how-to-change-the-world/.

publicly held companies at a time when those types of boards were going through a lot of change prompted by some scandals in the early 2000s," she says:

> When I started serving on not-for-profit boards, there was definitely a need for strong governance at the board level. In 2018 I heard about what Scott was doing and was intrigued and interested in being involved at the startup level of a social enterprise because it's different from the boards I've been on before. In a non-profit, mission is always the key. In a commercial business, the duty of the board is to maximize profit for shareholders. The tandem hybrid model rises mission to a higher level than it would be in a for-profit business, and it's an interesting balance between the commercial success of the organization and the mission behind it.

Jim Milligan also joined the OWP board in 2018 and currently chairs the audit committee. "My attraction to OWP is similar to Carol's," he says:

> It's the unique combination of a mission being served by a financial enterprise. I wanted to learn from, and help, a smaller organization looking to grow and do some very meaningful things. I've seen the importance of an effective board with the private companies I've been involved with and the value a diverse and experienced board can provide to help an organization fulfill its vision.

Kurt Florian has been involved with the Epilepsy Foundation of America since the mid-1980s:

> I met Scott while I was president of the Epilepsy Foundation of Greater Chicago. He explained what OWP and ROW were doing and I thought it was a really interesting way to not only produce epilepsy medications, but also to help the rest of the world in terms of epilepsy treatment. As I got to know Scott, I introduced him to many of the epileptologists and neurologists in the Chicagoland area.
>
> When OWP was formalizing an outside board, Scott asked me to join. I was also on the advisory board of ROW. The biggest difference I saw from other not-for-profit boards is they all had a charitable mission as their focus, but not any kind of fiduciary duty to shareholders. With OWP, board members have fiduciary duties to shareholders, the main one being Scott and his mission for ROW. Focusing on maximizing returns to OWP ultimately ends up funding all the wonderful work ROW does.

Stockholders

An average startup won't have stock, but may have some legal instrument that communicates an equity position. These should be documented in a capitalization table (cap table):

[A cap table] is a list of all the securities your company has issued and who owns them. Securities include stock, convertible notes, warrants, and equity grants. Cap tables are important because they tell you who owns how much of your company. This can affect everything from how you price future fundraising rounds to who needs to sign off on major company decisions.[9]

When stock is needed, there are several kinds to choose from: A, B, preferred, common, voting, super voting, etc. As far as a tandem hybrid, the stock type doesn't matter as long as the founder retains control of the company to protect the initial vision and mission. A company doesn't have to go public to issue stock. Stock isn't a requirement to grow, but it will make it a lot easier to attract the right people to invest in you and work with you. People at the higher levels expect restricted stock options as part of their comp packages.

If you decide to do an IPO in an attempt to become a multimillion-dollar company, you don't have to give up control. You can do a low-float IPO, meaning that you're not floating the entire company, maybe only 10 or 20 percent of the commercial enterprise. You can still maintain control, either through voting stock or by holding at least 51 percent of common stock.

Investors

We looked at various types of investors in Chapter 6. These can range from family and friends to VCs and private equity firms. Each will have their own reasons for investing and their own expectations for return on investment (ROI). You must know the strings that are attached to the capital and make sure you want to pay the price when they are pulled. "Vetting investors is always a challenge," writes Rupert Scofield, CEO of FINCA International:

> While the prospect of any investment capital can be tempting, it is important to be certain that potential investors share your priorities. Not only will their funding sow the seeds for your future success, investors will play a major role in the shape and direction of your company. If your values are aligned, investors may serve as a sounding board for ideas, a mentor in times of trouble, and a facilitator to other investor or business relationships to build your company.[10]

---

9 Jenna Lee, "What is a cap table?" Carta, October 8, 2019, https://carta.com/blog/what-is-a-cap-table/.

10 Rupert Scofield, "Finding the Right Impact Investor for Your Social Enterprise," *Pioneers Post*, April 16, 2019, www.pioneerspost.com/business-school/20190416/finding-the-right-impact-investor-your-social-enterprise.

"The current shareholders of OWP have bought in with our mission in mind," says Jim Milligan. "Of course they want an acceptable return, but they're aligned with the overall mission, which involves a good portion of the profits of OWP going to ROW. They invested in the social mission to serve the world through ROW."

Employees

Talented people are key to the success of any organization. You want to work with good people and the closer and more critical they are to the core of your enterprise, the more important it is that they be aligned with your mission. When it comes to a tandem hybrid, you need people who are committed to the company and the cause, whether they are working for the business or the non-profit side of the organization. As Marc Benioff, founder of Salesforce, says, "The secret to successful hiring is this: look for the people who want to change the world."[11]

You want to attract people who are better than you can afford at first and who have faith they will be rewarded later. You want people who will go the extra mile to help you succeed and who will stay with you long-term. Over time, not all employees will have this same level of commitment. If someone buys into your vision and mission, great. If they don't, they're still of value as employees and you should develop them and help them become better employees and pay them well for their services. However, mission buy-in is absolutely critical in the C-suite: the CEO, the president, the CFO, the COO, the four or five people at the top.

Scott's Story

At OWP we deferred some of the salary of early employees. We paid them less than market rate, but we accrued their salary until we reached a point where we could reimburse them the difference. We gave a few people some pretty big checks. We're now at the stage where we can attract people by paying good salaries, but initially we needed people with enough faith in what we were trying to do to make sacrifices.

My intent is to hire high caliber people to succeed me with the management of OWP and pay them fair market value salaries with incentives based on performance. There's a big difference between running a company and having the vision for that company. I'd like for the next generation of leaders to have been here during the formative years of the organization. Especially at the C-level, I want people who are aligned

11 Marc Benioff, "12 Lessons on Hiring From Larry Ellison and Marc Benioff," Recruiter.com, www.recruiter.com/recruiting/12-lessons-on-hiring-from-larry-el lison-and-marc-benioff/.

with the vision and mission of the Pharmaceutical Social Enterprise and who have been part of making it happen.

This doesn't mean we won't hire from outside, but they have to be people who are aligned with our vision and values. I'd rather hire people who are aligned with our mission and train them in pharma-related skills over two or three years and grow them into leadership positions than hire the people who have the professional skillsets we need but who don't buy into our values or mission.

Customers and Contractors

Your vision and mission should be part of your appeal to customers. The more they know about why you do what you do, the more likely they will support your company if your cause resonates with them. This might give you an advantage over the competition, but your product or service still has to make sense to customers. They will ask: is your product or service cost effective? Is it safe? Is it better than the competition? Of course, the bigger you are the easier it is for people to hear about what you're doing and to have more confidence in your company. Success over time confirms your authenticity and gives you credibility. Your social mission may also give you a slight advantage when it comes to contractors and vendors. A supplier who believes in what you're doing may give you a discount on supplies as a way to support your mission. It doesn't hurt to ask.

When it comes to social enterprises, we can make a broad distinction between customers and beneficiaries. Customers are those who pay for your goods or services while clients are those who benefit from your goods and services without covering their costs. The commercial business will have customers whose purchases cover the goods and services provided to the clients of the social entity. People in the U.S. buy pharmaceutical products from OWP, which allows it to donate medicines and capital to ROW, which then provides medications, equipment and training to healthcare partners and their patients around the world.

Coaches and Consultants

Scaling a company may be something you've never done before and you'll need experts, coaches, consultants, and mentors to guide you. The former will no doubt charge, the latter may offer their advice for free. If you have a business background, you may benefit from coaching on the dynamics of social enterprises. If your expertise is non-profits or charitable organizations, a business consultant could be well worth the money.

Coaches and consultants have slightly different roles. Jose Palomino, CEO of Value Prop Interactive explains:

Both a coach and a consultant are focused on helping you solve pro-blems in your business. The difference is in their approach. A business coach takes the approach of improving you as the leader of your busi-ness. A business consultant takes a more specialized hands-on approach, providing specific solutions for your business itself. ... coaching is "done with you" and consulting is "done for you."[12]

Local Community

Small and medium-size social enterprises can have a powerful impact on their neighborhoods and communities. When a tandem hybrid reaches large-scale, it can have an even more dynamic influence on its community by providing employment, paying taxes, participating in civic affairs and philanthropic ventures in the area. Its unique structure can keep the business from being sold out from under its mission and broken up or relocated.

Although not started as social enterprises, companies like Hershey and Hormel have provided jobs through their commercial businesses and supported extensive civic and educational programs through their foundations and charitable organi-zations. As you will learn in Part III, these companies have enriched their home-towns of Hershey, Pennsylvania (Chapter 9) and Austin, Minnesota (Chapter 10) for more than a century. The communities that hosted these companies were protected from having them being sold or relocated because company owners and leaders maintained control as one of their founding principles.

This was not the case with the Upjohn Company (Chapter 12), which can serve as a warning to tandem hybrids. The company no longer exists as a separate entity, having been swallowed up in multiple mergers. When Upjohn was subsumed by Pharmacia, and then Pfizer, it had a profound impact on Kalamazoo, Michigan by negatively affecting the city's tax base, job market, and many civic institutions.

Hershey, Hormel, and Upjohn are three of the eight large-cap companies we examine in Part III. None are social enterprises but all have been around for decades and have real-world lessons to teach social entrepreneurs about the commercial and non-profit sides of the tandem hybrid model.

---

12 Jose Palomino, "The Difference Between a Business Coach and a Consultant: Which Do I Need?" Value Prop, January 30, 2021, www.valueprop.com/blog/the-difference-between-a-business-coach-and-a-consultant-which-do-i-need.

ROW in Action

Medication Grants to Venezuela

ROW is currently granting OWP Pharmaceuticals' Roweepra and Subvenite through more than 20 partners globally. As part of these efforts, since 2018, ROW has been making large grants of Roweepra to Venezuela, a country that is experiencing a severe shortage of medicines that makes it very difficult for people to get essential medical care. The Pharmaceutical Federation of Venezuela estimates 85 percent of medicines are not available, and states: "The entire Venezuelan healthcare system is on the verge of collapse."[13] Anti-epileptic drugs are among the hardest to find. These grants have been made through the *Cuatro por Venezuela* Foundation and the Venezuelan chapter of the International League Against Epilepsy (LIVECE).

ROW has granted 64,000 patient prescription months of medication to Venezuela as of the time of writing.

Figure 8.1 Patient receiving medication from the Cuatro por Venezuela Foundation.

---

13 Samantha Raphelson, "Venezuela's Health Care System Ready To Collapse Amid Economic Crisis," NPR, February 1, 2018, www.npr.org/2018/02/01/582469305/venezuelas-health-care-system-ready-to-collapse-amid-economic-crisis.

Part III

Lessons from History

None of the eight multi-generational companies in Part III began, or function today, as social enterprises. So what are they doing in this book? As we've said elsewhere, the tandem hybrid's goal is to be a large-cap organization that uses the power of the market to fund its mission and create significant social impact. To envision large-scale impact, large-scale examples are needed. There aren't many social enterprises that meet this criterion to use as case studies, so we're doing the next best thing; looking at large companies that: started because of the vision of a founder, became financially successful enough to dominate their markets, found creative ways to keep control of the business through trying times, scaled up from local roots to international prominence, and sustained that growth for decades.

Our intent isn't to add to the volumes that have been written about these companies but to scan an abridged history and cherry-pick lessons that social entrepreneurs can apply to the commercial and non-profit sides of the tandem hybrid model. Imagine the impact of a social enterprise that mirrored the commercial success of these giants, but was built with a defined social purpose from the outset. This is the promise and potential of the tandem hybrid.

DOI: 10.4324/9781003325987-11

9 The Hershey Company and Mars Inc.

The Hershey Company and Mars Inc. dominate the same market, but represent polar opposites when it comes to fulfilling the vision of their founders. Milton Snavely Hershey built a community that still bears his name and created what is now one of the largest private foundations in the world. He gave away most of his wealth during his lifetime and donated the rest in his will. Frank C. Mars left behind one of the richest families in the world, with a handful of descendants worth $94 billion. The company's philanthropic efforts are connected to their communities and customers.

The Hershey Company

Milton Snavely Hershey started what is now the Hershey Company in 1894. It is one of the largest chocolate manufacturers in the world, with almost $10 billion in revenues in 2022.[1] It was #370 on the Fortune 500 list in 2021. But it's only one of four major entities started by this businessman, social entrepreneur, and philanthropist. The other three are the Hershey Trust Company (portfolio value in 2021, $11.9 billion,[2] down from $17.4 billion the year before), the Hershey Entertainment & Resorts Company (2020 revenues, $502 million[3]), and the M. S. Hershey Foundation (2019 revenues, $12.3 million[4]).

"Chocolate Is Permanent"

Milton's first two candy businesses failed and he started his third, the Lancaster Caramel Company, in 1886. The business grew and he bought a

1 "Revenue for The Hershey Company (HSY) Revenue in 2021," accessed April 19, 2022, https://companiesmarketcap.com/hershey-company/revenue/.
2 "Hershey Trust Co—Portfolio Holdings," Fintel, accessed April 20, 2022, https://fintel.io/i/hershey-trust.
3 "Hershey Entertainment & Resorts Revenue," Zippia, www.zippia.com/hershey-entertainment-resorts-careers-1574551/revenue/.
4 "The M S Hershey Foundation," ProPublicia, accessed April 19, 2022, https://projects.propublica.org/nonprofits/organizations/236242734.

DOI: 10.4324/9781003325987-12

home and property for a factory in Lancaster Pennsylvania and opened a factory in Chicago, where he got interested in chocolate. He started the Hershey Chocolate Company in 1894 as a subsidiary of the Lancaster Caramel Company. The business did well enough that he sold it five years later for $1 million. He retained the chocolate business and focused on that. He once told a friend, "Caramels are a fad, but chocolate is permanent. I'm going to make chocolate."[5]

Innovation has been a driver of success at Hershey from the beginning. All chocolate was handmade and expensive before Milton modernized the chocolate industry:

> By developing and using innovative machinery that eliminated the need to make and wrap chocolate by hand, Hershey introduced the first method for mass-producing chocolate at affordable prices, allowing everyone to experience the joys of his magical creation, the Hershey Bar.[6]

♦ **Create or improve a product or service that will have a large market and can generate significant revenue.**

More than a century later, Hershey is still known for innovation:

Hershey is pushing a lot of new concepts and innovations. The candy maker is launching new stand-up packaging for 150 items this year, reinventing the self-check queue, innovating for digital commerce, expanding manufacturing plants, renovating its corporate offices, and going viral on social media.[7]

♦ **Innovation is the key to capturing and maintaining market share. Management has to lead by example and create a culture that encourages and rewards innovation.**

Hershey bought his first chocolate-making machines in 1893 and built his own dairy-processing plant to supply his production process in 1901. Fifteen years later he bought land in Cuba and built a sugar mill to supply his growing business. In 1918, Hershey got an order from the U.S. Government for 2 million milk chocolate bars for soldiers on active duty during Christmas. This was a boon to business, but financial troubles hit in 1920 and Hershey signed a promissory note to save his company. When the note was paid off a few years later, he decided to divide his operations so that if

5 "Milton S. Hershey, The Candy Man," *Entrepreneur*, October 8, 2008, www. entrepreneur.com/article/197530.

6 Ibid.

7 Crystal Lindell, "How the 125-Year-Old Hershey Company Continues to Innovate," Candy Industry, May 14, 2019, www.candyindustry.com/articles/ 88674-how-the-125-year-old-hershey-company-continues-to-innovate.

the chocolate business ever failed, it wouldn't take his other ventures down with it. In 1927, he reorganized and incorporated as Hershey Chocolate Corporation, with an initial public offering of 350,000 shares. Hershey Estates was established to handle all non-chocolate business.

♦ **Organize in a way that protects your vision from the vicissitudes of the marketplace.**

Hershey, PA

On the personal front, Milton married Catherine "Kitty" Sweeney in 1898. That year he bought the place where he had been born, Homestead Farm, which included more than 65,000 acres. He invested in other property and improvements in Derry Church, as the community around Derry Township was called. He did so much for the community that it became known as Hershey, the ultimate company town. It has no legal status as an incorporated municipality, although more than half the population of the township lives there today. Hershey's interest extended to every aspect of his community. The Derry Township website summarizes his considerable contributions:

> Milton S. Hershey returned to his birthplace to build a new factory for the Hershey Chocolate Company in 1903. The Hershey Volunteer Fire Company was organized two years later. The area boomed with construction for the next 15 years with the development of a model industrial town. New structures included sites such as the Cocoa House (1905), Hersheypark (1907), Hershey Laundry (1908), Ballroom (1909), Hershey Department Store (1910), Hershey Park Pool (1912), Hershey Trust Company (1914), the M.S. Hershey Consolidated School (1914), and the Press Building (1916). Hershey Industrial School for disadvantaged orphaned boys was established 1909, today known as Milton Hershey School. During the Great Depression of the 1930s the Community Building, Hotel Hershey, Milton Hershey School Senior Hall, Hershey Sports Arena, Hershey Chocolate Corporation Windowless Office Building, and the Stadium were built.[8]

♦ **Invest in the well-being of others and take an interest in the whole person, not just in what goes on at work.**

A large part of what M.S. Hershey did for the community was handled through the Hershey Trust Company, set up in 1905 to provide banking for the town. The Hersheys loved children but couldn't have any of their

---

8 "The History of Derry Township," Derry Township, accessed March 9, 2022, www.derrytownship.org/community/history.

own so in 1909 they founded the Hershey Industrial School for Orphans. They donated 486 acres of farmland—which included Hershey's birthplace—where students lived and worked until they were eighteen. The school started with four boys the following year. It was renamed the Milton Hershey School in 1951. The Hershey Archives give a glimpse of Hershey's motivation:

> Sadly, Catherine Hershey passed away on March 25, 1915. That event, World War I, and a sugar crisis prompted Milton Hershey to place almost his entire fortune in a perpetual trust for the security of the school on November 13, 1918. News about the amazing gift did not become public until 1923. In an article in Fortune magazine in 1924, Milton Hershey explained why he gave his money away. "I never could see what happiness a rich man gets from contemplating a life of acquisition only, with the cold and legal distribution of his money after he is gone. For myself, would I find any further zest in accumulating wealth? No, but now I am more interested than ever in maintaining and improving the morale and efficiency of all my companies. I want to devote the rest of my life to that end, for the school."[9]

♦ **Decide how much is enough for you and yours, then use the rest to bless others.**

The School Trust received all of Hershey's chocolate company stock at a time when the company held his other business assets. The stock was valued at $60 million. The Hershey Trust Company was appointed trustee for the school. It not only managed the School Trust's assets, it also had responsibility for Hershey's land holdings and other financial investments. The Trust Company has been criticized for doing too little with Hershey's money. A 2021 article by investigative journalists for *Spotlight PA* addresses this:

> Beginning in 1909, Milton Hershey put his estate into the Milton Hershey School Trust, the legal entity that exists solely to hold the Hershey estate and to fund the school. Board members say they are bound by the school's founding document, the original deed signed by Hershey and his wife, Catherine. To ensure that the school will exist "in perpetuity," the deed says the board can spend only the income earned by the endowment, not the endowment itself. So while the school's total assets are worth $17.4 billion, $16 billion of that—Hershey Co. stock, real estate holdings and other investments—cannot be spent, according to the deed. ... Hershey's fortune, which

9   "History of Milton Hershey School," Hershey Community Archives, February 25, 2021, https://hersheyarchives.org/encyclopedia/history-of-milton-hershey-school/.

funds the school, has ballooned to be larger than that of the Ford Foundation. But the school has faced persistent criticism for helping only a fraction of the vulnerable children it could reach with its vast wealth.[10]

♦ **Build flexibility into your organization so leadership can adjust how they honor the original vision.**

Almost all of this wealth was in Hershey Company stock, but by 1981, the Hershey Trust Company's shares had shrunk to the slimmest of ownership margins, 50.1 percent, making the chocolate company vulnerable to hostile takeover. This was a possibility neither the business nor the trust could tolerate, so in 1984 the company divided its stock into two classes: Common Stock, which held one vote per share, and Class B Common Stock, which held ten votes per share. Of the 5,102,002 shares of Class B stock, the trust company acquired 5,051,001.[11]

In an interesting turn of events fifteen years later, the Trust asked the Company to explore a sale of the Company so the Trust could diversify its holdings. Trusts that had all their eggs in one basket were thought to be at risk. The Packard Foundation, with most of its assets concentrated in Hewlett-Packard stock, lost about two-thirds of its value in 2001. If that happened to the Hershey Company, the school for which the Trust was responsible would suffer, hence the interest in diversification.

An offer came from Wm. Wrigley Jr. Co to acquire Hershey for $12 billion. Many people and politicians in the town of Hershey opposed the sale. The courts temporarily blocked any sale and rather than continue the fight, the Trust dropped the idea. Another candy company tried to buy Hershey in 2016. Reuters reported, "Hershey Co said on Thursday it had rejected a $23 billion takeover bid by Mondelez International Inc. that would seek to expand the latter's limited U.S. footprint and create the world's largest confectioner." Mondelez said it would let Hershey keep its name and not cut jobs, but, "The board of directors of the company unanimously rejected the indication of interest and determined that it provided no basis for further discussion between Mondelez and the company."[12]

10 Bob Fernandez, Charlotte Keith, "America's Richest School Serves Low-Income Kids. But Much of its Hershey-Funded Fortune Isn't Being Spent," Spotlight PA, May 28, 2021, www.spotlightpa.org/news/2021/05/pa-milton-hershey-school-spending-students-surplus/.

11 "Hershey Facts," The Hershey Company, November 2019, www.thehersheycompany.com/content/dam/corporate-us/documents/investors/2019-fact-book.pdf.

12 Lauren Hirsch, "Hershey Rejects $23 Billion Mondelez Takeover Offer," Reuters, June 30, 2016, www.reuters.com/article/us-hershey-m-a-mondelez-intl/hershey-rejects-23-billion-mondelez-takeover-offer-idUSKCN0ZG24O.

♦   **Structure company ownership to keep control in the hands of the founder(s) to protect the original vision. Adjust the structure when circumstances require it.**

Foundations and Trusts

Hershey had a lifelong interest in helping the youth of his community. In addition to the school for orphans, he created the M. S. Hershey Foundation in 1935 to provide educational and cultural opportunities for the citizens of Derry Township. He endowed it with 5,000 shares of Hershey stock and appointed the Hershey Trust Company as trustee. The funds generated by the Foundation went to help the Derry Township Public Schools. In 1938, the Foundation endowed Hershey Junior College, which offered tuition-free education to all residents.[13]

Hershey had a new will drawn up in 1944 shortly before his death. The two-page document provided that most of his estate be put into a new trust fund. The Hershey Archives notes:

> At the time of his death his estate consisted of the wealth that he had accumulated since his endowment of the Milton Hershey School trust fund in 1918 [almost $900,000]. The beneficiary of this new trust fund would be the Derry Township School District. Milton Hershey had been very supportive of the community's public schools during his lifetime and he wanted to provide an enduring legacy for them.[14]

Milton Hershey died in 1945, age eighty-eight, leaving behind a legacy that has impacted millions. He organized his company and community in such a way as to direct its impact long after he was gone.

♦   **Consider what will happen to your wealth when you're gone, and proactively plan to share it in the most effective way.**

Tandem Hybrid Distinctives and Hershey

Driven by a Compelling Social Mission

The Hershey Company had a strong and visionary founder in M. S. Hershey. He didn't start with a social mission in mind but one quickly developed: to share the company's success with its employees and community. He did this generously and consistently throughout his life and after his death through his various bequests and foundations.

---

13   "The M.S. Hershey Foundation," Hershey Community Archives, September 7, 2018, https://hersheyarchives.org/encyclopedia/m-s-hershey-foundation/.
14   "One Last Gift," Hershey Community Archives, February 1, 2012, https://hersheyarchives.org/encyclopedia/one-last-gift/.

Financed by Commercial Success

Everything M. S. Hershey was able to do for his employees and neighbors was funded by the success of his commercial businesses. He was a visionary and innovative businessman who saw the potential chocolate market before anyone else and took risks to become its dominant player. The company consistently came up with new products and opened new markets. Hershey pursued vertical integration so he could control everything from raw supplies to international sales.

Structured to Retain Control

After Hershey had to sign a promissory note in 1920 to save his company, he subsequently divided his operations so that if the chocolate business ever failed, it wouldn't sink his philanthropic ventures. In 1927, he incorporated the Hershey Chocolate Corporation as a public company to run the business and established Hershey Estates to handle all non-chocolate endeavors, later controlled by the Hershey Trust. The Trust would always hold enough stock that the company could not be sold out from under its founding vision.

Scalable and Sustainable for the Long Haul

Hershey stayed ahead of the curve by building capacity before there was a demand for his products and by ensuring control of his business and social enterprises for perpetuity through the Hershey Trust. Years after his death, this arrangement prevented the company being sold or taken over and relocated from Hershey, PA. It also created one of the largest foundations in the world.

Mars Inc.

Mars Inc, is a privately owned family business with 2021 revenues of $40 billion. It is one of the largest food companies in the world. The company operates four business segments: Mars Petcare, Mars Food, Mars Wrigley, and Mars Edge. It is owned by the grandchildren of Frank Mars and employs 130,000 people in more than 80 countries.[15]

Frank C. Mars started his first candy company in Tacoma, Washington in 1911. The venture failed after a few years. He moved to Minneapolis and started The Nougat House in 1920. There he created the Mar-O-Bar and started the Mar-O-Bar Company, which later became Mars Inc. In 1923 the company came out with the Milky Way bar and the next year, sales topped $800,000. It went on to become the best-selling candy bar in America.

15 "Mars," *Forbes*, accessed April 20, 2022, www.forbes.com/companies/mars/?sh=16793e493bb7.

"Frank Mars hired his son Forrest E. Mars to work in the candy operation after his graduation from Yale, but the two reportedly had a stormy relationship," as noted in one history of the company:

> In the early 1930s, Frank, giving Forrest some money and the foreign rights to manufacturer Milky Way, ordered his son to start his own business abroad. Moving to England, Forrest established a confectionery and a canned pet food company, which met with great success.[16]

Frank and fellow candy magnate Milton Hershey had a friendly relationship and Mars was one of Hershey's biggest customers, purchasing as much as $7.5 million in chocolate annually. Their companies would later become fierce rivals. The lifestyles of their founders were quite different. Whereas Hershey invested heavily in his company and community, Mars spent lavishly on himself:

> Depression be damned, Chicago's new candy power couple purchased themselves a Duesenberg town car worth $20,000 (a ridiculous $300,000 in modern cash) and were gleefully chauffeured near and far, from the factory grounds to as far north as their new palatial estate in Minocqua, Wisconsin. Like many of the other leading Chicago tycoons of the period, Frank Mars also jumped into the ranching and horse breeding game, employing 100 people to run his nearly 3,000 acre "Milky Way Farms" in Tennessee[17].

Forrest E. Mars, Sr.

Frank lived on the farm until his untimely death in 1934, at age 50. He left the majority share of Mars Inc. to his wife and daughter, Patricia. Forrest returned to the States in 1940 but continued to run the U.K. company. He went into business with Bruce Murrie, son of the Hershey Company president, and they created a snack for American soldiers during World War II that wouldn't easily melt. It was called M&Ms for "Mars and Murrie." After the war, Forrest's company, M&M Ltd, bought Murrie out.

To candy and pet food, Forrest added rice with a commercial rice parboiling plant in Houston, Texas. He started what became known as Uncle Ben's. The company moved its corporate headquarters to Washington, D.C. in 1959. It would relocate to McLean, Virginia in 1984. In 1962 the company began food

16 "Mars, Inc.," Reference for Business, accessed April 2, 2022, www.refer enceforbusiness.com/history2/16/Mars-Inc.html.
17 Posted by Andrew Clayman, "Mars Inc., est. 1911," Made in Chicago Museum, accessed March 12, 2022, www.madeinchicagomuseum.com/sin gle-post/mars-inc/.

manufacturing operations in the Netherlands and England, and marketing campaigns in France and Sweden.

◆ **Expand your core business when it makes sense to do so. Explore new markets beyond your current borders.**

Forrest had been working since his return to the U.S. to gain control of his father's company. When Patricia Mars's husband retired as CEO in 1959, and Patricia was diagnosed with cancer, Forrest bought enough stock to become president and CEO in 1964. (Patricia died the following year.) He had some innovative ideas about how a business should be run:

> In 1967 Forrest merged his business with the Mars Company owned by his father and took over operation of the new company. He established a radically egalitarian system at the company in which workers were called associates and everyone—from the president down—punched a time clock. Offices were eliminated and desks were arranged in a wagon-wheel fashion, with the higher ranking executives in the center, to facilitate communication between individuals and functional areas. Notoriously demanding, Forrest rewarded his associates with salaries that were substantially higher than those in other comparably-sized companies.[18]

The Five Principles

Forrest retired in 1973 and lived another thirty years before dying at the age of 95. His elder sons, Forrest E. Mars, Jr., and John Mars, took over as co-presidents. In 1983 their sister Jacqueline (Jackie) joined them in the Office of President. That year Mars published its first booklet on The Five Principles: Quality, Responsibility, Mutuality, Efficiency, and Freedom. An article in *The Guardian* elaborates:

> A booklet signed by 13 members of the family gives a glimpse into their thinking. The pamphlet, the Five Principles of Mars, explains what makes the company 'different.' It lists quality, responsibility, mutuality, efficiency and freedom—of which the last is described in a curious way. Private ownership, says the pamphlet is crucial to Mars's 'freedom' as it means the firm is not answerable to anybody.[19]

18 Clayman, "Mars, Inc."
19 Andrew Clark, "Life in Mars: Reclusive Dynasty Behind One of World's Most Famous Brands," *The Guardian*, May 2, 2008, www.theguardian.com/business/2008/may/02/mars.wrigley.secretive.

♦ **Clearly define a set of core values and build a culture around them. Communicate them constantly and make sure they permeate every level of the organization.**

Former Mars chairman Stephen Badger, great-grandson of founder Frank Mars and son of Jacqueline Mars and David Badger, adds:

> If I had one piece of advice for other family businesses, it would be to really find the set of values that combine you together. Those [five] principles really bring us together. When you have disagreements, as you would in any family, they ground us ... and help us find common ground even if we disagree.[20]

One innovation Badger and other leadership have embraced is a more open engagement with the world. "We made a very conscious decision after quite a lot of discussion and disagreement over many years to fundamentally shift what had been a tradition for essentially 100 years, to pivot and engage the external world," Badger said. "We've also recognized that there are some issues that are so significant, they warrant our participation in terms of putting ourselves into the dialogue."[21]

♦ **Being socially responsible is expected of businesses today. Customers choose companies that are engaged with the larger issues that matter to them.**

Andy Pharoah, vice president of corporate affairs and strategic initiative, adds:

> Every area is changing with the world that we're operating in, whether you're in finance, whether you're in human resources, whether you're in logistics, whether you're an engineer in one of our plants. There is this perpetual disruption. For companies, you either disrupt or you will be disrupted. You cannot just sit back and say we've had a tremendous business for over 100 years. We have to be as hungry as when we sold our first chocolate bar, or when we first entered the pet food category in the 1930s.[22]

20 "Former Chairman Stephen Badger Talks Leadership, Life, Lessons," Mars, accessed April 16, 2022, www.mars.com/news-and-stories/articles/leadership-life-lessons-stephen-badger.

21 Robert J. Terry, "Why Mars Inc. Is Telling its Story after Decades of Avoiding the Spotlight," *Washington Business Journal*, March 4, 2018, www.bizjournals.com/washington/news/2018/03/01/why-mars-inc-is-telling-its-story-after-decades-of.html.

22 Ibid.

♦ **A successful past is no guarantee of a successful future. Stay agile and adapt to a disruptive world.**

But Badger makes one thing clear:

> The family is 100 percent committed to keeping the business private, and we spend a lot of time engaging the family to that end. The notion of subjecting ourselves to shareholders who would be nameless and faceless, and not to mention have a different set of goals and aspirations for the business than we do—there's just no reason we would want to subject ourselves to that.[23]

The company has passed from direct family leadership into non-family leadership. The current global CEO is Grant F. Reid, who came up through the ranks within Mars. The Mars family still owns and oversees the business and some members sit on its board of directors.

♦ **Don't subject your company's future to investors or shareholders who will always put money before mission.**

Private Foundations

In 2008, Mars Inc bought the Wrigley Company, and Mars Wrigley is now a wholly owned subsidiary of Mars Inc. What is now the Mars Wrigley Foundation began in 1987 as a 501(c)(3) organization, "to provide oral health education and care, improve lives in mint- and cocoa-growing regions, prevent litter and waste, and create vibrant communities. ... Since 2010, the Mars Wrigley Foundation has reached more than 6.5 million individuals [in 16 countries] through investments in oral health, including its signature Healthier Smiles grant program."[24]

"As philanthropists, the Marses set no records for generosity," says noted author Jan Pottker in a 2008 exposé of the family:

> In 1993, when its revenues were estimated at $12 billion, the company gave only $600,000 for distribution through the Mars Foundation. Checks from the foundation tend to be spread around and written for relatively small sums. Forrest Jr. and John are focused on business, so Mars charitable interests are usually administered by their wives or by Jackie. ... Mars answers allegations of cheapness by maintaining that it makes anonymous contributions.[25]

23 Ibid.
24 "Mars Wrigley Foundation," Mars, accessed April 20, 2022, www.mars. com/made-by-mars/mars-wrigley/foundation.
25 Jan Pottker, "Sweet Secrets: Opening Doors on the Very Private Lives of the Billionaire Mars Family," *Washingtonian*, April 29, 2008, www.washingtonian.

However, Jackie is a well-known philanthropist who serves on several boards including at the Smithsonian and the National Archives. She and her brother, John, run the Mars Foundation. A company spokesperson told *Business Insider*:

> The family has always believed that the biggest contribution toward the world we want tomorrow is through the good that Mars, Inc. can do every day, and the family reinvests the vast majority of any profit made back into the company.[26]

In response to the COVID-19 pandemic, Mars Inc. donated $20 million to support people and pets in communities where they work. Eight million went to global organizations like CARE ($5 million), the United Nation's World Food Program ($2 million), and the Humane Society International ($1 million):

> The balance of $12 million will come from a combination of cash and in-kind donations from across the markets where Mars operates as well as donations from its foundations including: The Mars Wrigley Foundation, the Banfield Foundation, the Pedigree Foundation and the Tasty Bite Foundation.[27]

The last three foundations are separate from, but partners with, Mars's subsidiaries. Mars Petcare works with the Banfield Foundation and the Pedigree Foundation. The Banfield Foundation is a 501(c)(3) non-profit organization that "funds programs that enable veterinary care, elevate the power of the human-animal bond, provide disaster relief for pets, and advance the science of veterinary medicine through fostering innovation and education."[28] They provided $2.6 million in funding in 2021.[29] The

com/2008/04/29/from-the-archives-sweet-secrets-opening-doors-on-the-very-private-lives-of-the-billionaire-mars-fami/.

26 Hillary Hoffower, "Meet the Mars Family, Heirs to the Snickers and M&M's Candy Empire, Who Spent Years Avoiding the Limelight and Are America's Third-Wealthiest Family 'Dynasty'," *Insider*, June 29, 2021, www.businessinsider.com/mars-inc-fam
ily-fortune-net-worth-lifestyle-snickers-twix-2019-3.

27 "Mars to Donate $20M toward COVID-19 Relief," Candy Industry, April 6, 2020, www.candyindustry.com/articles/89060-mars-to-donate-20m-toward-covid-19-relief.

28 "Banfield Foundation, About Us," Banfield Foundation, April 13, 2022, www.banfieldfoundation.org/Banfield-Foundation-About-us.

29 "Banfield Foundation Releases 2021 Impact Report Highlighting Support For 1.4 Million Pets And The People Who Love Them," Cision PR Newswire, March 8, 2022, www.prnewswire.com/news-releases/banfield-foundation-releases-2021-impact-report-highlighting-support-for-1-4-million-pets-and-the-people-who-love-them-301497465.html.

Tasty Bite Foundation was set up by Mars's subsidiary Tasty Bite Eatables Limited, based in India. Its objectives are "being a catalyst for accelerating sustainable and inclusive rural development," and "empowering farmers through infrastructure support and technology solutions."[30]

♦ **Share your success with those who helped make it happen. Beyond the local, be a responsible corporate citizen and help address global problems.**

Forbes lists the Mars as the third richest family in America—behind the Waltons and Koches—with a net worth of $94 billion in 2021.[31] When Forrest Sr. died in 1999, his three children inherited the company. Jacqueline (Jackie) and John are now worth $31.7 billion apiece, largely due to each owning about one-third of Mars. The third sibling, Forrest Jr., died in 2016 and his four daughters—Victoria, Valerie, Pamela, and Marijke—each got an estimated 8 percent of Mars, and are now worth $8 billion respectively. To put this in perspective, if these six people were the country of Mars, their 2020 GDP would be greater than 129 countries.[32]

Tandem Hybrid Distinctives and Mars

Driven by a Compelling Social Mission

Frank Mars was a sharp and successful businessman who laid the foundation for one of largest food companies in the world. He lived a lavish lifestyle and was not known for community involvement or philanthropy. Neither was his son and successor, Forrest Mars. The company has a very small social footprint for its size, with its massive profits going to a handful of family members.

Financed by Commercial Success

Mars has been commercially successful due to hard work and timely expansion into different markets, domestically and internationally. Forrest was a demanding but rewarding boss and the company has consistently outperformed many of its competitors. What the Mars family did with their commercial success was invest in the company and grow their personal fortunes. The company has had minimal social impact on any communities or causes.

30 "About Us," Tasty Bite Foundation. accessed April 16. 2022, www.tastybite foundation.com/about-us.

31 "America's Richest Families," Forbes, accessed April 20, 2022, www.forbes. com/families/list/.

32 "List of Countries by GDP," *Statistics Times*, accessed April 20, 2022, https:// statisticstimes.com/economy/countries-by-gdp.php.

Structured to Retain Control

Mars is one of the largest privately held companies in the world. Its organizational structure guarantees family control and its direction is dictated by the number of people who can sit around a conference table. As it says in their Five Principles booklet: "Private ownership is crucial to Mars's 'freedom' as it means the firm is not answerable to anybody."[33]

Scalable and Sustainable for the Long Haul

From the outset the Mars family has done what it takes to scale and grow their commercial enterprise from a candy bar with first-year sales of $800,000 to a global food giant with 2021 revenues of $40 billion. The Mars Wrigley Foundation is a private foundation and doesn't make its financial information available, but its impact is small and connected to Mars commercial businesses. The company's exceptional success has not spilled over in broad social good but has enriched a small family to the tune of $94 billion.

Hershey–Mars Comparison

Business

Both founders built very successful, innovative, and enduring companies that are good places to work and good corporate citizens. Mars was a four-generation dynasty and still very tightly controlled. Hershey had no kids and no heirs in the company.

Philanthropy and Foundations

Hershey's foundations were set up to help his workers and community. Mars's are connected to businesses they own. Jackie Mars helps upper-end groups like the Smithsonian and the National Archives. Nothing is known about the philanthropy of the other children or grandchildren. Hershey gave away everything. The Mars family kept everything. Hershey died with almost nothing and even had his belongings auctioned off for charity. The six Mars heirs are worth $94 billion!

Personal Lives

Both men had reputations for being "benevolent dictators," but they took better care of their employees than most other companies. Beyond work, Hershey invested in his community at all levels—some think too much so.

33 "The Five Principles," Mars, Inc., www.mars.com/about/five-principles.

The Mars family is very secretive and uninvolved, except in their business. They may be generous to causes, but it's not public.

Legacy

Hershey's legacy is various well-endowed foundations that have helped hundreds of thousands. The town he built still attracts more than 3 million visitors a year. Mars's legacy is a headquarters known as the Kremlin and an ultra-rich, reclusive family.

What Would They Think?

What would Milton S. Hershey and Frank C. Mars think about their businesses and foundations today? Hershey would probably think the initial charter for his foundation was too restrictive and would be shocked that it was sitting on $11 billion and not doing more to help as many people as possible, as he did during his life. Mars might say staying private was good for the company but all the profits going to a handful of descendants is bad for the family. The $94 billion generated by generations of dedicated people shouldn't all be in the hands of a few blood relatives.

Takeaways for Social Entrepreneurs

- Create or improve a product or service that will have a large market and can generate significant revenue.
- Innovation is the key to capturing and maintaining market share. Management has to lead by example and create a culture that encourages and rewards innovation.
- Organize in a way that protects your vision from the vicissitudes of the marketplace.
- Invest in the well-being of others and take an interest in the whole person, not just in what goes on at work.
- Decide how much is enough for you and yours, then use the rest to bless others.
- Build flexibility into your organization so leadership can adjust how they honor the original vision.
- Structure company ownership to keep control in the hands of the founder(s) to protect the original vision. Adjust the structure when circumstances require it.
- Consider what will happen to your wealth when you're gone, and proactively plan to share it in the most effective way.
- Expand your core business when it makes sense to do so. Explore new markets beyond your current borders.

- Clearly define a set of core values and build a culture around them. Communicate them constantly and make sure they permeate every level of the organization.
- Being socially responsible is expected of businesses today. Customers choose companies that are engaged with the larger issues that matter to them.
- A successful past is no guarantee of a successful future. Stay agile and adapt to a disruptive world.
- Don't subject your company's future to investors or shareholders who will always put money before mission.
- Share your success with those who helped make it happen. Beyond the local, be a responsible corporate citizen and help address global problems.

10 Hormel Foods Corporation and Tyson Foods

Most of the nationally known brands in the meat industry belong to two companies: Hormel Foods Corporation and Tyson Foods. Both companies grew to prominence through the efforts of the sons who succeeded their fathers. Commercially, Tyson is more than four times the size of Hormel—$47 billion in 2021 revenues[1] compared to $11 billion,[2] but it's just the opposite when it comes to their non-profit foundations—$1.3 billion in assets for the Hormel Foundation compared to $21 million for the Tyson Foundation in 2020. The founders were very involved with their communities, a heritage their companies continue. Their families have retained control and reaped the benefits of innovations and acquisitions over the decades.

Hormel Foods Corporation

George A. Hormel & Company started in 1891 with a single product: pork sausage. Today the Hormel Foods Corporation has more than 20,000 employees in more than 75 countries worldwide, with 64 subsidiaries and 2021 revenues of $11.3 billion.[3] Its market cap in April, 202 was $29.1 billion.[4] Products include SPAM, Skippy, Jenny-O, Planters, and more than thirty other well-known brands. Hormel is ranked #317 in the Fortune 500 and is regularly recognized as one of the 100 Best Corporate Citizens.

George Albert Hormel was born in 1860 in Buffalo, New York, the son of German immigrants. The family moved around and as a teen, George worked for his uncle Jacob at his meat market in Chicago where he learned how to butcher and pack meat. His uncle was a harsh employer and George often worked fourteen-hour days. As he recalled in his memoir, "I often

1 Kim Souza, "Tyson Foods Records 47% Gain in Fiscal Year Net Income," TD&P, November 15, 2021, https://talkbusiness.net/2021/11/tyson-foods-re cords-47-gain-in-fiscal-year-net-income/.
2 "Hormel Foods Revenue 2010–2021," Macrotrends, accessed April 16, 2022, www.macrotrends.net/stocks/charts/HRL/hormel-foods/revenue.
3 Ibid.
4 "Market Capitalization of Hormel Foods," Hormel, accessed April 16, 2022, https://companiesmarketcap.com/hormel-foods/marketcap/.

DOI: 10.4324/9781003325987-13

wonder how I stood that killing pace as well as I did. But I learned things working for my uncle I might otherwise never have learned so thoroughly."[5] He eventually quit and wound up as a traveling hide-buyer. When he tired of the travel he settled in one of his stops, Austin, Minnesota. He borrowed $500 and bought into a meat market with Albert Friedrich. The partnership didn't last, and Hormel started his own pork packinghouse and retail meat market in 1891. He used what he had learned about meat packing and sales to become successful as an independent local meatpacker.

In 1892 George married Lillian Belle Gleason, a teacher and the organist at the Presbyterian church he attended. They had a son, Jay Catherwood Hormel, that same year. George's younger brothers, Herman, John, and Ben, moved to Austin and joined him in the business, as did his parents. George paid good wages, did extensive training, and hired family and friends of employees, creating a sense of family at the company. He also had a reputation as a demanding employer who kept a sharp eye on every detail. As noted in one biography:

> George Hormel's autocratic approach, together with his concern for treating his workers fairly, made for a paternalistic leadership style best characterized as a "benevolent dictatorship." Although an exacting boss, Hormel maintained a good relationship with his employees because he was viewed as "one of them": he worked on the floor for the first decade of the plant's operation, lived in the community alongside his employees, married a local girl, attended the local Presbyterian church, periodically served on the Austin city council, and participated in community organizations such as the Masonic Lodge. As the local newspaper stated after his death, "he was always just 'George' during his life in this city."[6]

♦ **Maintain a balance between caring for employees and caring about the bottom line. People and profit are both important.**

By 1900 the company had grown to where George could no longer work on the floor but had to devote his full attention to the business side of Hormel. "The company was officially incorporated in 1901, with authorized capital of $250,000 consisting of 1,250 shares of preferred stock and 1,250 shares of common stock. Its net worth was $93 million."[7] In the early 1900s, Hormel

5 George A. Hormel, *The Open Road* (Austin, MN: TMs, Collection of the Mower County Historical Society), 37.
6 Anita Talsma Gaul, "George A. Hormel," Immigrant Entrepreneurship, accessed April 18, 2022, www.immigrantentrepreneurship.org/entries/george-a-hormel/.
7 Ibid.

invested in refrigerated railcars and opened distribution centers in eight other cities. (By the 1930s Hormel would have its own refrigerator car line with a fleet of 125 units.)

George Hormel took a trip to England to establish his export business and by the end of World War I, exports accounted for about 33 percent of the company's annual business. World War I also enabled Hormel to increase production and hire more people, so that by 1921 it had more than 1,000 employees.

♦ **Take advantage of difficult circumstances and look for ways to grow when markets are strained or in flux.**

Jay C. Hormel

Jay went to work at his father's company in 1914. In 1921, when he returned from military service, he discovered that assistant controller Cy Thomson had embezzled more than $1 million. Sweeping changes were instituted, several executives were fired, and in 1926 Jay was given more responsibility in running day-to-day operations. Researcher Anita Talsma Gaul notes:

> While George was a pragmatic leader who concentrated on product quality and plant efficiency, Jay was an "idea man" who envisioned new products, new distribution methods (the sausage trucks were his idea), new sales techniques, and new marketing strategies. In particular, Jay focused on products that could be marketed and sold directly to the consumer: ready-to-eat foods that did not need to be handled by a butcher.[8]

♦ **Find new ways to reach customers and to shorten the path between you and them whenever you can.**

Like his father, Jay found inspiration during an overseas trip. This led him to recruit a German meat processor to come to Austin and assist Hormel in producing America's first canned ham in 1926. Other canned meats followed, which opened up whole new markets. The 1930s saw more new brands like Dinty Moore beef stew, Hormel chili, and SPAM. Along with innovative ideas and products, Jay was quick to advertise and promote, something George was not expecting. One year, Jay spent $500,000 on advertising, which angered his father. But George also had the wisdom to recognize how the business was changing. He decided to retire and let his son take over. Jay became acting president in 1927. Another sign of George's wisdom was moving to Beverly Hills, despite his love for Austin. He

8 Ibid.

was a lifelong micromanager and knew he couldn't stay in Austin and stay away from the plant. As he told a reporter, "I felt that if I left the business it would go to pot, but if I did not leave it, I would not last long."[9]

♦ **Know when it's time to transition to new leadership that's more attuned to contemporary ideas and opportunities.**

Hormel went public in 1928 and immediately began paying dividends. As of January 2016, the company had split its stock 2-for-1 ten times.[10] Jay put together the Hormel Plan in the 1930s. It gave employees guaranteed annual wages—something unusual in what was a seasonal business—a joint-earnings plan, and employee profit sharing. This was good for employees and good for the business since the meatpacking industry had a high turnover rate. Jay believed the plan would reduce employee turnover and help Hormel retain a skilled workforce, which it did.

After George's death in 1946, Jay transitioned to chairman of the board and H. H. Corey became the first non-family president of Hormel in 1947, almost fifty years from the company's founding. By 1950, Hormel provided more than 90 percent of the manufacturing jobs in Austin.[11] When Jay died in 1954, Corey was named chairman of the board and R. F. Gray became president in 1955.

The company continued to grow in the 1960s and 1970s. It built ten domestic facilities and expanded international operations. In 1973, Hormel Foods became the first meatpacking company to include nutritional labels on meat products. In 1976, the company topped $1 billion in sales. A one-million-square-foot plant was opened in Austin in 1982. The $100 million building had state-of-the-art processing equipment. Hormel got out of the slaughtering business in 1988 and moved into microwaveable foods and ethnic foods. The changes in products led to a name change in 1993 when George A. Hormel & Company became Hormel Foods Corporation.

In the first fifteen years of the 21st century, Hormel made more than a dozen acquisitions, including well-known brands like Jenny-O, MegaMex Foods, Skippy Foods, and Applegate Farms. And in 2021, Hormel bought Planters from Kraft Heinz for $3.35 billion in cash.

♦ **Key acquisitions can expand products and services, increase vertical integration, and achieve economies of scale.**

---

9 Ibid.
10 Dan Caplinger, "Hormel Stock Split History: When Will the Dividend Aristocrat Split Again?" The Motley Fool, March 12, 2018, www.fool.com/investing/2018/03/12/hormel-stock-split-history-when-will-the-dividen-2.aspx.
11 Wilson J. Warren, *Tied to the Great Packing Machine: The Midwest and Meatpacking* (Iowa City, IA: University of Iowa Press, 2007), 83.

The Hormel Foundation and Institute

After reaching sales of $75 million in 1941, George and Jay established The Hormel Foundation, a non-profit 501(c)(3) organization. According to its website:

> The Foundation was created to fulfill three primary responsibilities: preserve the independence of the Hormel Foods Corporation, support the Austin, MN community and area, provide for the financial welfare of family heirs for the duration established by family trusts. ... The Foundation controls more than 48 percent of Hormel Foods' stock and would vote against any proposal to purchase the Corporation.[12]

♦ **If it's a family business, structure the ownership to keep the company in family hands in perpetuity.**

The Hormel Foundation is the fourth largest public foundation grant-maker in Minnesota, with net assets in 2020 of $1.3 billion. The Foundation was reorganized in 1980 from a 501(c)(3) organization to a 509(a)(3)—a supporting organization "operated for the benefit of those charitable or educational organizations represented on its board."[13] Total Foundation giving to the Austin community topped $300 million in 2021 with $10.6 million in grants given to fourteen local non-profits.

When asked in 2016 about the difference between the Hershey Trust and the Hormel Foundation, then chairman Gary Ray said:

> It's actually qualitatively different, and that also goes to the foresight of George A. and Jay C. Hormel in setting up the Foundation. The Foundation has a long standing and explicit responsibility—which includes both supporting the local Austin community and preserving the independence of Hormel Foods.[14]

(Actually, the Hershey Trust was set up along the same lines to benefit its home community. It owns more than 80 percent of Hershey Company voting stock, is committed to keeping the company from being sold, and has poured millions into its hometown of Hershey, Pennsylvania.)

---

12 "Home," The Hormel Foundation, accessed April 19, 2022, www.thehormelfoundation.com.
13 "About the Foundation," The Hormel Foundation, accessed April 19, 2022, www.thehormelfoundation.com/pages/about-us/#:~:text=In%20order%20to%20continue%20to,)(3)%20of%20the%20IRC.
14 "Interview with Gary Ray," The Hormel Foundation, accessed April 19, 2022, http://thehormelfoundation.com/pages/Interview.

The main recipient of The Hormel Foundation's giving is The Hormel Institute, a world-renowned cancer research center and part of University of Minnesota located in Austin. The Institute was established in 1942 by Jay Hormel.

Family and Community

Family played a big part in George's life and business:

> Besides the knowledge, skills, values, and habits he learned from his family, George also relied heavily on his family's assistance in the start-up and operation of his packinghouse. Three of his brothers and his parents moved to Austin to work in various capacities in his fledgling company, as did other family members, including a cousin and a brother-in-law. His father loaned him the money to expand the packing plant in 1892, and in 1895 he purchased the company's first delivery wagon. George's wife also played a vital supportive role during the company's initial years.[15]

Jay married Germaine Dubois in 1922 and they had three sons: George ("Geordie"), Thomas, and James. Geordie became a musician and started The Village Recorder Studio. Thomas was an artist, composer, and environmental philanthropist, James was a philanthropist and LGBT activist. He was the first openly gay man to become a U.S. ambassador, serving in Luxembourg from 1999 to 2001.

In 1992, Jay's sons went to court to force the Hormel Foundation to sell Hormel stock and diversify their holdings. AP News reported that Judge James Mork ordered the Hormel Foundation to sell 4.6 million shares worth about $108 million. "The heirs said they were not in financial trouble, but want to create financial stability for their children and grandchildren."[16]

Geordie certainly wasn't short of funds. He lived in a 54,000-square-foot mansion and bought the historic Wrigley Mansion as an anniversary gift for his wife.

For more than 130 years, Hormel and Austin—population 26,000 in 2020—have enjoyed a symbiotic relationship that continues to enrich both parties. "Austin wouldn't be the same community without Hormel here," says City Administrator Craig Clark. "When they have 800 to 900 people at the corporate office and research and development office and then between Hormel and QPP on the processing side, around 3,000 people, it's really a critical industry for the community."[17] Not to mention the millions poured into the area by the Hormel Foundation and Hormel Institute.

15 Gaul, "George A. Hormel."
16 "Judge Rules in Favor of Hormel Heirs," AP News, December 11, 1992, https://ap news.com/article/796baf80a36c604c09becbb5eec54f45.
17 Brett Bachtle, "How Hormel Defines the Image of Austin," ABC News, April 23, 2020, www.kaaltv.com/coronavirus/how-hormel-defies-the-image-of-a ustin/5709179/.

♦ **Cultivate a healthy symbiotic relationship between your company and your community.**

Tandem Hybrid Distinctives and Hormel

Driven by a Compelling Social Mission

There was no social mission connected to Hormel Foods for the first fifty years until The Hormel Foundation was founded in 1941. Even then the foundation's purpose wasn't philanthropy but preserving family control of the business and ensuring their financial welfare. Another forty years later the Foundation was reorganized as a "supporting organization" and has since grown into the fourth largest public foundation grant-maker in Minnesota, with the majority of its philanthropy focused on the Austin community, where Hormel is based.

Financed by Commercial Success

George built a solid and successful commercial business that his son Jay expanded. When sales topped $75 million in 1941, George and Jay set up The Hormel Foundation, which would eventually evolve into a billion-dollar philanthropic concern benefiting the community of Austin, the state of Minnesota, and the world through organizations like The Hormel Institute, a leading cancer research center. The commercial success of Hormel Foods continues to generate hundreds of millions of dollars for these civic and philanthropic ventures.

Structured to Retain Control

The Hormel family ran the company and the Hormel Foundation ensured the control and profits of the business would remain in Hormel hands. Family members who had nothing to do with the day-to-day operations still reaped the benefits that allowed for lavish lifestyles. Family control also means Hormel will stay rooted in Austin and continue to invest in the economic and cultural health of its home community.

Scalable and Sustainable for the Long Haul

Hormel Foods has grown from one meat market to an international giant doing business in more than 75 countries. From the outset, Hormel has constantly invested in new equipment, new markets, and new products via aggressive acquisitions. It shows no signs of slowing down and is in no danger of being taken over or uprooted from its family or community of origin.

Tyson Foods

Tyson Foods is one of the three largest meat-producing corporations in the world and the largest in the U.S. It produced twenty percent of all the chicken, beef, and pork consumed in the U.S. in 2021 and had sales in excess of $47 billion.[18] With more than 139,000 team members, it's ranked #73 among the Fortune 500 in 2021. Tyson's roots go back to a depression-era chicken-hauling business in Springdale, Arkansas, run by company namesake and founder John W. Tyson.

John W. Tyson

John William Tyson, son of Isaac and Anna Tyson, was born in Mound City, Missouri, in 1905. He grew up in Kansas City, where as a youth he started his own business selling chickens, eggs, and produce. As an adult, he focused on selling fruits and vegetables. When the Great Depression hit, John went to Springdale, Arkansas, in 1931 to buy apples. For the next few years he eked out a living hauling produce and chickens for locals. When he heard chickens were fetching better prices in other parts of the country he started taking chickens to other states. One online bio reports:

> In 1936, reading that chicken prices were higher in Chicago, Tyson took a $1,000 loan and $800 of his own money to purchase 500 spring chickens. Using his in-transit feeding system, the 1,400-mile roundtrip to Chicago generated $235 profit. He was soon driving to Cincinnati, Detroit, Cleveland, Memphis and Houston.[19]

To meet increasing demand, Tyson hatched his own chicks and sold them to local farmers. Then he sold these growers the feed they needed, and built a commercial mill to make the feed. He bought land and set up broiler houses. He began cross-breeding chickens to produce better stock. His innovative insight and intent was to control his product from the egg to the consumer. He incorporated Tyson Feed and Hatchery in 1947 and became a leading supplier of chickens to several major Midwest cities. By 1950, Tyson growers were producing 500,000 birds a year.

♦ **Own as many parts of your supply chain, production, and delivery systems as feasible to increase revenues.**

---

18 Souza, "Tyson Foods Records 47% Gain in Fiscal Year Net Income."
19 "John Tyson," University of Arkansas, accessed April 22, 2022, https://walton.uark.edu/abhf/john-tyson.php.

Donald J. Tyson

John had a son named Donald born in 1930 to his first wife, Mildred Rat-cliff. Don joined the company after college as a general manager. "I left the [University of Arkansas] in 1952, and from that day until 1963, the year I took the company public, I worked in the business six days a week and on Dad's farm on the seventh day."[20] Hard work paid off and by 1957 the company was processing ten million birds annually. Tyson opened its first processing plant in 1958. It came in over budget at $90,000, but completed the vertical integration of the company.

Not every new idea was a success:

> In the 1960s, Tyson planned to open a chain of fast-food chicken restaurants across the country. All 30 were dismal failures. Another idea that did not catch on was its Gizzard Burger, which contained leftover ground chicken gizzards supplemented with various beef and beef flavoring. "They did everything but sell," Tyson recalled.[21]

♦ **There are bad ideas, e.g., Gizzard Burgers, but don't be afraid of failure; it's part of success.**

The company went public as Tyson's Foods in 1963. It sold 100,000 shares of stock at $10.50. Tyson also made a key acquisition that year, buying Garrett Poultry Company in Rogers, Arkansas, home of Walmart. It would make 19 other acquisitions between 1966 and 1989.

Don became president of Tyson in 1966. The next year, his parents were killed when their car was struck by a train. Don and his half-brother, Randall, inherited the company. Randal had been born in 1952 to John's second wife, Helen Knoll, and died in 1986 at age thirty-four. His wife, Barbara has been involved with the company in various positions, including serving on the board.

Under Don's leadership, the company prospered and made its way into the Fortune 1000 by 1971. The next year the company became Tyson Foods, Inc. Additional acquisitions got Tyson into the hog-farming business. By the end of the 1970s, Tyson was selling 4.5 million chickens a week and was also America's leading hog producer. The company helped McDonald's develop Chicken McNuggets and also provided chicken products to other fast food chains, including Kentucky Fried Chicken. By 1995 Tyson was supplying 82 of the top 100 fast food chains.[22] And its CEO was on his way to becoming a billionaire, as reported in Forbes:

20 "Our History," Tyson, accessed April 22, 2022, www.tysonfoods.com/who-we-are/our-story/where-we-came-from/our-history.
21 "Tyson, Donald John," Encyclopedia.com, accessed April 22, 2022, www.encyclopedia.com/education/economics-magazines/tyson-donald-john.
22 Ibid.

Over the next three decades, Don built Tyson into one of the largest companies in America by gobbling up rival food processors. He first landed on the Forbes 400 list of the richest Americans in 1986 with a net worth of $275 million.[23]

By the end of the 1980s, Tyson was the world's largest fully integrated producer, processor, and marketer of poultry-based foods. The company also launched its international division with joint ventures in Mexico and Japan. The following decade it would expand into Asia, Central America, South America, the Caribbean, Japan, Hong Kong, Singapore, Canada, and Moscow.[24]

Don stepped down as CEO in 1991 and relinquished the day-to-day operations of the company in 1995. At that time he controlled 90 percent of the company's voting stock. He stayed active and remained on the board until his death in 2011 at age eighty.

♦ **Joint ventures and strategic partnerships can open up lucrative international markets.**

John H. Tyson

Don had married Mildred Ernst in 1952, the year he started fulltime at Tyson. The couple had three children before separating: John, Cheryl, and Carla, all of whom worked in the business. John H. Tyson succeeded his father as CEO in 2000. Born in 1953, John began working weekends at Tyson during high school. After college he went to work at the company in various positions. His struggles with drugs and alcohol kept him on the sidelines management-wise until he decided to get, and remain, sober in the late 1980s. He became chairman of the board in 1998. The company went on to make record profits, partly fueled by their purchase of rival IBP (Iowa Beef Processors, Inc) in 2001 for $4.7 billion, which made Tyson the world's largest meat producer at the time. In 2014 Tyson also acquired Hillshire Brands with an all-cash offer of $8.5 billion.

In 2000, with a strong push from John Tyson, the company began a chaplaincy program that's now one of the largest corporate chaplaincy programs in the U.S., with more than more than 100 chaplains of various faiths serving in twenty-two states. The chaplains provide pastoral care and counseling to team members and their families regardless of religious affiliation or beliefs. Tyson ranks second on the Corporate Religious Equity, Diversity & Inclusion (REDI) Index among Fortune 100

23 Dan Alexander, "Recovering-Alcoholic-Heir-Turned-Successful-Executive Debuts as Billionaire Thanks To Rising Tyson Foods Stock," Forbes, April 14, 2014, www.forbes.com/sites/danalexander/2014/04/14/recovering-alcoholic-heir-turned-successful-executive-debuts-as-billionaire-thanks-to-rising-tyson-foods-stock/?sh=64d19ff30444.
24 "Our History."

companies.[25] It is committed to creating inclusive, faith-friendly workplaces. This is one of the company's core values, along with striving "to honor God and be respectful of each other, our customers, and other stakeholders."[26]

This commitment to religious inclusion also led the company to create the Tyson Center for Faith and Spirituality in the Workplace. Tyson Foods and the Tyson Family Foundation established the Center in 2009 at Walton College at the University of Arkansas. Its mission is: "To make the workplace of tomorrow more faith-friendly by providing current and future business leaders with relevant learning experiences, knowledge, and opportunities for leadership and connection."[27]

♦ **If spirituality is important to you, include it in company culture without making it compulsory. Foster a faith-friendly workplace.**

John retired as CEO in 2006 but remains chairman of the board and the controlling shareholder of the company. His son, John Randal Tyson, became Tyson's Chief Sustainability Officer in 2019. He represents the fourth generation of Tysons in company leadership. His sister, Olivia, is president of the Tyson Family Foundation. 2019 is also the year Tyson expanded into the alternative protein field with its first plant-based and blended products, and a new Raised & Rooted brand. "Market research suggests that the global alternative meat industry will achieve $100 billion in sales by the year 2030," as reported by Mash:

> Current estimates of the alternative meat market place its value at around $2.5 billion. Compared to the global meat market which is worth $1.4 trillion, the alternative protein scene may seem like small potatoes, but given its rapid growth in popularity and market share in recent years, Tyson's involvement in the industry is yet another instance of it being ahead of the business curve.[28]

♦ **Do in-depth research to anticipate where your market is going and get there ahead of the competition.**

25 "Corporate Religious Equity, Diversity & Inclusion (REDI) Index," Religious Freedom & Business Foundation, accessed April 20, 2022, https://forumworkp laceinclusion.org/wp-content/uploads/2020/11/rediindex2020final.pdf.

26 "2005 Sustainability Report," Tyson Foods, accessed April 20, 2022, www. tysonfoods.com/sites/default/files/2017-12/SR2005.pdf.

27 "Tyson Center for Faith and Spirituality in the Workplace Praises Recognition for Tyson Foods," University of Arkansas, February 19, 2020, https://news.ua rk.edu/articles/52257/tyson-center-for-faith-and-spirituality-in-the-workpla ce-praises-recognition-for-tyson-foods.

28 Ben Fisher, "The Untold Truth of Tyson Foods," Mashed, April 21, 2020, www.mashed.com/205745/the-untold-truth-of-tyson-foods/.

Partnership and Foundation

Tyson Foods is still very much a family owned, and controlled, company. The Tyson Limited Partnership sees to that. Its FORM 10-K filed with the SEC notes:

> As of October 3, 2020, Tyson Limited Partnership (the "TLP") owns 99.985% of the outstanding shares of the Company's Class B Common Stock, $0.10 par value ("Class B stock") and the TLP and members of the Tyson family own, in the aggregate, 2.23% of the outstanding shares of the Company's Class A Common Stock, $0.10 par value ("Class A stock"), giving them, collectively, control of approximately 71.06% of the total voting power of the Company's outstanding voting stock. ... As a result of these holdings, positions and directorships, the partners in the TLP have the ability to exert substantial influence or actual control over our management and affairs and over substantially all matters requiring action by our stockholders.[29]

The Tyson Family Foundation is a private foundation founded in 1970 in Fayetteville, Arkansas. Their Form 990 for 2019 shows the foundation had $6.7 million in revenues, $21.2 million in assets, and gave $8 million in grants:[30]

> The Foundation supports efforts for education, health, arts and culture and youth programs as well as a scholarship program for Tyson Foods employees and their families. The foundation has endowed and supported local, regional and national organizations committed to furthering access to knowledge, promoting creativity and supporting communities. The Foundation is currently led by President Olivia Tyson.[31]

In 2020 Tyson donated more than 30 million pounds of food, or the equivalent of 120 million meals. This was part of more than $75 million invested in various programs to address hunger and support team members. Besides hunger relief, other programs included community grants to non-profits ($3.8 million), the Helping Hands Program—financial assistance to

29 "United States Securities and Exchange Commission FORM 10-K for Tyson for fiscal 2020," www.annualreports.com/HostedData/AnnualReports/PDF/NYSE_TSN_2020.pdf.

30 "Tyson Family Foundation," Cause, IQ, accessed April 20, 2022, www.causeiq.com/organizations/tyson-family-foundation,237087948/.

31 "Tyson Family Foundation Gift to Create Digital Library and Art Publication Funds," University of Arkansas, May 3, 2021, https://news.uark.edu/articles/56805/tyson-family-foundation-gift-to-create-digital-library-and-art-publication-funds.

team members ($6 million), and the Giving Together Program—matching team member gifts to non-profits ($700,000).[32]

♦ **Give generously to causes you and your people believe in, locally, nationally, and internationally.**

Tyson Foods was one of the companies hardest hit by the COVID-19 pandemic. At least 50,000 COVID-19 cases have been linked to meat and poultry processing facilities in 38 states, according to the Midwest Center for Investigative Reporting. That includes at least 259 reported worker deaths in at least 67 plants in 29 states.[33] Tyson has spent more than $700 million dealing with COVID as of summer, 2021. It required its entire U.S. workforce of more than 139,000 to get vaccinated by November 1, 2021.

Tyson works to fulfill its social, financial, and environmental responsibilities as a global business. It tries to address the spiritual, physical, social, and financial needs of its team members and the communities where it operates. And it returns a healthy profit to its investors. This latter class is still a fairly small group of Tyson family members.

Tandem Hybrid Distinctives and Tyson

Driven by a Compelling Social Mission

Today Tyson Foods has an earned reputation for generously addressing social causes like hunger relief and COVID-19 mitigation efforts. Internally it has programs for employees that include everything from spiritual care to employee-directed matching gift outreaches. These social missions weren't part of the original vision but have grown out of a corporate culture that seeks to, "honor God and be respectful of each other, our customers, and other stakeholders."

Financed by Commercial Success

Tyson's commercial success is apparent in the size and scope of its businesses. A portion of its profits and products are funneled into social causes such as hunger relief. In the U.S. the company donated more than 30 million pounds of food (120 million meals) in 2020 and more than 16 million pounds (64 million meals) in fiscal 2021 to the communities where it operates.

---

32 "In a Year of Unprecedented Need, Tyson Foods Donates Record Amount of Protein," Global Newswire, September 28, 2020, www.globenewswire.com/en/news-release/2020/09/28/2099767/7106/en/In-a-Year-of-Unprecedented-Need-Tyson-Foods-Donates-Record-Amount-of-Protein.html.

33 Kate Gibson, "Tyson Foods Requiring That All of its 139,000 Workers Get Vaccinated against COVID-19," CBS News, August 3, 2021, www.cbsnews.com/news/tyson-foods-covid-vaccine-employees-november/.

Structured to Retain Control

Tyson's has been, and will continue to be, family owned and operated. The Tyson Limited Partnership guarantees that by holding more than 70 percent of company voting stock. John Tyson is chairman of the board and the fourth generation of Tysons are in leadership positions. The same goes for the Tyson Family Foundation and the family's other philanthropic efforts. They control where the money is made and the causes to which a portion is given.

Scalable and Sustainable for the Long Haul

Tyson scaled up at every important juncture of its growth, often ahead of its competitors, paying special attention to vertical integration and owning all parts of its production and distribution networks. What it didn't develop on its own it picked up through key acquisitions to solidify its market dominance. As the third largest meat-producing company in the world, Tyson's not going anywhere.

Hormel–Tyson Comparison

Business

Both founders built very successful, innovative, and enduring companies that are good places to work and good corporate citizens. Tyson is a four-generation dynasty and still very tightly controlled. Hormel isn't family run but the family controls 48 percent of voting stock. Tyson includes the spiritual in their core values and has been recognized for their faith-friendly workplaces. But they've also had problems with worker safety and EPA violations.

Philanthropy and Foundations

Most philanthropy is in line with the business and in the communities they serve; Austin in the case of Hormel and Arkansas in the case of Tyson. Tyson is also big into hunger relief and often responds to natural disasters. Both companies set up foundations to give their families control of voting stock. This wasn't done to preserve the business so much as to guarantee control. Their non-profit foundations give primarily to causes related to the business.

Personal Lives

The founders didn't lead extravagant lives, but their descendants did, and do. The Tyson family is worth more than $3 billion. They are actively involved in the business. The Hormel descendants are in the millionaire class, not the billionaire class. They live their own lives away from the business.

Legacy

The founders left strong businesses to their families. The sons built the businesses into powerhouses and created outside organizations to preserve family control of the companies. The businesses are good places to work overall and they contribute to their communities.

What Would They Think?

What would George A. Hormel and John W. Tyson think about their businesses and foundations today? Hormel might be proud that his foresight and planning kept his company independent for the long term; otherwise it would have been acquired by IBP or Tyson. He might not be as proud of his descendants who reap the rewards of his hard work even though they don't participate in the business. John and Don Tyson also did a masterful job keeping their company independent by controlling the disposition of voting stock. Their family has stayed involved, and have billions to show for it.

Takeaways for Social Entrepreneurs

- Maintain a balance between caring for employees and caring about the bottom line. People and profit are both important.
- Take advantage of difficult circumstances and look for ways to grow when markets are strained or in flux.
- Find new ways to reach customers and to shorten the path between you and them whenever you can.
- Know when it's time to transition to new leadership that's more attuned to contemporary ideas and opportunities.
- Key acquisitions can expand products and services, increase vertical integration, and achieve economies of scale.
- If it's a family business, structure the ownership to keep the company in family hands in perpetuity.
- Cultivate a healthy symbiotic relationship between your company and your community.
- Own as many parts of your supply chain, production, and delivery systems as feasible to increase revenues.
- There are bad ideas, e.g., "Gizzard Burgers," but don't be afraid of failure; it's part of success.
- Joint ventures and strategic partnerships can open up lucrative international markets.

- If spirituality is important to you, include it in company culture without making it compulsory. Foster a faith-friendly workplace.
- Do in-depth research to anticipate where your market is going and get there ahead of the competition.
- Give generously to causes you and your people believe in, locally, nationally, and internationally.

11 H. Lundbeck & Co and Novo Nordisk

These global biopharmaceutical giants have a lot in common. They aren't controlled by founding families but by foundations structurally committed to keeping them in their home country of Denmark. They both dominate the markets on which they are laser-focused, disorders of the brain and central nervous system for Lundbeck, and diabetes and serious chronic diseases for Novo Nordisk. Millions of people benefit daily from their life-saving medications, but most outside Denmark don't know their names. Nor do people know the founders and scientists who built these companies. Unlike Hershey, Mars, Hormel, and Tyson, these entrepreneurs didn't put their names on what they created.

H. Lundbeck & Co

H. Lundbeck A/S (known simply as Lundbeck) is a global biopharmaceutical company specializing in treating disorders of the brain and central nervous system. Based in Copenhagen, Lundbeck does business in more than 50 countries—including the U.S.—and employs more than 5,600 people. It generated revenues of $2.8 billion in 2020 and is one of the top three pharma companies in Denmark, the others being Novo Nordisk A/S, and LEO Pharma A/S. The big three account for about 90 percent of the employees in the Danish pharmaceutical industry.[1]

Lundbeck is divided into six divisions and is managed by an executive management team and a board of directors. It makes and markets drugs for psychiatric and neurological disorders and claims to be the only fully integrated pharmaceutical company in the world solely devoted to the treatment of psychiatric and neurological disorders. It focuses on four areas: Restoring brain health, understanding brain diseases, neurology, and psychiatry. Lundbeck

---

1 "The Danish Pharmaceutical Industry and TTIP," Copenhagen Economics, accessed April 20, 2022, www.copenhageneconomics.com/dyn/resources/Pub lication/publicationPDF/7/297/1455614178/the-danish-pharmaceutical-indus trys-impact-from-ttip.pdf.

DOI: 10.4324/9781003325987-14

spends about 26 percent of its revenue on R&D ($695 million), which puts it at #8 on Pharma's top 20 R&D spenders in 2020.[2]

♦ **Determine how much your business depends on R&D and spend accordingly.**

Hans Lundbeck

H. Lundbeck & Co was founded by Hans Lundbeck in Copenhagen in 1915 as a trading company. It expanded his original import-export business in butter to a wide range of products. "Lundbeck set up a series of agencies to handle the buying and selling of goods," notes one company history, "which ranged from photographic equipment to production machinery to saccharin and even vacuum cleaners. Most of Lundbeck's operations were conducted from his office in Copenhagen, with no need for warehouse or manufacturing facilities, as Lundbeck acted primarily as a broker."[3]

Lundbeck got into pharmaceuticals in 1924 with the hiring of Eduard Goldschmidt. Goldschmidt had a background in the chemical and pharmaceutical industries that resulted in new business in these fields. In the 1930s, Lundbeck began manufacturing and selling pharmaceuticals in Denmark. In 1937, Lundbeck came out with its first original product called Epicutan, used for healing wounds. Two years later, the company expanded its manufacturing capabilities and set up a chemical research facility to pioneer new drugs.

Next came the painkiller, Ketogan, which was twice as strong as morphine. Lundbeck hired a microbiology researcher who helped develop its first antibiotic products in the early 1950s. In 1959, Lundbeck launched one of the first antipsychotics in the world: Truxal. This treatment for schizophrenia was among its bestselling drugs. In the early 1960s, Lundbeck introduced the antidepressant Saroten. It went on to develop the antidepressant Celexa (citalopram) and the Selective Serotonin Reuptake Inhibitor (SSRI) Cipramil.

By 1970, Lundbeck had around 700 employees, with about 100 of them working abroad. As international business grew, the company opened offices in New York, Paris, and the UK. Starting late in the 1970s, Lundbeck divested itself of all other businesses and concentrated on pharmaceuticals; a move that paid off handsomely. By the end of the century, it was

---

2 Brian Buntz, "Pharma's Top 20 R&D Spenders in 2020," *Drug Discovery and Development*, May 13, 2021, www.drugdiscoverytrends.com/pharmas-top -20-rd-spenders-in-2020/.

3 "H. Lundbeck A/S—Company Profile, Information, Business Description, History, Background Information on H. Lundbeck A/S," Reference for Business, accessed April 20, 2022, www.referenceforbusiness.com/history2/27/ H-Lundbeck-A-S.html#ixzz77lQB42IZ.

generating more than $37 million in sales. Cipralex/Lexapro was launched in 2002 and grew to be a large share of Lundbeck's business.

♦ **Double down on what you do best. Divest yourself of what isn't your core business.**

Lundbeck's narrow focus on brain and neurological disorders puts it in the vanguard in that field. In September 2021 it announced a partnership with Inscopix to use a camera to film neurons in the brain. "We are always assessing new methods to accelerate our research and development. With the ability to actually film brain activity on neuronal level I think we are exploring an interesting opportunity to gain new knowledge," says Benjamin Hall, director in circuit biology at Lundbeck.[4]

Lundbeck is also making headway against such scourges as Alzheimer's disease, which affects more than six million people in the U.S. Doug Williamson, chief medical officer and vice president of U.S. Medical at Lundbeck, explains:

> Alzheimer's still cannot be conclusively prevented, cured, or even slowed despite billions of dollars being invested in research. Between 1998 and 2017, just four new treatments for Alzheimer's appeared on the U.S. market, while an additional 146 attempts ended in failure. … For every Alzheimer's study that doesn't work out, or every new Alzheimer's drug that doesn't meet its end points, we learn something that moves us forward.[5]

● **Learn as much from failure—yours and others'—as from success.**

Lundbeck recently sold off its rights to one failed Alzheimer's drug but continued to research others in partnership with various pharmaceutical companies. Some companies they work with, others they have invested in or purchased outright. It acquired the biotechnology firm Synaptic Pharmaceutical in 2003 to establish a research presence in the U.S. It expanded that presence in 2009 when it bought Ovation Pharmaceuticals for $900 million. Prior to this, Lundbeck had bought Saegis Pharma for $820 million (2006). Other key acquisitions followed: Chelsea Therapeutics for $658 million (2014), Prexton Therapeutics for $1.1 billion (2018), Alder BioPharmaceuticals for almost $2 billion (2019), and Abide Therapeutics for $200 million (2019).[6]

4 "Lundbeck to Use New Technology that Can Photograph Neurons in the Brain," Lundbeck, September 20, 2021, www.lundbeck.com/global/press/news-archive/2021/a-family-portrait-of-the-brain.
5 Maryellen Kennedy Duckett, "Brain Hackers," *National Geographic*, December 2, 2019, www.nationalgeographic.com/science/article/partner-content-brain-hackers.
6 "Acquisitions by Lundbeck," Trackn, February 18, 2022, https://tracxn.com/d/acquisitions/acquisitionsbyLundbeck.

Lundbeck has about 1000 U.S. employees. Headquartered in suburban Chicago, the company has been consistently recognized among the top life science companies for corporate reputation. The PatientView Corporate Reputation of Pharma, USA Edition, reports: "Lundbeck US ranked in the top tier for corporate reputation, and #1 in both overall reputation and patient support during the COVID-19 crisis among companies focused on brain health."[7] Ninety percent of employees at Lundbeck say it's a great place to work compared to 57 percent of employees at a typical U.S.-based company.[8]

♦ **Earn and keep a stellar reputation by treating people well, both inside and outside your organization.**

However, this doesn't mean the company is above some of the illegal tactics common in Big Pharma. As reported by Reuters in March 2021:

> Danish drugmaker Lundbeck on Thursday lost its fight against a 2013 EU antitrust fine imposed for deals with rivals to delay sales of generic copies of its anti-depressant citalopram after Europe's top court sided with EU enforcers. The case is one of several in the European Commission's decade-long crackdown against pay-for-delay deals which it says hurt competition and hold back innovation. The EU competition enforcer had imposed a combined fine of 146 million euros ($172 million) on Lundbeck and five generic drugmakers for such deals, prompting the companies to challenge the ruling at the General Court which upheld the EU decision in 2016.[9]

Lundbeck Foundation

The Lundbeck Foundation exists because of a visionary businesswoman, Grete Lundbeck. At age 19, Grete Sterregaard was Hans Lundbeck's first hire. She went on to reach a key position in the company, and in 1940 she and Hans were married. The union was short-lived as Hans died three years later. In 1950, Grete became chair of the board of Lundbeck and was one

---

7 "Patient Groups Recognize Lundbeck as a Top Company for Corporate Reputation for 6th Straight Year," Lundbeck, May 13, 2021, www.newsroom. lundbeckus.com/news-release/2021/patient-groups-recognize-lundbeck-a s-top-company-for-corporate-reputation-for-6th-straight-year?utm_source= LundUS&utm_page=LuUS&utm_loc=ftrdbanner.

8 "Lundbeck," Great Places to Work, November 2020, www.greatplacetowork. com/certified-company/1244197.

9 Foo Yun Chee, "Lundbeck Loses Fight against EU Antitrust Fine in Pay-for-Delay Deals," Reuters, March 25, 2021, www.reuters.com/article/us-eu-lundbeck-antitrust/lundbeck-loses-fight-against-eu-antitrust-fine-in-pay-for-delay-deals-idUSKBN2BH17R.

of only a handful of female business executives in Denmark at the time. And one of the most powerful.

That same year the company reincorporated as a limited company, with Grete having 50.5 percent of company stock and the Eduard Goldschmidt family holding the rest. Grete established the Lundbeck Foundation in 1954, endowing it with most of her Lundbeck stock and willing the rest upon her death, which occurred in 1965. In 1967, the Foundation bought out the Goldschmidt family. Its holdings were reduced to 70 percent in 1999 when the company was listed on the Copenhagen stock exchange. The Foundation still retains 70 percent ownership today. Its goal is to ensure a clear purpose and governance for the company in the future as well as provide financial support for scientific research. The Lundbecks had no children, so ensuring family control of the company was never part of the equation.

♦ **It's never too late to create a structure for preserving a company's ownership and founding vision.**

"Our job is to invent and bring innovative treatments to patients, thereby creating value for patients, society and our shareholders," says Peter Anastasiou, Lundbeck's executive vice president and head of North America:

> The foundation model is unique and an immense benefit to people impacted by brain diseases. Developing new therapies for brain diseases is complex, time consuming and costly. Despite the significant challenges in CNS (central nervous system) drug development, the stability of our unique ownership structure allows us to stay focused on patient needs and pursuing innovative solutions to restore brain health.[10]

Lene Skole, Lundbeck Foundation CEO, explains:

> We are an industrial foundation, which means we are a combination of a business and a charity. We do not have owners, and income from our commercial activities—usually dividends from the companies we own—is channeled back into society through donations for various purposes.[11]

Industrial foundations are illegal in the U.S. because they were seen as serving the interests of the rich rather than charities. "These tax-exempt

10 "The Brain Foundation: How the Lundbeck Foundation is Shaping the Future of Brain Science," Lundbeck, accessed April 18, 2022, https://newsroom.lundbeckus.com/our-impact/the-brain-foundation-how-the-lundbeck-foundation-is-shaping-the-future-of-brain-science.

11 "Lundbeck's Largest Shareholder," Lundbeck, accessed April 18, 2022, www.lundbeck.com/us/about-us/this-is-lundbeck/the-lundbeck-foundation.

foundations exist globally," reports Scott McCulloch, "yet Denmark is a leader with some 1,300 in operation. Some experts estimate the value of listed companies controlled by Danish foundations at about 68 percent of the total market capitalisation of the Copenhagen Stock Exchange."[12]

Lundbeck Foundation's strategy includes investing in healthcare companies based in Denmark that have the potential to become global leaders. Its portfolio includes H. Lundbeck (70 percent ownership), Falck (59 percent ownership), and ALK-Abelló (40 percent ownership).[13] It also aggressively invests in research and awards grants for public biomedical sciences research at Danish universities.[14]

♦ Synchronize your commercial and social enterprises to maximize your impact.

The Foundation started Lundbeckfonden Ventures in 2009 and is wholly owned by the Lundbeck Foundation. "Our current portfolio is around 18 companies, which represent a broad spectrum of therapeutic fields in the life science industry," explains its website. "We have invested between 350 to 400 million Danish kroner annually since our start in 2009. Going forward towards 2030, we will grow our international investments and grow the amount we invest in both private and public companies."[15]

The Lundbeck Foundation is worth about $10.2 billion and grants at least $79.4 million each year to Danish-based neuroscience research.[16] In 2019, the Foundation made 382 grants totaling $105.8 million; equivalent to the salaries of almost 900 full-time researchers. This includes the annual Brain Prize of $1.6 million to one or more brain researchers who have had a significant impact on brain research.

Lundbeck grants don't go directly to patients, but to Danish universities and Danish university hospitals: "We want to play a part in making Danish research a world leader, and our aim with our grants is to create the best possible conditions for researchers at all stages of their careers."[17] The Lundbeck Foundation has a deep taproot—its parent company—but it has also diversified into similar companies to guarantee a broader and more stable base. Above ground, it has a singular focus: understanding and

12 Scott McCulloch, "Industrial Foundations: The Imperfect Solution to Long-Term Prosperity?" Campden FB, August 1, 2018, www.campdenfb.com/article/industrial-foundations-imperfect-solution-long-term-prosperity.

13 "Strategic Investments," Lundbeckfonden, accessed April 20, 2022, https://lundbeckfonden.com/en/business-activities/strategic-investments.

14 "The Organisation," Lundbeckfonden, accessed April 20, 2022, https://lundbeckfonden.com/en/about-us/the-organisation.

15 "About Lundbeckfonden Ventures," Lundbeckfonden, accessed April 18, 2022, https://lundbeckfonden.com/about-lundbeckfonden-ventures.

16 "The Organisation."

17 "What We Have Funded," Lundbeckfonden, accessed April 22, 2022, https://lundbeckfonden.com/en/grants-and-prizes/what-we-have-funded.

treating brain disorders. The relentless pursuit of this mission through business, research, education, philanthropy, and charity has made it the world leader in restoring brain health. These efforts have benefited millions, although most outside of Denmark have never heard of Lundbeck.

Lundbeck Foundation and Neurotorium

The Lundbeck International Neuroscience Foundation (LINF) was launched in 1997. Its mission is to support and approve non-product related educational activities that improve the quality of life of patients within psychiatry and neurology. The Lundbeck Institute was also started that year. Its activities are controlled by LINF and focused on education. In 2021 the Institute was subsumed in a knowledge platform called Neurotorium. Neurotorium's mission is as follows:

> to improve awareness and knowledge of the brain and its diseases through online educational content created for clinicians, educators and all who are interested in learning more about the brain. We offer high-quality materials that are curated and reviewed by leading experts within the fields of psychiatry, neurology and neuroscience.[18]

♦ **The relentless pursuit of your founding mission should drive everything you do in business and philanthropy.**

H. Lundbeck & Co is the second largest drug company in Denmark, but it's only a midrange company in the global pharmaceuticals market. Still, it's the world leader in its niche of choice, treatment for diseases and disorders of the brain and central nervous system. That's the ranking that means the most to the company, the foundation, and the millions of patients they serve.

Tandem Hybrid Distinctives and Lundbeck

Driven by a Compelling Social Mission

Lundbeck started as a trading company and got into pharmaceuticals because it was profitable. Today the company is a world leader in treating disorders of the brain and central nervous system. It flourishes in more than 50 countries, but it is firmly rooted in Denmark. Staying put and enriching its home country is Lundbeck's primary social mission, which it carries out through its commercial and charitable organizations.

18 "About Neurotorium," Neurotorium, accessed April 22, 2022, https://neurotorium.org/about/.

Financed by Commercial Success

Lundbeck's considerable profits are used to fund research, develop products, advance education, and pioneer treatments for neurological disorders. It does this directly through its company and foundations and indirectly through its investment in other life science companies via Lundbeckfonden Ventures. Lundbeck doesn't suffer from NIH ("not invented here") syndrome and it expects a healthy ROI for its core mission.

Structured to Retain Control

Hans and Grete Lundbeck didn't have children so there's no family interest in the business. In its place is a strong national identity that is guarded by the Lundbeck Foundation that Greta started after Han's death. She endowed it with enough stock that the foundation still owns 70 percent of the company today even after going public in 1999. The foundation's goal is to keep the company focused on brain health and firmly in Danish hands.

Scalable and Sustainable for the Long Haul

Lundbeck has grown by focusing its commercial and social efforts on a single medical niche: addressing disorders of the brain and central nervous system. It has become the world leader in the field and impacts millions of lives daily although it's only a midsized pharma company. In Denmark, however, it's the second largest drug company and has an outsized influence on everything from employment to education, and will for the foreseeable future.

Novo Nordisk

Novo Nordisk A/S, is the largest pharmaceutical company in Denmark, more than six times bigger than its nearest rival, Lundbeck. It was the world's ninth largest biopharma company in 2021, with a market cap of $173 billion:[19] "Diabetes treatment products generated most of Novo Nordisk's sales, but they also focus on areas such as hormone replacement therapy and pharmaceuticals for treatment of other serious chronic diseases, like obesity, hemophilia, growth disorders."[20] Novo Nordisk produces half the world's insulin supply, which is

19 Heather McKenzie, "Q1 2021: A Look at Top 25 Biopharma Companies by Market Cap," BioSpace, May 3, 2021, www.biospace.com/article/q1-2021-an-in-depth-look-at-biopharma-s-top-25-/.

20 "Pharmaceutical Industry in Denmark—Statistics & Facts," Statista Research Department, April 23, 2021, www.statista.com/topics/5971/pharmaceutical-industry-in-denmark/.

used by more than 34 million people.[21] It has more than 45,000 employees, with about 6,000 employees in the U.S.[22]

Novo Nordisk is the result of the 1989 merger between Nordisk Insulinlaboratorium and Novo Terapeutisk Laboratorium, two fierce competitors who finally decided to unite and dominate.

Rivals from Birth

Professor August Krogh (1874–1949) won the Nobel Prize in Physiology or Medicine in 1920. His wife, Marie (1874–1943), was also a renowned scientist and physician. In 1907, she became only the fourth woman in Denmark to earn a medical degree. Marie developed type 2 diabetes and had patients with type 1 diabetes. On a lecture tour of America in 1922, the Kroghs heard about two Canadian scientists who had succeeded in producing active insulin. They took a side trip to Toronto where they sought and received permission to develop and sell insulin in Scandinavia.

The Kroghs, along with Dr. Hans Christian Hagedorn, a colleague of Marie's, began working together in 1923. Hagedorn quit his medical practice to run the new laboratory. The trio had deep knowledge, but not deep pockets. August Kongsted, owner of Leo Pharmaceuticals, provided financial support in return for having the first product named after his company: Insulin Leo. In February 1924, Nordisk Insulinlaboratorium was set up under the management of Krogh, Hagedorn, and Kongsted. They agreed that profits should be used for scientific and humanitarian purposes.

♦ **Making money is necessary but not sufficient as a mission; be clear up front how profits will be used.**

The Pederson brothers, Harald and Thorvald, had been hired to help in the insulin production process. When Thorvald, a chemist, was fired in 1924 after a dispute with Hagedorn, his brother quit. On their own, the Pederson's developed a stable liquid insulin product, which they called Insulin Novo. They also developed the Novo Syringe to deliver the appropriate amount of insulin per shot. They approached Nordisk about a collaborative effort to market their creations but were rebuffed, so Harald and Thorvald started their own company in 1925: Novo Terapeutisk Laboratorium (later Novo Industri). As noted in one online history:

> The die was now cast for decades of rivalry between two companies, two images and two cultures, but both with the same overall objective:

21 "What We Do," Novo Nordisk, accessed April 23, 2022, www.novonordisk. com/about/what-we-do.html.

22 "Who We Are," Novo Nordisk, accessed April 21, 2022, www.novo nordisk-us.com/about/who-we-are.html.

to develop and manufacture world-class diabetes medicine. … although the Pedersen brothers starting the Novo branch did not have the same thorough understanding of diabetes, the same scientific background or even the same knowledge about manufacturing and selling pharmaceutical products as the Nordisk branch, their entrepreneurial spirit, inventiveness and perseverance compensated for these disadvantages.[23]

The Pederson families gave financial support and worked in the fledgling business. They sought to maintain a family feel as they hired more employees and provided benefits that were ahead of their time. Since Nordisk was already well-established in the Scandinavian countries, Novo went after other markets. By 1936, it had fifty-six employees and 90 percent of its production was exported to forty countries.

♦ **If you can't bloom where you're planted, it might be time to start your own garden.**

Nordisk was continuing to innovate. In 1936, it introduced a new, longer-acting insulin product. Ten years later it came up with a neutral insulin called Neutral Protamine Hagedorn (NPH), which soon accounted for the majority of longer-acting insulin used in the Western world.

Novo began marketing its own long-lasting insulin product in 1938: zinc-protamine-insulin (ZPI). This triggered a patent lawsuit from Nordisk that went to the Supreme Court and was decided in Nordisk's favor. Novo had to pay Nordisk a share of the profits earned from sales of ZPI.

In 1953, Novo launched Lente, an insulin-zinc suspension that captured up to a third of the world's insulin market. Profits enabled Novo to build laboratories in Bagsværd in 1959. The city became Novo's headquarters. In 1973, Novo introduced Monocomponent (MC) insulin, the purest insulin then available. A decade later, they came out with a new version called Human Monocomponent insulin. It was the world's first insulin preparation identical to human insulin.

In 1974, Novo Industri A/S was listed on the Copenhagen Stock Exchange, with the Novo Foundation retaining a controlling interest. Novo became the first Scandinavian company to be listed on the New York Stock Exchange in 1981.

Nordisk shifted its management in the 1970s and the company was restructured in 1980. It spun off production, sales, and research into a separate unit called Nordisk Gentofte. This unit became a public company in 1984 and was listed on the Copenhagen Stock Exchange in 1986. Around this time Nordisk also began marketing Nanormon for the

---

23 "The History of Novo Nordisk Foundation," Novo Nordisk Fonden, accessed April 30, 2022, https://novonordiskfonden.dk/en/about-the-foundation/history/.

treatment of growth hormone deficiency. Nordisk became one of the world's largest manufacturers and exporters of human growth hormone.

♦ **Modify your organizational structure as you grow to increase capitalization and expand markets.**

Novo introduced the NovoPen in 1985. It dispensed the right dose of insulin several times a day. Nordisk answered a year later with their own insulin pen, the Insuject. Three years after that, Novo came out with the world's first disposable insulin syringe, NovoLet. This high level of competition couldn't go on forever:

> With their highly purified insulin products, human insulin, elegant pen devices and mastery of the new genetic engineering techniques, the two Danish companies were now in a strong position as international competition increased. Before long, however, they had to admit that they could achieve even better results by combining their efforts.[24]

Merger

The 1989 merger of Novo and Nordisk created the world's largest manufacturer of insulin:

> Two pharmaceutical companies, large by Danish standards but small in global terms, were operating within a few kilometers of each other, both manufacturing insulin as their core business. Both companies were pursuing the same markets, the same researchers and the same scientific personnel, which were vital to the future development of the companies. There was talk of a possible merger in the circles around the two companies and their respective [controlling] foundations. The discreet feelers came to nothing, at least at first. The historical, cultural and personal barriers were too great. ... Nevertheless, in January 1989, the boards of the two foundations with corporate interests, Novo Foundation and Nordisk Insulinlaboratorium, issued a press release that ... was short and sweet: "The Boards of the Novo Foundation and Nordisk Insulinlaboratorium have agreed to merge the two foundations into the Novo Nordisk Foundation."[25]

Since Novo and Nordisk were controlled by their respective foundations, the foundations merged before the companies did. Nordisk's foundation had been started in 1926 to support diabetes research. It held a controlling interest in the company, with Krogh, Hagedorn, and Kongsted comprising

24 Ibid.
25 Ibid.

the leadership of both company and foundation. The Novo Foundation was created in 1951. Its goals were ensuring the growth of Novo and providing financial support for scientific, humanitarian, and social causes.

Eleven years after the merger, Novo Nordisk divided into three entities:

> the company's two core businesses, Health Care and Enzyme Business, became independent legal entities. The name Novo Nordisk A/S was carried on by the former Health Care, while Enzyme Business took the name Novozymes A/S. The holding company Novo A/S was established at the same time to manage the funds of the Novo Nordisk Foundation. ... The three new companies are today part of the Novo Group.[26]

◆ Competition is good for business, but sometimes cooperation is even better.

In 2001, Novo Nordisk established the World Diabetes Foundation to improve diabetes care in developing countries. The Novo Nordisk Hemophilia Foundation was set up in 2005 to improve hemophilia treatment in the developing world. Novo Nordisk had a long history of serving diabetics. In 1932 the Nordisk Foundation had founded the Steno Memorial Hospital to treat diabetics and research the disease. It became the largest diabetes center in Scandinavia. A research laboratory was attached to the hospital in 1957. Novo had started its own sanatorium in 1938, the Hvidovre Diabetes Sanatorium, for diabetic research and clinical testing of Novo's products. The name was changed to Hvidovre Hospital in 1949. The Steno Memorial Hospital and Hvidovre Hospital merged in 1992, after the corporate merger, to form the Steno Diabetes Center.

Despite all the good the Novo Nordisk Foundation is doing, the company is not above illegal business tactics like price-fixing. Novo Nordisk, Eli Lilly, and Sanofi produce 99 percent of the world's insulin, which has proved a temptation to profiteering that they haven't resisted. That's why the three companies are being investigated by the U.S. Congress and sued by the state of Mississippi:

> Attorney General Lynn Fitch says that over the last 10 years, the companies have raised prices as much as 1000 percent, within days of each other. She adds this has happened even as insulin production costs have decreased. Fitch notes that in 2016, the average diabetic spent just over $5700 per year. Fitch further alleges that the increases are part of a

26 "Novo Nordisk History," Novo Nordisk, accessed April 20, 2022, www. novonordisk.co.in/content/dam/Denmark/HQ/aboutus/documents/History Book_UK.pdf.

"fraudulent conspiracy" between the companies and pharmacy benefit managers—who are also named in the suit.[27]

All three companies lowered prices on their generic options and offered free emergency supply options, but in August 2021, the House Energy & Commerce Committee sent letters to executives of the companies, "raising concerns that despite their supposed concern over the past two years with the price of insulin, the price still remains unacceptably high. ... the price of insulin in the U.S. is more than 10 times that of 33 other countries."[28]

♦ **Remember Luke 8:17: "For there is nothing hidden that will not be disclosed, and nothing concealed that will not be known or brought out into the open."**

World's Largest Foundation

The Novo Nordisk Foundation objectives are to create a solid basis for the operation of Novo Nordisk and to support scientific, humanitarian, and social causes. It owns all Novo Nordisk's A shares, which ensures that Novo Nordisk will remain an independent company in Danish hands. In terms of assets, the Novo Nordisk Foundation is the largest foundation in the world, with a net worth of $73.1 billion in 2020. That year it dispensed more than $1.6 billion in awards and grants.[29] "Yes, it is bigger than the Gates Foundation in terms of assets," says Kasim Kutay, the chief of Novo Holdings, the investment fund that manages the assets and investments for the foundation:

> The reason is that we are an enterprise foundation that both owns companies and at the same time also has a charitable purpose. However, Gates Foundation is by far the biggest foundation in the world when it comes to grant giving with a five times higher activity level than us.[30]

27 Jonathan M Block, "Eli Lilly, Sanofi, and Novo Nordisk Sued Over Insulin Prices," Seeking Alpha, June 16, 2021, https://seekingalpha.com/news/3706905-eli-lilly-sanofi-and-novo-nordisk-sued-over-insulin-prices.

28 Vandana Singh, "House Committee Questions Eli Lilly, Sanofi, Novo Nordisk On 'Unacceptably High' Insulin Prices," Yahoo, August 20, 2021, www.yahoo.com/now/house-committee-questions-eli-lilly-183433152.html.

29 "Highlights from the 2020 Report," Novo Nordisk Fonden, accessed April 20, 2022, https://novonordiskfonden.dk/wp-content/uploads/NNF-pixie-annual-report-UK-2020-FINAL.pdf.

30 Maija Palmer, "Meet the World's Largest Biotech Investor with $65bn Under Management," Sifted, December 8, 2020, https://sifted.eu/articles/novo-holdings-largest-biotech-investor/.

Half the Foundation's money comes from Novo Nordisk profits; the other half is generated by Novo Holdings' investments in almost 100 life sciences companies, which averaged 13 percent ROI over the last ten years[31]. In 2017, the Novo Nordisk Foundation created the BioInnovation Institute (BII) to support innovative entrepreneurs and researchers in further developing research projects and new solutions that benefit society. In 2020 it spun off BII as a separate foundation. As of June, 2021, BII had invested in 68 startups to the tune of more than $40 million.[32]

♦ **Plow profits back into the fields where they originated when it comes to R&D, investments, and giving.**

Novo Nordisk is the largest pharmaceutical company in Denmark, and one of the Big Three in the world when it comes to diabetes and other chronic diseases like hemophilia and human growth disorders. The Novo Nordisk Foundation is the largest foundation in the world. Both company and foundation are firmly rooted in Denmark but their markets and investments are global, with a growing interest in developing countries. Both are dominant because of their disciplined and narrow focus on the diseases they are working so hard to eradicate.

Tandem Hybrid Distinctives and Novo Nordisk

Driven by a Compelling Social Mission

The Novo part of Novo Nordisk was started by a trio of renowned scientists and physicians. One of them, Dr. Marie Krogh, suffered from diabetes. Understanding and treating the disease was the company's mission and its profits were to be used for scientific and humanitarian purposes. The Nordisk part of the equation splintered off from Novo early on but pursued the same goals in the same fields. Their 1989 merger made them the world leader in diabetes research and treatment and led to the creation of the largest foundation in the world; accomplishments that would have made the founders very proud.

Financed by Commercial Success

Novo Nordisk has been able to do so much to improve the lives of millions with diabetes and other serious chronic diseases because of its laser focus from the beginning. Everything it has done commercially and charitably is to eradicate these disorders. By eventually combining their efforts instead of

31 Ibid.
32 "Establishing BII as an independent Foundation," BioInnovation Institute, June 3, 2021, www.pwc.dk/da/arrangementer/2021/bii.pdf.

constantly competing, they have multiplied their commercial and philanthropic successes.

Structured to retain Control

Both Novo and Nordisk were controlled by their respective foundations, who had to merge before the companies could. The organizations weren't diluted by the merger but supercharged since both were committed to the same market and the same country—Denmark. There has been some reorganization since the merger but all the entities are still part of the Novo Group and aligned with the founders' original vision.

Scalable and Sustainable for the Long Haul

Novo and Nordisk did well as rivals and some of their success was driven by the fierce competition and bad blood between the companies. Their merger put the new organization in a class by itself and made it the undisputed world leader in diabetic research and treatment. It also made them the biggest pharma company in Denmark and funded the largest foundation in the world. Novo Nordisk has no plans to slow down on either front.

Lundbeck–Novo Nordisk Comparison

Business

Lundbeck and Novo Nordisk are innovative and enduring companies that are good places to work and good corporate citizens. While they market and invest in other countries, they are determined to remain Danish companies with a Denmark-first philosophy. They are the leading companies in the world in their markets because their companies and foundations are narrowly focused. They are also guilty of some of the sins of Big Pharma (e.g. price-fixing and pay-for-delay deals).

Philanthropy and Foundations

Neither the founders nor their companies are known for philanthropy. Their foundations are for preserving ownership of the companies and keeping them in Danish hands. The foundations don't give directly to patients but invest in research in the fields where they are the world leaders.

Personal Lives

Little is known of the founders' personal lives. The subject isn't mentioned in the comprehensive histories of the companies or foundations.

Legacy

The legacy of both companies is geographically rooted in Denmark and committed to remain so, which has greatly benefited the country. But their impact has been global and improved the lives of millions of people with neurological disorders and diabetes because of their intense focus on these diseases, both commercially and philanthropically.

What Would They Think?

What would Hans and Grete Lundbeck, August and Marie Krogh, and Hans Christian Hagedorn think about their businesses and foundations today? Grete Lundbeck was a visionary woman who changed the trajectory of Lundbeck by setting up the Lundbeck Foundation, which keeps the company focused on brain research and firmly tied to Denmark. But she might not approve of all the restrictions it now has. The Kroghs and Hagedorn accomplished the same with their foundation, keeping the original focus on diabetes and chronic diseases, along with a fierce loyalty to Denmark. They could be somewhat frustrated that their foundation—the largest in the world—doesn't give directly to people.

Takeaways for Social Entrepreneurs

- Determine how much your business depends on R&D and spend accordingly.
- Double down on what you do best. Divest yourself of what isn't your core business.
- Learn as much from failure—yours and others'—as from success.
- Earn and keep a stellar reputation by treating people well, both inside and outside your organization.
- It's never too late to create a structure for preserving a company's ownership and founding vision.
- Synchronize your commercial and social enterprises to maximize your impact.
- The relentless pursuit of your founding mission should drive everything you do in business and philanthropy.
- Making money is necessary but not sufficient as a mission; be clear up front how profits will be used.
- If you can't bloom where you're planted, it might be time to start your own garden.
- Modify your organizational structure as you grow to increase capitalization and expand markets.
- Competition is good for business, but sometimes cooperation is even better.

- Remember Luke 8:17: "For there is nothing hidden that will not be disclosed, and nothing concealed that will not be known or brought out into the open."
- Plow profits back into the fields where they originated when it comes to R&D, investments, and giving.

12 AstraZeneca and the Upjohn Company

AstraZeneca and Upjohn are in the same global marketplace but they got into pharmaceuticals in completely different ways. Dr. Will Upjohn created and patented a product to launch the company that bore his name. For more than a century his family led the company to commercial success and community impact before a series of mergers absorbed Upjohn, name and all. AstraZeneca is more conglomerate than company; a group effort from the start with no mission except to make money. Which it's been exceptionally good at; enough so to become one of the largest pharmaceutical companies in the world. Whereas the Upjohn Company had deep roots in one family and location, AstraZeneca has broad branches, mostly grafted onto a thick trunk.

AstraZeneca

AstraZeneca is the merger of Sweden's Astra AB, and the U.K.'s Zeneca Group. The two joined forces in 1999 to create the leading pharmaceutical company in Scandinavia and the tenth largest in the world in 2021, with revenues of $37.4 billion and more than 76,000 employees.[1] Neither company had noted individual founders but both have had dynamic presidents and CEOs along the way who were key to their success.

Astra AB

A group of more than 400 doctors and apothecaries joined together in 1913 and established Astra AB to manufacture drugs in Sweden. Their first products were a heart medication and a nutritional supplement, followed by more medical and chemical compounds. World War I boosted sales because of restrictions on imports but the company floundered after the war. At various points it was acquired by another company, faced bankruptcy, was

1 Kevin Dunleavy, "The Top 20 Pharma Companies by 2021 Revenue," Fierce Pharma, April 12, 2022, www.fiercepharma.com/special-reports/top-20-pharma-companies-2021-revenue/.

DOI: 10.4324/9781003325987-15

bailed out by the government, and eventually was bought by a private consortium in 1925. Two years later Bîrje Gabrielsson became president, a post he held for thirty years. Under his leadership Astra reorganized and created its own distribution network. It built research and production facilities in the 1930s and introduced new drugs like Hepaforte for anemia and Nitropent for angina.

Astra prospered during World War II as it had during World War I, but there was no postwar slump. On the home front, the company introduced penicillin in Sweden and came out with a local anesthetic called Xylocaine. Healthy profits fueled more drug development. Manufacturing was increased and consolidated to a modernized plant at Södertälje. R&D spending was increased, resulting in new drugs. Xylocaine became internationally popular during the 1950s and helped Astra expand its overseas business. In the 1960s and 1970s it branched into separate divisions for pharmaceuticals, agricultural, nutritional, and recreational products, among others. But by 1980, Astra refocused on pharmaceuticals and sold off its other businesses.

Astra brought in a new CEO in 1988. Håkan Mogren strengthened sales and distribution networks, hiring 1,000 reps worldwide to triple the salesforce within his first two years. Sales increased by almost 50 percent and pretax earnings topped $114 million. Four thousand more reps were added in the next three years and subsidiaries expanded into forty countries. One history notes:

> Håkan Mogren transformed Astra from, "a cautious, slow-moving outfit" into "a true global player". Sales multiplied from SKr6.1 billion [$948 million] in 1988, Mogren's first year at the helm, to SKr38.4 billion [$5.9 billion] in 1996. By this time, Astra's drug portfolio included the world's best-selling drug, the peptic ulcer treatment Losec (known as Prilosec in the U.S.), which alone generated US$3.5 billion in annual sales.[2]

♦ **Build your salesforce and distribution networks for where you want to be, not for where you are.**

Astra also ramped up its R&D efforts in the 1990s and came out with several new medications to address gastrointestinal, respiratory, cardiovascular, and central nervous system disorders. But the exorbitant cost of developing and marketing new drugs in the 1990s caused many pharma companies to look for international partners to help them compete in the global market.

---

2 "Astra AB—Company Profile, Information, Business Description, History, Background Information on Astra AB," Reference for Business, accessed April 22, 2022, www.referenceforbusiness.com/history2/76/Astra-AB.html#ixzz78oO8KRJW.

Zeneca

Zeneca's roots don't go as deep as Astra's. Its core came from the breakup of Imperial Chemical Industries (ICI) in 1993. ICI was one of Britain's largest manufacturers. It made everything from chemicals and pharmaceuticals, to plastics and paints, to food and fragrances. In the early 1990s it sold off various product divisions. Pharmaceuticals, bioscience, biological products, and agrochemicals became a new company with the made-up name of Zeneca.

Zeneca quickly moved to acquire Salick Health Care, with its string of cancer care centers in the U.S., as part of a strategic focus on oncology. In 1998, it sold its non-oncology divisions to make itself ready for a possible merger with another pharma company. "In December 1998, Zeneca bought Astra for $35 billion," as reported by Drugwatch. "The new company, AstraZeneca, was the fourth-largest in the world, with a value of $67 billion, when the merger was completed in 1999."[3]

Corporate headquarters was established in London and R&D was based in Sweden, with major centers in the U.K. and U.S. Internally, AZ focused on five areas of research: cardiovascular, gastrointestinal, respiratory, oncology, and anesthesia. (Later, these would be reduced to oncology, cardiovascular, respiratory, and immunology.) Externally, they began partnering with, or acquiring, other pharma and biotechnology companies at a brisk pace:

- KuDOS Pharmaceuticals for $163 million (2005).
- Cambridge Antibody Technology for $955 million (2006).
- MedImmune for $15.2 billion (2007).
- Ardea Biosciences for $1.26 billion (2012).
- Part of Almirall for $2 billion (2014).
- Part of Takeda for $575 million (2016).
- ZS Pharma for $2.7 billion (2020).
- Alexion Pharmaceuticals for $39 billion (2021).

♦ **Mergers and acquisitions (M&A) are key growth strategies, but they can also conflict with your founding mission.**

Successful product launches in the early 2000s included such blockbusters like Nexium (acid reflux) and Crestor (cardiovascular). The good news came in the form of record profits. The bad news came when these drugs went off patent and revenues plummeted. In 2012 AZ hired a new CEO, Pascal Soriot, to slow the bleeding. Jobs were cut, facilities were relocated

---

3 Michelle Llamas, "AstraZeneca," Drugwatch, accessed October 12, 2021, www.drugwatch.com/manufacturers/astrazeneca/.

or closed, R&D was prioritized and improved. "This new approach to R&D seems to have paid off," reports a 2020 History of AstraZeneca. "Between 2005 and 2010 AstraZeneca's success rates for taking drugs from candidate nomination to phase III completion were at 4%, below an already-low industry standard of 5%, but since then they have risen dramatically to 19% in 2012–2016."[4]

According to IDEA Pharma's 11th annual Pharmaceutical Innovation Index (2022), AstraZeneca ranked first in invention and second in innovation among thirty-two top pharma companies.[5] IDEA Pharma makes the following distinction between invention and innovation: Invention: Bringing ideas or technologies together in a novel way to create something that did not exist before. Innovation: Return on invention; creation of meaningful value from invention.

♦ **Bring new products to market through invention or innovation. Either make something new or make something better.**

COVID-19

Typical for Big Pharma, AZ has had ongoing legal problems and has paid out more than $1 billion in federal fines and legal settlements.[6] One area where AZ has experienced both ends of the pharma spectrum—adulation and criticism—has been its response to COVID-19.

The COVID-19 pandemic hit in early 2020 and changed the world. AstraZeneca has played a leading role in meeting the challenge, as recounted by pharmaphorum:

> With no countries able to completely eliminate the virus, it quickly became clear that the only viable way to both keep people safe and prevent widespread economic disruption was to produce a vaccine against the SARS-COV-2 coronavirus that causes the disease. This resulted in AstraZeneca becoming possibly the most talked-about pharma company in the world when its own vaccine emerged as the frontrunning candidate. The AZD1222 vaccine was invented by the University of Oxford and its spin-out company Vaccitech, then later licensed by AZ.[7]

4 Michelle Llamas, "AstraZeneca."
5 Sy Mukheruee, Idea Pharma, "The Most Innovative and Inventive Drug Companies of 2022 Set the Foundation for Success Before the Pandemic," *Fortune*, April 20, 2022, https://fortune.com/2022/04/20/top-pharmaceutical-companies-innovation-invention-2022/.
6 Michelle Llamas, "AstraZeneca."
7 "A History of AstraZeneca," pharmaphorum, September 18, 2020, https://pharmaphorum.com/views-analysis-sales-marketing/a_history_of-_astrazeneca/.

But it has been anything but smooth sailing for AZ since then:

> The company penned deals to deliver billions of vaccines around the world. Yet, of the major vaccine in the global market, AstraZeneca's has had the roughest ride. Between halted trials, confusing data, and communication mishaps, the company is now facing suspended vaccinations and a decrease in trust in its vaccine.[8]

AZ adjusted to the pushback and has regained some lost ground. As of December 1, 2021, two billion doses of the vaccine, now called Vaxzevria, have been released to more than 170 countries. It has not yet been approved in the U.S. "because the one large-scale trial of the vaccine conducted so far used outdated data":

> The FDA found that in initial trials, some participants mistakenly got half doses of the vaccine. It also found that the trial did not include enough people over 55 years old. It asked the company to do a larger trial in order to get clearer data.[9]

♦ **Use your assets and expertise to address global crises and alleviate human suffering.**

Community Support

AstraZeneca doesn't have its own foundation, except in the U.S., where the AstraZeneca HealthCare Foundation has been in existence since 1993. (No explanation is given as to how the foundation was established six years before the company.) The Foundation's purposes are "to promote public awareness of healthcare issues, to promote public education of medical knowledge, and to support or contribute to charitable and qualified exempt organizations consistent with its charitable purpose." In 2020 the Foundation awarded $1.2 million in grants to nine non-profits that reached more than 11,000 people.[10]

---

8 Jeremy Kahn, "A Complete Timeline of What's Going on with the AstraZeneca COVID Vaccine," *Fortune*, April 8, 2021, https://fortune.com/2021/04/01/astrazeneca-covid-vaccine-timeline-news-latest-update/.

9 "What You Should Know about the AstraZeneca COVID-19 Vaccine," Healthline, accessed April 23, 2022, www.healthline.com/health/adult-vaccines/astrazeneca-vaccine#approval-in-the-u-s.

10 "2020 Annual Report, AstraZeneca HealthCare Foundation," AstraZeneca HealthCare Foundation, accessed April 20, 2022, www.astrazeneca-us.com/content/dam/az-us/Documents/AZHCF/2020-AZHCF-Annual-Report-FINAL.pdf.

Worldwide in 2020, AstraZeneca made more than $76 million in financial and non-financial contributions to 1,339 organizations in 88 countries. The AZ website explains:

> Our work is done with non-profit organizations, associations and societies from around the world. ... We aim to make a significant financial and non-financial contribution to the communities in which we operate. This comprises our medicines for patients and our focus on sustainability for people and the environment.[11]

A significant chunk of AZ's donations went to mitigate the effects of the pandemic.

AZ's Young Health Programme was founded in 2010 to help young people aged 10–24 combat long-term conditions such as cancers, diabetes, respiratory and heart diseases, and mental health issues. It has been active in more than thirty countries and partnered with more than thirty non-profits in its first decade.[12] AZ also helped create TransCelerate BioPharma Inc. Its ten founding partners agreed to "combine financial and other resources, including personnel, to solve industry-wide challenges in a collaborative environment."[13]

♦ **You don't have to reinvent the wheel when it comes to social and philanthropic ventures; you can work with reputable partners to maximize impact.**

One of its highest priorities has been COVID-19. CEO Dalvir Gill says:

> [T]he DataCelerate platform now includes a rapidly created COVID-19 module, with the capability to make research data from COVID-19 clinical trials around the world accessible not only to Member Companies, but also, for the first time, to non-members. Having a shared foundation of knowledge about the virus is key to accelerating the timeline for solutions—and not just for this virus but the next one that may emerge at any time.[14]

11　"Supporting Our Communities," AstraZeneca, accessed April 20, 2022, www.astrazeneca.com/sustainability/supporting-our-communities.html.

12　"Young Health Programme," AstraZeneca, accessed April 20, 2022, www.younghealthprogrammeyhp.com.

13　Thomas Sullivan, "Ten BioPharmaceutical Companies Launch TransCelerate BioPharm, Inc. to Accelerate Product Development," Policy & Medicine, May 6, 2018, www.policymed.com/2012/09/ten-biopharmaceutical-companies-launch-transcelerate-biopharm-inc-to-accelerate-product-development.html.

14　"2020 Year-End Achievements," TransCelerate Biopharma, accessed March 30, 2022, www.transceleratebiopharmainc.com/wp-content/uploads/2020/12/TransCelerate_2020_EOY-Report-FINAL.pdf.

AstraZeneca has become one of the largest biopharmaceutical companies on the planet the same way the other pharma giants have: through rigorous R&D and relentless—and expensive—M&A. AZ doesn't have a storied past that shapes its culture like Lundbeck or Novo Nordisk, but it has a clear focus on the future, with 160 projects in its development pipeline at the time of this writing. AZ is also a key player in the COVID crisis, which is in keeping with its commitment to "deliver life-changing medicines that create enduring value for patients and society."[15]

Tandem Hybrid Distinctives and AstraZeneca

Driven by a Compelling Social Mission

AstraZeneca has the lowest profile in this regard of any of the other companies we've looked at. Neither Sweden's Astra AB nor the U.K.'s Zeneca Group had noted founders or founding visions, other than to make money. Both went through various iterations until their merger in 1999. Even though AZ is one of the largest pharma companies in the world it doesn't have its own foundation but gives financial and non-financial support to other organizations.

Financed by Commercial Success

AZ's commercial success has been fueled by R&D and M&A, resulting in a broad range of profitable products and promising projects in development. And now it's making what it calls "modest profits" from its COVID-19 vaccine—more than $2 billion in the first three quarters of 2021—despite saying it would not sell the shot on a for-profit basis during the pandemic. However, it will still supply vaccine to poorer nations on a not-for-profit basis.[16]

Structured to Retain Control

AstraZeneca is a publicly traded company on several stock exchanges. There is no controlling organization outside the company and no majority stockholders. According to the shareholder registry, 50 percent of the ownership is controlled by the top 21 shareholders. BlackRock, Inc. is currently the largest shareholder, with 8.4 percent of shares outstanding. Company

---

15 "Our Company," AstraZeneca, www.astrazeneca.com/our-company.html.
16 Robert Hart, "AstraZeneca Will Now Profit from Covid Vaccine after Pledge to Sell at Cost during Pandemic," Forbes, November 12, 2021, www.forbes.com/sites/roberthart/2021/11/12/astrazeneca-will-now-profit-from-covid-va ccine-after-pledge-to-sell-at-cost-during-pandemic/?sh=76947de1779d.

executives, board members, and other insiders own less than 1 percent of the company.[17]

Scalable and Sustainable for the Long Haul

As one of the largest pharma companies in the world, and one of the few makers of Covid vaccines, AZ stock prices are projected to continue rising. It will keep doing what it's always done: invent, innovate, and acquire.

The Upjohn Company

The Upjohn Company no longer exists as a separate entity, but for more than a century it invented, innovated, and marketed its way into a global pharmaceutical powerhouse. Its deep roots and significant contributions to pharmacology have been swallowed up in multiple mergers. It joined with Sweden-based Pharmacia in 1995 to form Pharmacia & Upjohn. Twenty years later, Pharmacia & Upjohn was acquired by Pfizer Inc. This section will look at Upjohn prior to these mergers.

Dr. Will

William E. Upjohn (1853–1932) was one of twelve children born to Dr. Uriah Upjohn in Kalamazoo, Michigan. After graduating medical school in 1875, he moved to nearby Hastings, Michigan to practice medicine. A local history of Kalamazoo gives the colorful details of what happened next:

> Known by his contemporaries as a dreamer and a tinkerer, Dr. Upjohn saw a need to improve the means of administering medicine ... Dr. Upjohn began experimenting with making better pills in the attic of his home. Eventually he invented his "friable" pill. Friable meant that the pill could easily be crushed to a powder. The pill was patented in 1885, and its reputation quickly spread within the medical community, thanks greatly to Dr. Upjohn's marketing strategy. He sent small pine boards to thousands of physicians along with samples of his rival's hard pills, and his own friable pills. He invited doctors to hammer the pills into the boards to see which one would be the most digestible.[18]

---

17 "What Kind of Shareholders Hold the Majority in AstraZeneca PLC's (LON: AZN) Shares?" Yahoo, January 19, 2022, www.yahoo.com/video/kind-sha reholders-hold-majority-astrazeneca-043418976.html.

18 Martha Lohrstorfer and Catherine Larson, "William E. Upjohn, Person of the Century: 1853–1932," Kalamazoo Public Library, June 3, 2010, www.kpl. gov/local-history/kalamazoo-history/biographies/upjohn-william-e/.

◆   **Encourage head-to-head competition when your products and services are superior.**

Dr. Will (as William was called) moved back to Kalamazoo, where, along with his brother, Henry—also a doctor—and their two wives, they started making and selling pills and granule products. In their first year they hired twelve employees and offered 186 pills they had made friable. Sales reached $50,000, but disaster struck in 1887 with Henry's death from typhoid fever. Two other brothers, Frederick and James, joined Dr. Will to start the Upjohn Pill and Granule Co. with $60,000 in capital stock. William served as president, James as vice president, and Frederick as treasurer. Neither brother stayed with the company long-term.

Upjohn began hiring sales reps and recruited agents to represent the company in big cities like New York and Chicago. Sales topped $94,000 in 1889 and $132,000 the following year. Employees shared in the success, receiving one-week vacation and a Christmas bonus. New buildings were built in Kalamazoo as the product list reached 500. Dr. Will was elected to the Village Council in 1892, reflective of a lifetime camaraderie between company and city.

Upjohn made a big splash at the Chicago World's Fair in 1893, with Dr. Will manning the exhibit. Business expanded from coast to coast and by the end of the century, the company had sixty employees, half of them sales-people. In 1902 the business reorganized as The Upjohn Company. Annual sales reached a quarter million. The employee workweek was shortened from sixty to fifty hours at the same pay. Dr. Will's nephew, Lawrence N. Upjohn—another doctor—joined the company in 1904 and would later become its president and chairman. Sales exceeded $1 million for the first time in 1912. Employees now had two-week's vacation and access to a company cafeteria. In 1915 an additional benefit was added, life insurance for employees and dependents.

◆   **Share your success with those who help create it in practical ways that are meaningful to them.**

Upjohn hired its first research scientist in 1913, Dr. Frederick W. Heyl. Heyl developed an effervescent antacid and later came up with a digitalis tablet for heart disease. That year Dr. Will married Carrie Sherwood Gilmore, his neighbor and the widow of James Gilmore, one of the founders of the largest department store in the city. Dr. Will was active in city affairs and was voted Kalamazoo's first mayor in 1918. He helped establish a commission-manager form of government and led the city to pay off its debt load. In 1925 he gave $1,000 to start the Kalamazoo Foundation (now the Kalamazoo Community Foundation).

By 1928 Upjohn had twenty buildings and more than $6 million in sales. Employees were rewarded with a 45-hour work week at the same pay. (It would go down to 40 in 1931.) A Nutritional Research Lab was started. William Harold Upjohn, a brother who had joined the company in 1907 and risen to become General Manager died unexpectedly in 1928 and Dr. Will talked his stepson and son-in-law, Donald S. Gilmore, into joining the company. (Donald, who was Carrie Gilmore's son, married Dr. Will's daughter.) Gilmore came on the board of directors in 1929 and was made vice-president in 1931.

That same year, Dr. Will bought 1,262 acres of farmland and started the Upjohn Richmond Farms as a work project to counter the effects of the Great Depression. It later became home to Upjohn's Agricultural Division. It would be his last acquisition. Dr. William died in 1932, age seventy-nine, having spent half his life at the helm of the company he'd started. His granddaughter, Martha Gilmore Parfet, said of him, "He had a wonderful quote about believing God had given him this great wealth, but that he was just a steward of the wealth to see it disbursed and used for everybody responsibly."[19] Dr. Will's stewardship was so appreciated by his company and community that almost 70 years after his death he was named the "Person of the Century" by the *Kalamazoo Gazette* at the turn of the millennium.[20]

◆ **Remember that you're a steward (manager) of all you have, not the owner, even if the company bears your name.**

Next Generation

Dr. Will's nephew, Dr. Lawrence N. Upjohn, took over for the next eleven years, after which Donald Gilmore became president. Under Lawrence and Donald, the company expanded its R&D staff and facilities. It began a research fellowship program to attract young scientists, which paid off in the coming years. Despite the Depression, sales topped $10 million, generated by more than 1,500 employees, a third of whom were in sales. Multivitamins were introduced in 1940 and grew to generate 30 percent of sales. Total revenues that year were more than $15 million.

Like many other pharmaceutical companies during World War II, Upjohn developed its own lines of antibiotics such as penicillin and streptomycin. It did so well that by 1958 it was the sixth largest manufacturer of antibiotics in the world. Upjohn expanded internationally after the war and did well in foreign markets. The R&D department had more than 300 scientists in 1949 and came up with a method to synthetize Folic Acid. Another big breakthrough came with the production of cortisone.

19 Emily Monacelli, "15 Ways the Upjohn Family's Impact Lives on in Kalamazoo," MLive, February 23, 2017, www.mlive.com/news/kalamazoo/2017/02/upjohn_familys_influence_on_ka.html.
20 Lohrstorfer and Larson "William E. Upjohn."

The 1950s were a decade of growth. Upjohn opened manufacturing plants and subsidiaries outside the U.S. It acquired other companies. It got into the veterinary market. Revenues neared $150 million in 1958, with products less than five years old accounting for 58 percent of sales. The board voted to take the company public and authorized a twenty-five to one stock split, and on January 5, 1959, Upjohn was listed on the New York Stock Exchange.

In 1962, Ray T. Parfet became company president. Known as "Ted," he added chairman and CEO to his titles in 1969. Ted was part of the Upjohn family. He had married Gilmore's daughter, Martha, who was also Dr. Will's granddaughter. Keeping company leadership in the family was important, and prior to 1968 only family members or employees were allowed on the board of directors.

♦ **Family-owned businesses can be family run, as long as succeeding generations are properly trained and qualified.**

Ted reorganized the company into four divisions: Pharmaceutical, International, Chemical & Plastics, and Agricultural Products. Upjohn got into the personal healthcare market in 1969 with the purchase of Homemakers Inc., eventually to become Upjohn Healthcare Services. A Consumer Products division was created two years later. Motrin hit the market in 1974 and had the highest first-year sales of a pharmaceutical product in U. S. history: $55 million, boosting company sales to more than $1 billion in 1976. One hundred million of that went into research in 1977. Introduced in 1981, Xanax was another product that did well from the outset, earning $12.6 million its first year and more than $400 million by the end of the 1980s. Other blockbuster products launched in the 80s included Halcion (sleep medication), Nuprin (anti-inflammatory), and Rogaine (baldness treatment).

In 1987, Ted Parfet retired as CEO but stayed on the board until 1994. Dr. Theodore Cooper assumed control of Upjohn. Although the company had had several physicians at the helm, Dr. Cooper was one of the few medical doctors heading a U.S.-based pharmaceutical company at the time. His major focus was on improving Upjohn's quality control. Heading into the 1990s, the patents on many of Upjohn's major products were due to expire. The company intensified its R&D and got FDA approval for eight new drugs in 1992. It also put more effort into generics.

Commitment to Kalamazoo

Through the generations the Upjohn family had invested personally and financially in their hometown of Kalamazoo. In her article titled "15 Ways the Upjohn Family Impacts Lives in Kalamazoo," Emily Monacelli mentions:

Kalamazoo Community Foundation: One of the largest community foundations in the U.S., it was started with a donation from W.E. Upjohn. When he died, he left half his wealth, $1.3 million, to the Foundation.

W.E. Upjohn Institute for Employment Research: W.E. Upjohn bought land in Richland for displaced workers to farm and provide for their families. He created the W.E. Upjohn Unemployment Trustee Corp. to support the effort.

Dorothy U. Dalton Foundation: Dorothy was a daughter of W.E. Upjohn. Her Foundation supports civic, cultural, education, health, housing and human services causes.

Harold and Grace Upjohn Foundation: The Foundation was established in 1958 ... and supports the Kalamazoo Symphony Orchestra, Arts Council of Greater Kalamazoo, and many other causes.[21]

Then there's the Kalamazoo Nature Center, the Kalamazoo Institute of Arts, the Kalamazoo Civic Auditorium and Theatre, and the Foundation for Excellence. The list goes on and on.[22]

♦ **Invest in more than just jobs in the communities where you do business.**

Pharmacia & Upjohn

Consolidation in the pharmaceutical industry put pressure on Upjohn to compete with global rivals. It made sizeable investments in facilities and sold off unprofitable businesses. The Swedish company Pharmacia was a major player, but in the mid-1980s, it was cash-strapped and had to borrow money to meet payroll. A new chairman, Jan Ekberg, was brought on in 1986 to turn things around. He reorganized and expanded Pharmacia through key mergers and acquisitions so that by 1993 it was the third largest pharma company in the world, with sales above $3 billion.

Pharmacia had a new drug for the treatment of glaucoma but lacked production and marketing capabilities in the U.S. Upjohn was strong in these areas and Ekberg met with his counterpart at Upjohn, John Zabriskie, to discuss a possible merger, which took place in 1995. All did not go as expected. A case study of the merger offers the following summary:

In 1997, it was undeniable: the merger was failing badly, exceeding cost expectations by US$200 million, and a drop in stock prices of 25 percent. In April 2000, Pharmacia-Upjohn merged with Monsanto, creating a company known as Pharmacia Corporation. In 2001,

21   Monacelli, "15 ways."
22   Ibid.

Pharmacia announced that it was spinning off its agricultural business, Monsanto. In July 2002, Pharmacia agreed to a US$53 billion acquisition by US pharmaceutical giant Pfizer, which was completed in April 2003. ... Pharmacia no longer existed in name, and it was thus erased as an entity, subsumed by Pfizer.[23]

The loss of the Upjohn Company as a primary source of philanthropy required the not-for-profits in the Kalamazoo area to adjust to a new paradigm. It also affected the city's tax base and job market. Upjohn had around 8,000 employees in Kalamazoo in 1993. Pfizer's footprint would be much smaller but still sizable. In 2019, "While Pfizer employs 2,202 colleagues (workers), its activities also support more than an estimated 1,200 supplier jobs," according to a report by the W. E. Upjohn Institute for Employment Research.[24] "The activities of the direct and indirect jobs, support more than 1,600 jobs supplying goods and services to workers," according to the analysis. "Additionally, 631 government jobs are supported by Pfizer, and the economy [is] driven through the indirect and induced employment. That amounts to about 5,680 jobs, ... the output resulting from all that to be about $2.2 billion."[25]

Journalist Tom Chmielewski asked and answered the question: What happens when a city's "big employer" gets bought? "The end of Upjohn as an independent entity was a shock," he notes. "But it was not a disaster."[26]

♦ **Nothing lasts forever, so do life and business in such a way that you'll be missed when you're gone.**

Tandem Hybrid Distinctives and Upjohn

Driven by a Compelling Social Mission

The Upjohn Company always had an interest in serving its community and championing causes it believed in. Company founder, Dr. Will, had a sense of stewardship over the wealth God had given him and he used it to bless others. This was demonstrated in the way he ran his company and conducted his personal life. His descendants carried on in the same spirit.

---

23 Sophie Coughlan and Piero Morosini, "A Failure to Integrate: Pharmacia & Upjohn: Abstract," *Case Centre*, 2007, www.thecasecentre.org/products/view?id=74017.

24 Al Jones, "Pfizer Means $2.2 billion, 5,680 Jobs to Kalamazoo Area, Study Finds," *MLive*, October 14, 2016, www.mlive.com/news/kalamazoo/2016/10/pfizer_means_22_billion_in_cap.html.

25 Ibid.

26 Tom Chmielewski, "Case Study: What Happens When a City's 'Big Employer' Gets Bought?," October 20, 2017, www.thegazette.com/business/case-study-what-happens-when-a-citys-big-employer-gets-bought/.

Financed by Commercial Success

Dr. Will invented the company's first product and aggressively marketed it. This aggressiveness was a hallmark of the company's approach to research, product development, sales, and new markets. As the business grew, it enriched the Kalamazoo community, both corporately and charitably. Wealth wasn't hoarded by the Upjohns but stewarded and channeled into many civic and philanthropic endeavors.

Structured to Retain Control

The Upjohn family controlled and ran the company for its first eight decades. Prior to 1968, only family members or employees could sit on the board. It would be another twenty years before the company had its first non-family CEO. And less than ten years after that, Upjohn merged with Pharmacia. There was no outside organization or foundation set up to keep control in family hands; no outside mechanism to safeguard family and community interest in the company. This lack of foresight and preparation led to the demise of a respected firm, to the detriment of its employees and community.

Scalable and Sustainable for the Long Haul

The global pharmaceutical market is extremely competitive and smaller successful companies are acquired by larger ones. The Upjohn Company was extremely successful for more than a century. It scaled up to advance medical science and develop and market many life-changing medications. During that time it took good care of its employees and enriched its community. Much of this positive impact continued as Upjohn's people and products were merged into Pharmacia and later Pfizer.

AstraZeneca–Upjohn Comparison

Business

AstraZeneca and Upjohn are both victors and victims of the relentless M&A feeding frenzy that characterizes the global pharmaceutical industry, whose motto is: Swallow or be swallowed! The cost in time and money of coming up with new drugs and shepherding them through the approval process into the international marketplace is a very high barrier to entry that only a few businesses can hurdle.

Philanthropy and Foundations

AstraZeneca doesn't do much in its own name but gives to other foundations in the communities where it operates and to groups working on causes it cares about like COVID relief and helping young people with chronic diseases. The Upjohn family had several foundations, many focused on their hometown of Kalamazoo, Michigan. Most of these disappeared after the company was subsumed into Pfizer.

Personal Lives

AstraZeneca didn't have individual founders but the Swedish branch had more than 400 midwives and the English branch came from a broken home as the result of divorce. Its corporate culture has no patron saints. Upjohn had a dynamic founder and family at its core for most of its existence. Dr. Will had an outsized impact on his community that blessed multitudes in his generation and beyond.

Legacy

Even though it's a global giant, no individuals or families are associated with AstraZeneca when it comes to legacy. Dr. Will, on the other hand, was honored as the Person of the Century in his hometown. His family followed in his footsteps. Much of their work was discontinued when the company was merged out of existence, but they are fondly remembered.

What Would They Think?

AstraZeneca had no individual founders. It has always been about mergers and acquisitions and has grown large enough to have a major influence in Sweden and England. Upjohn had a legendary founder whose faith and family positively impacted the company's hometown of Kalamazoo, Michigan for decades. Dr. John would be deeply disappointed that his life's work lost its identity and influence when it was subsumed by larger pharma conglomerates, much to the detriment of the people and community he loved.

Takeaways for Social Entrepreneurs

- Build your salesforce and distribution networks for where you want to be, not for where you are.
- Mergers and acquisitions (M&A) are key growth strategies, but they can also conflict with your founding mission.
- Bring new products to market through invention or innovation. Either make something new or make something better.
- Use your assets and expertise to address global crises and alleviate human suffering.

- You don't have to reinvent the wheel when it comes to social and philanthropic ventures; you can work with reputable partners to maximize impact.
- Encourage head-to-head competition when your products and services are superior.
- Share your success with those who help create it in practical ways that are meaningful to them.
- Remember that you're a steward (manager) of all you have, not the owner, even if the company bears your name.
- Family-owned businesses can be family run, as long as succeeding generations are properly trained and qualified.
- Invest in more than just jobs in the communities where you do business.
- Nothing lasts forever, so do life and business in such a way that you'll be missed when you're gone.

ROW in Action

TeleEEG Epilepsy Clinics

To improve diagnosis of epilepsy, ROW is partnering with TeleEEG to establish and support epilepsy clinics in under-resourced countries to properly diagnose epilepsy and develop treatment plans using a low-cost, replicable approach. TeleEEG's telemedicine infrastructure connects TeleEEG clinics, predominantly in university hospitals and paediatric clinics, to their global team of consultant neurophysiologists for remote diagnosis. For each clinic, TeleEEG:

- Provides an EEG machine (necessary equipment to properly diagnose epilepsy).
- Trains local healthcare professionals in competently performing EEG tests.
- Offers ongoing interpretation of EEG tests through their team of 45 volunteer consultant neurophysiologists.

Once correctly diagnosed, patients can be properly treated with medication, which can reduce seizures from several times a day to once a month, and in some cases stop seizures altogether. Because of the partnership with OWP Pharmaceuticals, ROW is able to offer Roweepra (Levetiracetam) to qualified recipients. Levetiracetam is the number one generic anti-seizure medication in the U.S., but often not available in under-resourced areas. For patients that are non-responsive to locally available medication, ROW can often provide a sustainable supply of Roweepra. This often makes the critical difference in controlling seizures.

Figure 12.1 TeleEEG equipment in the field.

Part IV

A Call to Action

13 Move the Needle

How You Can Advance the Social Enterprise Movement

We are living in an era where profit and purpose are finally converging. We can see the result of the shifting landscape through the ground we've covered in this book. We've looked at how commercial enterprises are moving from a primary focus on stakeholders to shareholders and are improving the planet and its people. We've looked at social enterprises that are built for a specific social purpose, and relentlessly pursue their mission to create desperately needed change. We've shared our unique approach to large-scale social impact through the tandem hybrid model, and learned lessons from historic companies that dominate their markets. Now it's time to consider *your* role in the future of the social enterprise movement. What impact will you make? How are you best positioned to harness business as a force for good? We invite you to consider the action you can take to apply the principles we've discussed.

But first, a warning.

"Please Don't Start Another Social Enterprise!"

Wait ... what? This might not be the advice you were expecting. However, before starting something new, it's worth considering the alternatives. Cheryl Dorsey, President of Echoing Green—an organization that helps start social enterprises—often starts her talks at universities by exclaiming: "Please don't start another social enterprise!" She goes on to explain:

> Young people have equated success with being a founder. That's the Achilles heel of our movement. We're heading in the wrong direction if we let a million flowers bloom. It's not enough to have these tiny centers for excellence that never amount to anything. They're too fragmented, too balkanized to ever move the needle.[1]

---

1 Cheryl Dorsey, "Quotes." GoodReads, www.goodreads.com/author/quotes/4624465.Cheryl_Dorsey.

DOI: 10.4324/9781003325987-17

If the goal is social progress, we have to be clear-eyed about what will get us there. The honest truth is that not everyone is a social entrepreneur. Not everyone should start a social enterprise. And that's a good thing. We need smart, purposeful, innovative "intrapreneurs" and co-conspirators working at all levels and in all roles in existing organizations to truly move the needle on the complex social challenges that exist in our world today. You don't have to be a founder to make a profound difference.

No one has articulated the well-intentioned but misguided efforts of aspiring social entrepreneurs better than Daniella Papi-Thornton, former deputy director of the Skoll Centre for Social Entrepreneurship at the University of Oxford's Said School of Business. Her research and corresponding report, "Tackling Heropreneurship," shines a realistic light on what skills are needed to produce meaningful social impact. Papi-Thornton writes:

> To really change a system, I believe people need a more holistic set of skills, including systems thinking, an understanding of collaboration tools to further collective impact, and lateral leadership skills such as the ability to lead without power and to galvanize movement toward a common goal across a diverse and disjointed solutions ecosystem. They also need a grounded understanding of themselves and their skills, such as how they like to work, which roles in a team best fit their skills, and if/how their risk tolerance fits with the range of social impact career options. Finally, if they plan to take a leadership or strategic role in solving a problem, they need a deep understanding of the reality of that problem.[2]

To help ambitious innovators assess the need for their possible contribution to a particular social challenge, Papi-Thornton created a tool called the Impact Gaps Canvas.[3] The three-part exercise leads the participant through a process to (1) map the identified problem, (2) map any existing solutions, and (3) consider what gaps exist in the system. By mapping the problem, you develop a thorough understanding of the history, root causes, impacted people or organizations, and other interconnected issues and complexities. By mapping existing solutions, you learn who is already working on solving the problem, what has been tried, what has succeeded or failed, and what opportunities for collaboration and partnership might exist. Finally, you are then able to intelligently identify "gaps," things that are missing, inefficient, or otherwise not connected that could meet a need and contribute to meaningful change. A new social enterprise could be the answer. Or, you might find that working within or between existing efforts might be the best fit for your particular involvement.

2 Daniella Papi-Thornton, "Tackling Heropreneurship," Stanford Social Innovation Review, February 2016, https://ssir.org/articles/entry/tackling_heropreneurship.
3 Daniella Papi-Thornton, "Using the Impact Gaps Canvas," Tackling Heropreneurship, https://tacklingheropreneurship.com/the-impact-gaps-canvas/.

If You Do Start a Social Enterprise

Once you've confirmed that starting a new venture is necessary for addressing the particular social challenge that drives you, you'll need to consider the options for how you will structure your efforts. While we've highlighted the power of the tandem hybrid model to harness the best of both the for-profit and non-profit worlds, we know that effective social enterprises come in all shapes and sizes. Just as there's a need for both immediate aid and long-term development after a natural disaster, every form of intervention is needed in a world fraught with so many urgent problems. We need to stop the bleeding *and* stop what caused the wound. We need to rescue people from the river *and* go upstream to figure out why they're falling in. There's no one right model for all social enterprises, but there's probably one that's right for yours.

First Things First

Any social enterprise, tandem hybrid or not, must be driven by a compelling social mission. We discussed in Chapter 5 how to identify a meaningful issue that your venture can address—something that's right for you and good for the world. While guiding you through the complete design of your business model is not within the scope of this book (there are other great resources for that), we do believe having a solid grasp on your theory of change is important before choosing your model and structure.

As introduced in Chapter 2, a theory of change is simply the articulation of the impact you desire to make, and how you intend to make it. In other words, how will your products or services lead to your desired outcomes—positive changes in people or the planet? You'll want to identify your assumptions and do some market research, testing, and prototyping before you commit a large amount of your (and other people's) time and money to build the business. Through your initial research (and the Impact Gaps Canvas process mentioned above), you can learn a lot about which interventions have the potential to be effective in your specific situation. Incorporating the process of human-centered design can be especially helpful in defining your challenge, brainstorming ideas, and prototyping solutions (we like the tools at IDEO-ORG[4]).

Once you have confidence that your products or services have strong potential to be an effective solution for your chosen issue, you can start thinking about formalizing your structure. It may be helpful to review Chapter 2 and 3 to consider the pros and cons of various for-profit, non-profit, and hybrid structures. Specifically, you should answer the list of questions posed by Jim Fruchterman in Chapter 2 around Motivation,

---

4 "Human-Centered Design Sits at the Intersection of Empathy and Creativity," Ideo-org, www.ideo.org/tools.

Market, Capital, and Control. Among the longer list of questions, he asks founders to consider:

- What is your motivation for starting the venture?
- What market are you targeting?
- How do you plan to raise capital?
- What type of control do you want over the venture?

The answers to these and other questions will help guide you to the structure that will work best to accomplish your mission. Of course, consultation with an experienced lawyer is always recommended. Here's a brief summary of the factors to consider when choosing among for-profit, non-profit, and tandem hybrid models.

For-Profit Structures

The most common for-profit structures include a C-corp, S-corp, LLC, or partnership. Remember, with these traditional structures you'll need to ensure the social mission is baked into the fabric of the business and its people, because the structure does not legally require it. The newer for-profit social enterprise structures (L3C and benefit corporation), available in some locations, make it easier for companies to legally prioritize a social mission. Any for-profit company can also choose to pursue certification as a B Corp after a rigorous assessment by B Labs, providing a third-party stamp of approval for its social and environmental commitments. You may want to choose a for-profit structure if:

- You have a product or service that can generate revenue to sustain the enterprise.
- You want to have some degree of personal ownership and control of the company.
- You need to attract capital through equity investments and debt to launch and/or grow.
- You value the image of a socially responsible business rather than a charity.
- You don't need or want to fundraise by offering tax-deductible donations.
- You have confidence that your governance structure will prioritize the social mission.

Non-Profit Structures

The most common non-profit structure is a 501(c)3 charity or foundation, although there are many varieties to choose from. There are actually 29 different 501(c) options in the IRS Publication 557 for tax-exempt organizations.[5] Non-profit organizations have a clear and recognizable public purpose, so prioritizing the social mission is expected and required. Non-profit organizations can generate revenue, but the revenue needs to be related to, and reinvested in, the mission. Non-profits may also choose to pursue designations from groups like Charity Navigator or GuideStar to vouch for their efficiency and effectiveness. You may want to choose a non-profit structure if:

- Your product or service is not sustainable through market-driven revenue.
- You don't need to have personal ownership or control of the organization.
- You will be able to raise money through grants or tax-deductible donations.
- You want to avoid paying tax on mission-related income and property.
- You value the image of a public-focused charity rather than a business.
- You can grow the organization sufficiently without investment capital.

Tandem Hybrid Model

If neither the for-profit structure nor the non-profit structure seems like the perfect fit, you might be a candidate for the tandem hybrid model. Despite recent efforts to incentivize blending profit and purpose, the above options highlight the fact that our systems were built for one or the other. Instead of fighting the system, the tandem hybrid model harnesses it to offer the best of both worlds. Like a tandem bicycle, it requires a bit more effort to build and operate, but when it hits the road it has incredible power and speed. Chapters 5–8 explained in detail what the tandem hybrid looks like in action. It requires a social entrepreneur with a large and generous vision, and the foresight and humility to let the purpose outlive the person. Here, we offer a few reasons why the tandem hybrid model might be right for you:

- Your compelling social mission has the potential for large-scale impact.
- Your innovative business plan has the potential for large-scale growth.
- You want access to investment capital from both traditional and impact investors.
- You aim to provide a financial return and a social return on investment.
- You want revenue from your business to fund your mission.
- You want grants and tax-deductible donations to fund your mission.
- You want to attract and retain top talent by paying competitive wages.
- You want to hire experts to drive the business and experts to drive the mission.

5 "Tax Exempt Status for Your Organization," Publication 557, Internal Revenue Service, www.irs.gov/pub/irs-pdf/p557.pdf.

- You value the image of a profitable business and the image of a related charity.
- You can build and manage two organizations, keeping them separate but mutually dependent.
- You want the impact of your social enterprise to continue in perpetuity.

Is it Too Late to Start a Tandem Hybrid Social Enterprise?

While it's ideal if you can build the tandem hybrid model from scratch, it's never too late. In fact, with the surge of interest in corporate social responsibility, now is a great time for existing businesses and non-profits to consider how jumping on the tandem hybrid model might accelerate their impact. Just as OWP and ROW went through their own iterations in structure, it's not uncommon for organizations to modify their legal or organizational identity after launch. Here are a few scenarios for consideration:

For Business Owners

Perhaps you didn't launch your company with a social mission, but over time you've developed a desire to make social impact the top priority for your business. You may have recognized a social or environmental need in your industry, or an underserved population you could reach through your products or profits. What are your options? You could certainly advance your CSR or corporate giving efforts. You could pursue B Corp designation to prove your commitments. You could even change your legal registration from a traditional structure to a benefit corporation (like Patagonia).

But ... if you want to create a structure with all the benefits we've discussed, you could form a tandem hybrid by adding a connected non-profit organization (public charity or foundation) to manage purpose-related activities. This allows the existing business to focus on generating revenue, which can in turn be funneled to the non-profit to fuel the mission. You may need to transition, train, or recruit staff to manage the new entity, but your mission-related impact could grow exponentially. Keep in mind that you'll need to be the owner with majority control of the company to alter the structure.

If you're the majority owner and you're thinking about an exit, that's also a good time to consider transitioning to the tandem hybrid model. Typical exits happen through a sale or a transition to others in the family. Many owners who are philanthropically minded choose to exit, realize a large profit, and use some of the funds to support their charitable objectives through a family foundation or a donor-advised fund. We suggest an additional option—transitioning the company to a tandem hybrid social enterprise. A larger business has a larger capital requirement for an exit, but it can be significantly reduced by putting a percentage of the company into a hybrid model that supports a cause or calling that inspires you or your family. More money goes directly into the mission and the cause becomes sustainably connected to a profitable business for the long haul.

For Non-Profit Leaders

Perhaps you've realized the challenge of generating consistent and reliable funding for your charitable efforts. The ebb and flow of the market and the uncertainly of grant and donor dollars have stalled your growth and effectiveness. What are your options? You could start or expand some revenue-generating activities to complement your donor funding. Be careful here; too much unrelated business income could threaten your tax-exempt status. You could work to form a corporate partnership with an existing local business that provides sponsorship dollars and employee engagement.

But if you had your own separate financial engine, you could provide the long-term fuel for your mission to grow and scale. You could keep your donor base engaged and you wouldn't have to completely rely on outside support for your existence. You could form a tandem hybrid by starting a connected for-profit business. You'll likely need to recruit talent to establish, manage, and grow the business—and of course, have a legitimate and profitable product or service—but your current team would be freed up to do what they do best.

Why the World Needs More Social Enterprises

The world is re-defining "business as usual." Gone are the days of the narrow, short-term focus on shareholder primacy. A broad and inclusive stakeholder approach has taken root, and social and environmental responsibility is now an expectation for commercial as well as social enterprises. The public expects companies to comment on, respond to, and advocate for the pressing issues of the day—from domestic concerns about racial and gender equity to geopolitical issues of war and climate change. We have reached the point where doing good is good for business.

The world needs even more socially responsible companies, more sustainable charities, and more innovative public policies to actually turn the tide on the challenges we face in this generation. And we need the public and private sectors working together, not in competition over scare resources. We're convinced that what will really move the needle is a wave of high-profit, high-purpose social enterprises. Regardless of the model and structure, a growing social enterprise movement is needed for three simple reasons:

Problems Need Solving

Despite the best effort of governments, non-profits, capitalists, and philanthropists, the nature of global social concerns remains broad and deep.

Whether it's poverty, health care, education, human rights, or the environment, the problems are complex and systemic. Social entrepreneurs, through the mechanism of a social enterprise, have a unique way of working across sectors—and even across political divides—to solve problems at their root. This market-based, mission-first approach can rally supporters from across the ideological spectrum. Because social entrepreneurs often work in interdisciplinary and collaborative ways, they can spark the action needed to move markets and change policy.

For example, the World Economic Forum—as part of the Davos Agenda 2021—identified social entrepreneurs as viable partners for governments in creating lasting change. They note:

> In the current high-pressure situation, "systems social entrepreneurs" —actors who develop innovative approaches to persistent, complex social problems by employing systems thinking—can be crucial allies for governments. They are a source of proven innovations for the good of all and create the conditions and support for sustainable, equitable systems change through their participative methods, entrepreneurial mindset, and trusted relationships with affected communities.[6]

Planet Earth Needs Saving

There is no planet B, as many environmental advocates remind us. What was once reserved for the agendas of tree-huggers and progressive activists, environmental sustainability has quickly become a mainstream priority for the global community. As noted in the UN Environment Programme's State of the Climate:

> The world is in a climate emergency—"a code red for humanity" according to the UN Secretary-General. The concentration of greenhouse gas emissions in the atmosphere is wreaking havoc across the world and threatening lives, economies, health and food.[7]

Large businesses can and must act to reduce their environmental impacts, and innovation is needed at every level of every sector to combat this threat. But a social enterprise—particularly of the tandem hybrid variety—is especially equipped to help mitigate this existential crisis.

6 Victor van Vuuren, François Bonnici, Diana Wells, Koen Vermeltfoort, "These New Allies for Government Can Help Attain Equitable, Lasting Change," World Economic Forum, www.weforum.org/agenda/2021/01/systems-social-entrepreneurs-are-the-new-allies-for-governments-to-achieve-equitable-lasting-change/.
7 "State of the Climate," UN Environment Programme, www.unep.org/explore-topics/climate-action/what-we-do/climate-action-note/state-of-climate.html.

Ahead of the 2021 United Nations Climate Change Conference, also known as COP26, the Social Enterprise World Forum sent a message advocating for the important role social enterprises can play. It begins:

> The global changes needed to combat the Climate Emergency are huge. While most social enterprises are small, the philosophical foundation from which we operate is profound enough to help immediately. Social enterprise is a climate-friendly new way of doing business, and as the visionary Paul Hawken said in his book *The Ecology of Commerce*, "we don't need to save the Earth, we need to save business because it is killing the Earth."[8]

The message went on the suggest policy change in the areas of social procurement, social enterprise contracting, and local climate resiliency, which collectively would maximize the involvement of social enterprises that exist to improve the planet.

People Need Meaning

The millennial generation—born between 1981 and 1996—now accounts for the largest percentage of the global workforce. It's a group well-known for their social consciousness. "Millennials want to work for organizations with a purpose and a reason for being that goes beyond merely making a profit," notes one human resources report.[9] Gen Z, on their heels, is now entering the workforce and is no less socially inclined. Not only are these generations poised to launch more social enterprises, they are also the ones who will be looking to work for them. Why? Because the up-front mission of a social enterprise clearly aligns with their personal values and provides the sense of meaning they desire in their work.

The need for meaning isn't limited to emerging generations. Viktor Frankl, survivor of three Nazi concentration camps and author of the 1959 book *Man's Search for Meaning*, cited in his book a survey of nearly 8,000 college students at 48 colleges. "Asked what they considered 'very important' to them now, 16 percent of the students checked 'making a lot of money;' 78 percent said their first goal was 'finding a purpose and meaning to my life.'"[10] The search for meaning is universal, and a social enterprise provides it for more than just the founder—for the funders, partners, suppliers, employees, customers, and most important, the beneficiaries.

8 Maeve Curtin, "SEWF Message to COP26," Social Enterprise World Forum, https://sewfonline.com/sewf-message-to-cop26/.
9 Arthur Wilson, "What Millennials Want from Work: 7 Research-Backed Truths," Workstars, www.workstars.com/recognition-and-engagement-blog/2019/10/21/what-millennials-want-from-work-7-research-backed-truths/.
10 Victor Frankl, *Man's Search for Meaning* (Boston, MA: Beacon Press, 2006).

The Tandem Hybrid Promise

While all social enterprise models have the potential to address some of the world's most pressing problems, we believe the tandem hybrid model is especially promising because of the scale at which profit and purpose coalesce. Just imagine a world where a significant percentage of business revenues are intentionally directed to solve our collective social challenges. When the force of the market drives the heart of the mission, large-scale change can happen. And while the pharmaceutical industry happens to be the market that OWP and ROW are leveraging, any industry can be harnessed for good. Countless products and services in countless markets can be used to build a business that is driven by a compelling social mission, financed by commercial success, structured to retain control, and scalable and sustainable for the long haul. Wherever you find yourself on the social enterprise journey, we hope you can apply these principles in your efforts to make a difference in the world.

Scott's Story

Where do I see OWP and ROW in 50 years? I want OWP Pharma to be like Hershey, Hormel, Novo Nordisk, and Lundbeck—still relevant in our market, still innovative, and still profitable. My hope is that ROW has grown and evolved as well, and is receiving significant support apart from OWP, attracting funds from individuals, donor-advised funds, foundations, and corporations. Such a broad and diversified funding stream could support an expansion of ROW beyond neurological disorders, perhaps into diabetes and oncology.

Any leader at OWP or ROW—or other social enterprises for that matter—should answer the critical personal questions we've raised in this book. First, how much is enough? What is your monetary cap—the number beyond which you find money unnecessary? A Founder's Pledge isn't a vow of poverty. In fact, my number is big enough that I'll live comfortably and enjoy a nice house and exciting vacations. But it's not so much that I'll accumulate a surfeit of possessions that will only rust or rot in the future. If your only goal is to make as much as possible, the tandem hybrid model is not for you. You'll be lured by the sirens of the market to follow the money and chase after possessions and recognition. You'll be in good company, but eventually you'll find yourself unfulfilled and empty. However, if you want to wake up each day with a passion for a purpose that's bigger than you and that will last longer than your time on earth, consider taking the road less traveled.

Another question you need to answer if you want to run a social enterprise is, "What's your why?" What motivates you to pursue purpose over profit? For me, I can't ignore the medical and pharmaceutical injustice that exists today, especially in low- and middle-income countries. Addressing this situation is why we started OWP and ROW. Our "why" is in our mission statement: "We envision a world where all people receive the best level of medical and pharmaceutical care regardless of who they are or where they live."

Even though I'm doing similar work to what I did at Abbott Labs and Bristol-Myers Squibb, the feeling I get is totally different. I sign business development deals and I file new medication applications with the FDA, but then I get to hear about a young woman is Sierra Leone, who after a decade of suffering is now seizure-free and unleashed to discover her full potential. Lives all around the world are being completely changed because of our tandem hybrid social enterprise. The stories of our impact bring tears to my eyes and get me out of bed each morning. I've found my "why." I hope you find yours and pursue it with everything you have.

ROW in Action

Zambia Community Health Worker Project

While under-resourced urban communities face a myriad of challenges, it is the individuals from outlying rural and peri-urban communities who are the last to afford and have access to a wide range of services, including healthcare. Community health workers (CHWs) have been instrumental in getting low-cost care for those without previous access.

While CHWs are generally not equipped to support epilepsy care, ROW believes they hold great potential for helping reduce the harmful stigma, identifying children in need, and connecting parents and caregivers with treatment options. This shifting of epilepsy care is essential given the absence of specialists in child neurology globally, with less than 0.4 neurologists per 100,000 population, and much less in low-resource regions. Many low-resource countries have just one or two neurologists, with none focused on pediatric neurology.

ROW is partnering with Boston Children's Hospital (BCH), focusing on impacting children with epilepsy using a CHW approach in Zambia. *U.S. News & World Report* has ranked BCH as the number one pediatric hospital in the country for nine years in a row (2014–2022).[11] Through this partnership, ROW targeted a community near the capital city of Lusaka that's receiving training in epilepsy care and support. CHWs are trained to reach out to families with children affected by epilepsy and

Figure 13.1 Community health workers visiting rural community.

11 "Boston Children's Hospital," U.S. News & World Report Rankings, www. childrenshospital.org/about-us/us-news-world-report-rankings.

teach them when to access care, how to take medication, as well as seizure first-aid and precautions.

ROW is testing the approach using research methodologies for possible large-scale replication. Results so far have exceeded expectations, with the number of participating households being triple what was planned for.

Index

Note: Locators in *italic* indicate figures and in ***italic-bold*** boxes.

Printed in the United States
by Baker & Taylor Publisher Services